# WHEN
# YOUR WORLD
# FALLS APART

OTHER BOOKS BY DAVID JEREMIAH

*Escape the Coming Night*

*The Handwriting on the Wall*

*Invasion of Other Gods*

*Jesus' Final Warning*

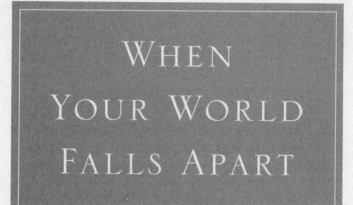

# WHEN YOUR WORLD FALLS APART

# DAVID JEREMIAH

W PUBLISHING GROUP
A Division of Thomas Nelson Publishers
*Since 1798*

www.wpublishinggroup.com

*This book is dedicated to the faithful members of the
Shadow Mountain Community Church.
Their prayers carried me through my bend in the road
and continue to sustain me to this day!*

# Contents

# Acknowledgments

When I first encountered my bend in the road in the fall of 1994, I did not think I would write a book about my experience. But the lessons I learned have been too valuable to keep to myself. This is not primarily a story about me; it is a record of God's dealings with me during these traumatic years. As always, He works best through the people He brings next to us at such crucial times.

I cannot say enough about the medical professionals who ministered to me during the crucial days of my illness. Dr. Thomas Witzig was part of the diagnostic team at the Mayo Clinic that walked me through the first stages of lymphoma. His Christian faith and his encouraging words helped me over the first hurdle.

When I returned to San Diego, I was placed in the capable care of Dr. Alan Saven at the Scripps Clinic. He directed the first chemical treatments and diagnosed the disease when it returned in 1998. Dr. Saven is a highly regarded oncologist who takes an aggressive approach to the treatment of cancer and a gentle approach to the treatment of his patients. Dr. James Mason, also of the Scripps Clinic, took me through the stem cell transplant. His upbeat approach to healing and health was a great encouragement to me. I am also indebted to Dr. Richard Furman, a thoracic surgeon from Boone, North Carolina.

His friendship and counsel have been a source of great strength, and his love for the Word of God has been a great example.

When I was released from the Scripps Clinic in March 1999, I was made aware of the importance of taking better care of my body. After some research into the options, I signed on with Mike Douglas, a former NFL prayer, who is now a physical trainer. I began working out every day under Mike's guidance and have gradually begun to implement some of the nutritional advice that he tries to pound into my head every morning. Mike has given me a new appreciation for the importance of physical fitness, even at the age of fifty-nine.

During the days that I was recovering from the stem cell transplant, several Christian leaders took time out of their busy schedules to call me repeatedly, sharing their love and concern. I want to thank especially Tim LaHaye, Jim Cymbala, John MacArthur, and John Maxwell for their prayers and encouragement.

Several friends provided tremendous assistance as I began to pull together the notes in preparation for this book. Helen Barnhart helped to administrate the project, keeping everything in proper order in the computer. Brenda Josee organized the material, and Rob Suggs produced the final manuscript. As always, my literary agent, Sealy Yates, walked with me through the entire process. He visited me in the hospital and helped me formulate the strategy for this book. I respect Sealy as a professional, and I love him as my friend.

I also want to express my deep appreciation to the people who allowed their stories to be told in this book: Helen Barnhart, Carole Carlson, John Hovey, Marv Eastlund, Sharon Paul, Glenda Palmer, and Steve Garrison.

The leaders who surround me at Shadow Mountain Community Church have demonstrated their love and support from the very beginning of this episode in my life. Thanks to Ken Nichols, Gary Coombs, Steve Caudill, Brian Rickard, Max Baumgartner, Ray Benton, Vance Yoder, and Roger Wiles. A special thanks to Glenda Parker, my administrative assistant, who spent many hours during my illness and recovery coordinating things between my family, the church, and *Turning Point.*

All of my children have ministered to me in a special way during the journey around the bend in the road. David and Cami, John and Jan, Daniel and Merae, and Jennifer and Emmanuel have found creative and expressive ways to encourage me.

Finally, I want to express my love for my wife, Donna. Together we have negotiated several bends in life's road. The closeness we experienced during those times will never be forgotten. Our love for each other has grown deeper, and our faith in Almighty God has been strengthened. I think you will capture something of the special relationship we enjoy as you read her foreword to this book.

—David Jeremiah
El Cajon, California

# Foreword

Being married to David Jeremiah has been quite an adventure. Our journey together these past thirty-seven years has brought us both great joy and pain. But no matter what the circumstances of our lives, we have always been grateful for the abundant grace of God, even during our darkest hours. Today, as I listen to Dave preach, see him playing with our grandchildren, or watch him jump with excitement at a ball game, my heart is filled with gratitude for the mercy of God.

Jesus Christ became my personal Savior when I was nine years old. Only when Dave considered becoming the pastor of Shadow Mountain Community Church in El Cajon, California, did I discover that the evangelist who preached the message during which I accepted the Lord once served as pastor in the pulpit that Dave now fills.

Cheerleading for Cedarville College positioned me close to the court and to a tall, lanky player named David Jeremiah. Dave and I shared an interest in radio, and along with Paul Gathany, we launched WCDR radio for Cedarville College. I love to tell people I was a disc jockey for a one-hour music program—I just don't tell them the limited scope of the radio station.

My decision to accept Dave's marriage proposal involved a lot of heart searching. I knew Dave planned to be a minister, and I had great reservations about being a pastor's wife. When I accepted the reality that God's plan for me could include the role of a pastor's wife, Dave and I launched into married life with eager anticipation for what God had in store for us.

Dave is an optimistic person who grasps every situation with confidence. Through the years, his optimism has influenced me, and I have learned to choose hope no matter the circumstances. That has been the single most important factor as we have faced each bend in the road the last few years.

Pastoring our first small church required a large amount of faith and provided many opportunities to choose hope. Moving to California from the Midwest with our little family filled our lives with excitement. Being part of a growing church and launching a broadcast ministry kept us facing each new day with a curious anticipation. The launching of *Turning Point* also brought an opportunity for me to work alongside Dave and motivated me with the joy of seeing his ministry's extended impact on so many lives.

I realize there is never a good time for bad news; however, the timing of the discovery of Dave's cancer forced both of us to internalize many of our emotions. Our oldest son, David Michael, was a newlywed and living on the East Coast; Jennifer was in her first year at Cedarville College and suffering from homesickness; and Daniel, our youngest son, had major decisions to make regarding his upcoming college plans. Only our daughter Jan was close by in Coronado!

Dave was strong and gave me the courage to choose hope rather than despair. I knew all the Bible passages about faith and trust, yet when the man I loved, my husband, the father of my children, the man who preached boldly about faith, could be dying, I wasn't sure that I could find the faith to carry on.

I wish I could tell you there is an easy way to survive any bend in the road of life, but that would not be true. I can tell you that each day held its own level of anxiety and that each day the Lord provided just enough strength and hope for that day.

As a wife and mother, I attempted to keep life as normal as possible. Celebrating holidays and birthdays, attending sports events, and mingling with our church family kept me hopeful. On the few days when I felt completely overwhelmed, I would drive up into the mountains east of our home. Getting out by myself gave me time to gain perspective alone with the Lord and realize that the choice I made to hope was not a once-for-all choice, but a moment-by-moment choice.

During these times, I discovered that hope, as the writer of Hebrews said, is the "anchor of the soul" (6:19). Hope was the anchor that brought me back to the God I had trusted with my life as a child. Now I had to trust God with the life of my husband.

In our private moments, Dave and I would draw strength from each other. Over the years, I have prayed for many people and circumstances. But how could I hold the man I loved in my arms and pray for God to spare his life without giving in to a sense of quiet desperation? Dave could sense when I was feeling down and knew what to say to lift my spirits and to help me regain a sense of hope.

Today, our journey together is continuing. In the course of Dave's recovery, two of our children have married, more grandchildren have been born, and *Turning Point* has launched a television program. We have discovered that looking forward is the only way to live.

No matter what your circumstances may be, please read this book with the awareness that the man who wrote it is a living testimony to the sustaining power of hope found only in the Lord Jesus Christ. The prophet Jeremiah's confession of faith is recorded in Lamentations 3:21–24:

> *This I recall to my mind,*
> *Therefore I have hope.*
> *Through the LORD'S mercies we are not consumed,*
> *Because His compassions fail not.*
> *They are new every morning;*
> *Great is Your faithfulness.*
> *"The LORD is my portion," says my soul,*
> *"Therefore I hope in Him!"*

Living with hope,
Donna Jeremiah

# 1

# A Bend in the Road

*Sometimes we come to life's crossroads*
*And we view what we think is the end.*
*But God has a much wider vision*
*And He knows that it's only a bend—*
*The road will go on and get smoother*
*And after we've stopped for a rest,*
*The path that lies hidden beyond us*
*Is often the path that is best.*
*So rest and relax and grow stronger,*
*Let go and let God share your load*
*And have faith in a brighter tomorrow.*
*You've just come to a bend in the road.*

It all began on an ordinary Monday morning.

I pulled the van out of my garage, turned onto the road, and drove toward the highway, where I merged into the familiar flow of traffic. How many times in my life had I performed this simple action—thousands? Tens of thousands?

I had no particularly pressing concerns during the forty-minute drive to La Jolla, California. I glided by the trees and shops and traffic lights that formed the reassuring backdrop of my world. I was thinking typical Monday-morning thoughts, reflecting on how tired I was.

How had I let myself get roped into this excursion to be poked and prodded by doctors? Mondays were good for many things: getting a jump-start into a new week, collecting my thoughts, reviewing another Lord's day, and catching my breath before thinking about the next one. Physical examinations weren't on my list of preferred Monday-morning activities. (To be honest, I have yet to find a suitable day for visiting the doctor.) But on this particular bright morning—September 26, 1994—I was thinking about Sunday's three sermons and the toll they had taken on my tired blood. I was reflecting dolefully on the rest and rehabilitation I could have been enjoying at that moment, instead of a forty-minute drive to Scripps Clinic for a full physical.

Those were my idle thoughts during a mundane drive on a Monday morning. But the clock was ticking: Forty minutes of peace and contentment were draining away before chaos struck.

On this day, the road of life on which I was traveling led to a sudden, sharp turn for which I was completely unprepared. I had no dark premonitions, no particular reason to cherish the simple securities and comforts that would be stripped away from me at the end of this journey. I was blissfully unaware of the rapid approach of a bend in the road.

It was still early as I arrived at the Center for Executive Health in La Jolla. The exam got underway at 7:45 A.M. with the interview, and I handled the usual barrage of questions from the nurses armed with their clipboards. Then I was ushered over into another part of the clinic for an EKG stress test. It went smoothly, and I could tell my numbers were good ones.

So far, so good. I smiled with satisfaction as the doctors nodded and made little checks on their notepads. They stroked their chins and admitted that I was in pretty fair shape for a grizzled fifty-three-year-old veteran of life's trenches. Better still, the physical exam was downhill all the way after the EKG. I had been through all this before, and it was easy to tell that I was checking out fine on the remaining tests. The men in the white coats gave me the thumbs-up at every point; I was beginning to think that maybe this was a smart way to spend a Monday after all.

Late in the morning, I was taken to an examining room, where I met the head physician. He asked me to lie faceup on the table, and I complied. The doctor began to go over my body from head to toe.

*Soon I'll have this whole thing behind me,* I thought. *It will feel good to have another successful physical in the books. The white-coats will hand me the bill and show me the door. I'll be free to climb into my van, drive back down the highway, and get on with my crowded agenda. And I'll have a little extra spring in my step, knowing that for one more round, I've come out victorious in the battle against time and corruption.*

Those were my thoughts.

That's when the bomb fell.

As the doctor probed the left side of my abdomen, he said, "Dr. Jeremiah, you have a mass here in your abdomen that causes me some concern. It feels to me as if your spleen is greatly enlarged."

I felt my heart skip a beat. "What do you think it is?" I asked.

"I can't say," he replied quietly, "until we see a CAT scan of that part of your body."

That's it. Two sentences—a handful of words—brought a crowded, thriving life to a screeching halt. As I sat up and dressed myself, I struggled to absorb the doctor's words. My mind launched into "spin-control" mode, searching for positive angles.

I had my scan late that afternoon in the radiology center across the street and was informed that results would be available the following day. At least the suspense wouldn't be prolonged; within hours I would be given words of comfort—or something else.

I was shell-shocked that afternoon as I went through the motions of the scan and closed out my business with the clinic. I was still in a daze as I made my way back to my home in El Cajon.

How was I going to handle this news bulletin there? This was something I needed to handle carefully—it was, after all, a bomb. I knew that Donna, my wife, planned to leave the next day to visit her mother in New Hampshire. She would be scrambling around the house, packing suitcases and orchestrating last-minute arrangements. She'd have that happy, busy glow about her, energized by the anticipation of her trip.

That's why I decided to keep silent. Why rain on her parade? At this point, everything was preliminary and tentative. I decided to let this evening be a bright one for at least one of us. I refused to ruin a pleasant trip for my loving wife.

So I kept the curtains tightly shut on the black clouds inside me. I smiled and made the best I could of the situation. The next morning, I drove Donna to the airport and watched her plane disappear into the blue, trouble-free sky that still existed for other people. Then I headed to my office, where I sat and watched my telephone, waiting for the call that would reveal my earthly fate. The moments ticked by slowly, and every ring was a false alarm.

Finally that afternoon, I picked up the receiver and heard the doctor's calm voice on the other end of the line. I listened desperately for a victorious affirmation—words about tests that came back negative, about lumps that were less than they seemed. I wanted those words desperately, and I poured out my soul praying for them.

But those words were not available to me. Instead, the doctor's fears were confirmed—I had a mass on my spleen.

The doctor carefully explained to me that three radiologists examined the scan and shared the firm opinion that I had lymphoma, a cancer that attacks the lymphatic system, of which the spleen is the center. We talked for a few minutes, then I returned the receiver to the cradle of the telephone. The most terrible phone call of my life was over. I felt emptiness and despair rising up inside me.

It was Tuesday, the day for staff meeting at our church—another difficult hurdle in my current state of turmoil. I kept the meeting short, dismissing it after a brief time of prayer. Then I sought out my close friend and staff member Dr. Ken Nichols and beckoned him into my office. I closed the door carefully, sat down beside him, and shared with him the details of my physical and the prognosis. He was the first person with whom I shared the crisis. We cried, embraced, and prayed. Then we pulled ourselves together and began to think about what to do.

Ken had an idea. He remembered a longtime friend of mine—Dr. Marv Eastlund of Fort Wayne, Indiana. I've known him since I was a pastor there many years ago. Dr. Eastlund is not only a knowledgeable physician, but he is also an experienced sufferer who spent six weeks in Mayo Clinic for a pancreatic disorder. (I'll give you his story in greater detail in chapter 9.)

Ken thought Dr. Eastlund might be able to help, and that sounded good to me. I made the call, and Dr. Eastlund didn't hesitate before issuing a directive: Go to Mayo Clinic immediately. My kind friend promised to make a phone call to expedite things for me. And in a matter of hours, I had an appointment at the Mayo Clinic.

On Thursday morning of that same week, I boarded a plane heading eastward. I was traveling on business—I was scheduled to speak at rallies in New Hampshire and Maine to support our *Turning Point* radio ministry. My friends Steve and Susan Caudill were flying with me. The plan was for Donna to meet us in Manchester, New Hampshire, at the first rally. As so often happens with air travel, the connections were perilously tight; we arrived at the rally with just enough time for me to kiss Donna hello and hurry to the platform.

The event was thrilling, and it lifted my spirits. The building was packed with fifteen hundred excited listeners. Several of them gave their hearts to Christ that night, securing their eternal destinies. Just at the time I was having a close encounter with death, these wonderful souls were having their first encounters with eternal life. I shook hands, chatted with folks, and signed books and Bibles until the last of the crowd went home.

---

*When God permits His children to go through the furnace,*
*He keeps His eye on the clock and His hand on the thermostat.*
*His loving heart knows how much and how long* (1 Peter 1:6–7).

**—Warren Wiersbe**

---

On the way back to the hotel, Donna and I stopped for a late dinner. That's where the thrill of the evening wore off. I became pensive over my plate because I knew that the time had come to level with my wife about the week's events.

We found our hotel and settled into the room, unpacking our things and turning down the sheets. Then I sat down on the bed and opened to Donna those dark curtains of my soul. I told her the whole story of three days of despair. When I finished, we cried and prayed and held each other through most of the night.

A bend in the road took us to that room. There, far from our home, on the other side of the continent—there, in a strange hotel—we huddled together to face the most challenging moment of thirty-plus years of marriage.

### "You're Going to the Mayo Clinic!"

The rallies came to an end, and Donna and I returned home at last. There were more doctors' examinations and troublesome hours of sorting out insurance questions. Our ministry had begun a new insurance plan at the beginning of October, and that coverage would not extend to a trip to Mayo. It looked as if we'd have to settle for surgery in San Diego. I had a date with the doctors for Tuesday morning at Sharp Hospital, at which time my spleen would be removed.

My condition was no longer a secret; I'd begun to call some of my network of ministry friends around the country. I coveted their prayers. One of these men was Lowell Davey, president of the Bible Broadcasting Network. When I called him and described my situation, he responded without hesitation, "David, you are going to Mayo Clinic! If your insurance will not cover it, I'll raise the money myself."

I think you'll understand that by this time, Donna and I were spent. The emotional roller coaster had left us dizzy and exhausted. I told Lowell that my surgery was scheduled for Tuesday morning at 7:45—only five days from now. I set a condition. "If you can get me into Mayo Clinic on Monday morning," I said, "then I'll go."

Two hours later, I received a phone call from a doctor at Mayo Clinic, calling to confirm my appointment at 7:45 Monday morning. I was astounded, to put it mildly. True friendship is a powerful force for strength and encouragement.

With our minds finally set on a course of action, I began to prepare myself for the weekend. I was scheduled to officiate at a wedding for the daughter of my administrative secretary on Saturday afternoon at 3:00. Once again, I was mindful of my personal situation casting a pall over someone else's joyful occasion—particularly in the case of a wedding. I asked for the couple to be kept in the dark about my crisis until after the ceremony. This was their once-in-a-lifetime day, and it should be filled with joy.

The next morning, I preached at both services. The Lord once again honored His Word. But this was not just another Sunday for me. Afterward, I told Donna that in twenty-five years of preaching, I'd never felt the presence of the Lord as I did that day. Other preachers know this feeling—at times it was almost as if I were sitting on a pew in the back of my mind, listening to someone else preach. I was deeply aware of Paul's statement, "When I am weak, then I am strong" (2 Cor. 12:10). I'd never been so weak, and He'd never seemed so strong.

That afternoon, we flew east, this time toward Mayo Clinic.

During my first appointment, there were rounds of blood tests, physical examinations, and more questions. Finally I met with the first doctor. She went over the results and confirmed the diagnosis of lymphoma. She also made the arrangements for my next appointment, in the department of hematology.

When she called hematology, she was told that no opening would be available until Thursday. My heart sank. This was Monday! Three days seemed like an eternity, and I had work to do back home. How could we wait here for seventy-two hours? The doctor sensed my desperation. She considered quietly for a minute and finally said, "I know one of the doctors in that department. Let me call him."

The doctor called her friend, and I heard her say into the phone, "He's a pastor from San Diego. His name is David Jeremiah." Then a look of surprise splashed across her face. She put her hand over the mouthpiece and turned to me. "He knows you!" she said. Speaking into the phone, she said, "Does that mean you'll see him this afternoon?"

It did. I was instructed to head right over.

My doctor had been speaking to a colleague named Dr. Thomas Witzig, who had once heard me speak at Moody Founder's Week. Dr. Witzig is a wonderful Christ-follower, and it pleased me greatly to discover that he would be the lead physician. When we sat down to talk, he walked me through the procedures to come during the next few days. Dr. Witzig agreed that surgery was required, and it was scheduled for Tuesday morning at the Methodist Hospital in the Mayo Clinic complex.

That's where I went the next morning. The surgery lasted about two hours and revealed that the lymphoma was centered in the area immediately around my spleen. The surgeons decided to leave the spleen in place; it was actually not as diseased as they had anticipated. This was the first tentatively hopeful medical news we'd received, and you can imagine our gratitude.

The doctors patiently educated Donna and me about my condition. They explained that lymphoma is a treatable form of cancer. There are never any guarantees with this dreaded enemy, but we at least had the possibility for recovery through chemotherapy—and that made hope possible.

We held tightly to that hope. Our spirits basked in the prayers, support, and encouragement of our church family and friends; we fed on their support and felt strengthened for the battle ahead. But in the midst of all the love and affirmation, it was the Lord, "a stronghold in the day of trouble" (Nah. 1:7), who knew the needs of my body and soul most deeply. It was He who walked with me through the valley of the shadow, He who lavished upon me a deeper, more personal experience of His presence than I'd ever known before. As I sought refuge in His Word, I found consolation beyond description for my troubled spirit.

Again and again I was reminded of the words of the apostle Paul. Long ago he was confronted with death and fear, and perhaps he experienced emotions a bit like my own. Paul was so gifted and had a heart eager to minister, yet he was forced to bide his time in a dark prison. I know Paul asked God the same questions I have asked, and I'm grateful he recorded God's answers: "And He said to me, 'My grace

A BEND IN THE ROAD

is sufficient for you, for My strength is made perfect in weakness.' Therefore most gladly I will rather boast in my infirmities, that the power of Christ may rest upon me" (2 Cor. 12:9).

God's grace is sufficient—I can tell you it's true.


## Life Is Difficult

Somewhere along your own path, you've likely encountered a bend in the road too. Suddenly you faced circumstances you never expected or wished to encounter. I hope you've found it helpful, as I have, to read encouraging words from fellow strugglers.

Gordon MacDonald is a friend and fellow struggler. His fine book *The Life God Blesses* has ministered to me more richly than I can tell you. Gordon writes with wonderful insight about the methods God uses to bring blessing into the lives of His servants. In one chapter, he coins a term to describe one of those tools. He calls them "disruptive moments." According to Gordon, disruptive moments are "those unanticipated events, most of which one would usually have chosen to avoid had it been possible."

He adds, "We don't like disruptive moments; they are too often associated with pain and inconvenience, failure and humiliation. Not that they have to be, but that seems the way of the human condition."[1]

Few of us ever fully grasp that simple but painful biblical truth—the heat of suffering is a refiner's fire, purifying the gold of godly character and wisdom. Wouldn't we rather it be a simpler, more comfortable process? But we know life simply doesn't play out that way. Everything worthy in this world comes at a price.

The Russian writer Aleksandr Solzhenitsyn understood the fullest implications of that idea. The point was driven home for him during long years of solitude and suffering in prison, the price he paid for writing a few words of truth about his government. He knew something of disruptive moments and wrote, "It was only when I lay there on rotting prison straw that I sensed within myself the first stirrings of good. Gradually it was disclosed to me that the line separating good and evil passes, not through states, nor between classes, nor between political parties either, but right through every human heart, and through all human hearts. So bless you, prison, for having been in my life."[2]

Can I say, "Bless you, prison," about my deepest trials? Can you bless the prisons that loom in the bend of your road? It takes a deep

---

### Tried for a season, pure for eternity.

### —Warren Wiersbe

---

spiritual wisdom to cultivate that ability—a profound faith that God loves us and that His purposes are truly right for us.

M. Scott Peck begins his bestseller *The Road Less Traveled* with three simple, indisputable words: "Life is difficult." Who will argue with that? Life *is* difficult.

My cancer diagnosis confirmed Peck's words. It was a profoundly disruptive moment in my life. This was no mere bump in the road; it felt like a gigantic and bottomless pothole. It opened up in my road quite suddenly, with no highway markers to warn me, and I plunged into its darkness. I had not been offered alternate routes or given a vote on the matter.

Life is difficult, and difficulty is the only path to wisdom.

## One Great Challenge, Two Indispensable Passages

None of us enjoy suffering, but we can know one thing for certain: Disruptive moments are occasions for comforting one another. For example, I cherish the hope that my own disruptive moments will enable me to comfort you in yours. Perhaps I can pass along some nuggets of wisdom that came at the price of suffering in my own life.

Pain draws me to God's Word, and in the midst of my trials, I've spent countless hours in deep personal reflection upon Scripture.

I've been drawn repeatedly to two passages of Scripture: 2 Corinthians 12:7–10 and Hebrews 12:5–11. I invite you to take a few moments to reflect upon these passages with me; I think you'll see a recurring pattern in both texts.

Let's first look at 2 Corinthians 12:7–10:

> And lest I should be exalted above measure by the abundance of the revelations, a thorn in the flesh was given to me, a messenger of Satan to buffet me, lest I be exalted above measure. Concerning this thing I pleaded with the Lord three times that it might depart from me. And He said to me, "My grace is sufficient for you, for My strength is made perfect in weakness." Therefore most gladly I will rather boast in my infirmities, that the power of Christ may rest upon me. Therefore I take pleasure in infirmities, in reproaches, in needs, in persecutions, in distresses, for Christ's sake. For when I am weak, then I am strong.

This passage of Scripture describes a disruptive moment in the life of the apostle Paul. As we will see, Paul outlines for us the purpose, pain, provision, product, and perspective of this disruptive moment.

### The Purpose of the Disruptive Moment

"Lest I should be exalted above measure by the abundance of the revelations . . ." (v. 7).

Paul clearly states that the purpose of his suffering was to protect him from the sin of pride. In the preceding verses, Paul described a time in the past when he had been granted an opportunity to be caught up into the very heavens with God. Now that's certainly a remarkable opportunity! Such an experience had been granted to no other person, and Paul could have easily been filled with pride over his unique privilege. If Paul had a press agent, he would have most certainly billed Paul as the only man who had visited heaven and lived to tell about it. But God uses disruptive moments to help us keep things in perspective.

## The Pain of the Disruptive Moment

"A thorn in the flesh was given to me, a messenger of Satan to buffet me" (v. 7).

Scholars have spent untold hours speculating on the nature of Paul's problem. What was the affliction he was referring to? Some have suggested that Paul had developed eye problems, since we know that he began to dictate his letters to others. Another theory is that Paul was suffering from epileptic seizures. Sir William Ramsey even suggested that Paul had some recurring strain of malaria. You could fill a medical encyclopedia with other ideas that have been advanced: hysteria, hypochondria, gallstones, gout, rheumatism, sciatica, gastritis, leprosy, lice, deafness, dental infection, or remorse. Remorse? Don't forget that Paul had persecuted and tortured many Christians prior to his conversion.

Although we cannot be sure about Paul's "thorn," we can say this: The word used for *thorn* carries the literal meaning of *stake*. So what Paul wants to suggest to us is that he'd had a stake driven into his flesh—quite a disruptive moment, wouldn't you agree?

We're not told the specific nature of Paul's suffering, so we must conclude that the details are beside the point. What matters is that Paul did suffer in such a way that he compared it to the pain of a stake being pounded through his flesh. If we'd been told the exact nature of his affliction, this passage might have just seemed to be a story about Paul. We wouldn't be able to fill in the blank with our own personal afflictions, and our own "thorns" might seem outside the reach of God's grace. Instead, we're invited by 2 Corinthians 12:7–10 to identify with Paul's suffering. We're given the opportunity to realize that if God's grace was sufficient for him—whatever the nature of his suffering—it is sufficient for us as well.

## The Provision in the Disruptive Moment

"My grace is sufficient for you, for My strength is made perfect in weakness" (v. 9).

Paul didn't relish painful experiences any more than you or I do. In fact, he asked God three times to remove the thorn from his flesh. But God refused his request. He would not remove the thorn, but He would do something else—in the midst of the ordeal, He would give Paul all the grace he needed to continue his work. He also told Paul that His strength would be made perfect in this time of weakness.

Think of that: strength enshrined in weakness, power in pain. It completely defies and undermines the human approach to things— and that's why it glorifies God.

### The Product of the Disruptive Moment

"That the power of Christ may rest upon me. . . . For when I am weak, then I am strong" (vv. 9–10).

What God told Paul was merely this: "You won't lack the grace to do your job. You won't lack the strength to be my ambassador. But the creative difference will be this: Your weakness will serve to magnify the glory of My power in such a way that no one will ever again be able to explain your experience in human terms."

The weaker we are, the stronger His grace is revealed.

Or to put it another way: When "this little light of mine" becomes dimmer, His great floodlight shines all the more brightly.

### The Perspective of the Disruptive Moment

"Therefore most gladly I will rather boast in my infirmities, that the power of Christ may rest upon me" (v. 9).

What a perspective! Paul sees himself in the midst of this disruptive moment and says, "I'm not the same man that I used to be. I've suffered, and I've felt my share of pain, yet now I find within myself an inner depth, a spiritual dynamic I've never known before. I've entered into the deepest mystery of life—the fellowship of Christ's sufferings. And now that I see the meaning of it all, I wouldn't trade a moment of misery for pure gold. In the end, you see, our pain offers us a far greater wealth. I've had a thorn in my flesh, and I claim it as a badge of honor."

So the apostle Paul has told us all about his weakness. Was he simply a passive person? Don't even consider it! The briefest study of his life demonstrates that there was nothing passive about Paul. This was the man who had scoured the countryside in search of Christians to intimidate. This was the man who had successfully debated the apostles on the question of Gentile salvation. This was the man who had faced stonings and beatings for the sake of the gospel.

Paul chose the most hostile settings in which to preach the gospel and plant churches. He scattered seeds of the gospel throughout Asia Minor and along the Aegean Sea. As the seeds grew, he trained the first pastors and elders in all the new churches. And then, in his spare time, he wrote half the New Testament!

So please don't call him "passive." Paul was a mover and a shaker, a human dynamo. How, then, do we reconcile that with his claim to weakness? How can a man be both weak and strong?

The answer lies in the phrase, "when I am weak, then I am strong." That statement bears careful scrutiny. Listen well to Charles Stanley's eloquent paraphrase: "When I, Paul, in and of my own strength, am weak, then I, Paul, relying on the power of Christ in me, become strong, capable of whatever the Lord requires of me, full of energy and zeal to accomplish His will."[3]

Keep these principles in mind as we move to our second passage, Hebrews 12:5–11:

And you have forgotten the exhortation which speaks to you as to sons:

> "My son, do not despise the chastening of the LORD,
> Nor be discouraged when you are rebuked by Him;
> For whom the LORD loves He chastens,
> And scourges every son whom He receives."

If you endure chastening, God deals with you as with sons; for what son is there whom a father does not chasten? But if you are without

chastening, of which all have become partakers, then you are illegiti-
mate and not sons. Furthermore, we have had human fathers who corrected us, and we paid them respect. Shall we not much more readily be
in subjection to the Father of spirits and live? For they indeed for a few
days chastened us as seemed best to them, but He for our profit, that we
may be partakers of His holiness. Now no chastening seems to be joyful for the present, but grievous; nevertheless, afterward it yields the
peaceable fruit of righteousness to those who have been trained by it.


### The Purpose of the Disruptive Moment

"God deals with you as sons" (v. 7).

Can you remember facing a disruptive moment as a child? Perhaps
you fell from your bicycle and skinned your knee. What was your first
impulse? To call for help, of course. And perhaps when you did that,
your mother or father called out, "Stay right where you are—I'm coming to help you!"

That's precisely what God says to us: *Stay where you are. I'll be there with
you.* When life wounds us and we're in deep pain, we instinctively cry
out to God. And it is then that we hear Him and feel His presence so
clearly. In the midst of tragic circumstances, we can have the richest
fellowship with Christ afforded to us. That's when our faith becomes
fully real, and we experience the assurance of things we've hoped for.
We have confirmation in our hearts for what we've always believed
with our minds. We may have talked for a lifetime about being a child
of the Father, but now, as helpless creatures who have stumbled and
been wounded, it becomes true for us: *I am a child; He is my Father.*

He is your Father. You'll find it out at the bend in the road. At the
point of your own disruptive event, remember this truth. Engrave it
on your mind, and hold fast to it: *He is there for His children. He has always
been there, and He always will be there.* Can there be any doubt He will be
there in this place, and in this moment, for you?

The purpose of the disruptive moment is to demonstrate that we
are truly the children of God. There is no training and learning

without pain in the process. As we take our first steps as children, we stumble and fall. And every child that the Father loves will experience His training methods. No discipline, no growth—it's as simple as that. "Whom the LORD loves," He disciplines, chastens, and trains.

### The Pain of the Disruptive Moment

"He chastens, and scourges . . ." (v. 6).

Let's be clear: God's Word never claims that times of pain and suffering should be eagerly anticipated. These are not times we have chosen. At the point of suffering, we don't feel joy; we feel genuine human pain. But that's not the end of the story.

### The Provision of the Disruptive Moment

"For whom the LORD loves He chastens" (v. 6).

We find comfort in knowing the Father is watching over us. He sees us walk through the bend in the road, and though we don't anticipate the disruptive moment, He does. He is attentive, but He does more than watch us; He walks with us. And never does He walk closer to His children than those times when we're experiencing deep pain and misery.

### The Product of the Disruptive Moment

"He [disciplines us] for our profit, that we may be partakers of His holiness" (v. 10).

God's discipline is "for our profit," although it seems anything but profitable at the time. Just as earthly parents discipline their children so they will grow up to be well-adjusted and successful, our heavenly Father disciplines us so that we will "grow up" to "be partakers of His holiness."

*The Perspective of the Disruptive Moment*

The writer of Hebrews offers three possible choices we can make in response to the disruptive moments we face.

1. **We can despise the moment and rail against it (v. 5).** "Why did this happen to me? Why am I going through this? Why would God allow me to have this experience?" How quickly we're prone to strike out against God when we come to a bend in the road. Those who choose this course of action, of course, are shortsighted. They have probably forgotten all about God on those occasions when there were nice surprises around the bend. But now, disaster strikes. They don't know what else to do, so they curse God. The writer of Hebrews tells us not to do that. He says, "Do not despise the chastening of the LORD."

2. **We can become discouraged by the event, lose heart, and give up (v. 5).** The writer of Hebrews instructs us not to be discouraged when we are rebuked. That's far too easy a response. Discouragement makes us want to give up, to throw in the towel and surrender to despair. That's not the spirit God wants in us. His goal is our perseverance, for it leads to growth and maturity, as we shall see.

3. **We can endure it and be trained by it (vv. 7, 11).** Finally—the right response. The Scriptures show us so clearly that nothing in life is wasted if we love and serve God. No matter how sharp the bend in the road, no matter how disruptive the moment, *everything* that happens to us is for the eternal purposes of God. He is training us through the process. Like any worthy parent, He wants to teach us what we cannot learn in any other way.

British journalist Malcolm Muggeridge wisely explained this concept to William F. Buckley: "As an old man, Bill, looking back on one's life, it's one of the things that strikes you most forcibly—that the only thing that's taught one anything is suffering. Not success, not happiness, not anything like that. The only thing that really teaches one what life's about—the joy of understanding, the joy of coming in contact with what life really signifies—is suffering, affliction."[4]

The only road that leads to the destination God desires for us has its sharp bends. All attempted shortcuts lead into wilderness.

Where are you, traveler? Perhaps you're facing a disruptive moment in your life, one you could never have anticipated. Perhaps your road has led to a divorce, a death, a financial disaster, a physical or mental sickness, or the heartbreak of seeing a fellow traveler wander away from the path. Maybe the bend in your road is something so disappointing and devastating that you can hardly bear to acknowledge

---

*I bear willing witness that I owe more to the fire, and the hammer, and the file, than to anything else in my Lord's workshop. I sometimes question whether I have ever learned anything except through the rod. When my schoolroom is darkened, I see most.*

**—Charles Spurgeon**

---

it. You could be standing by the side of your path, so overcome by pain that you believe you can't move on.

Please remember this: Your crisis is important to God. Could it be that you're looking at it from your own perspective? That's not the way our Father behaves toward us. Whatever struggle or setback you face is intended to empower and purify you. Your situation is important to Him, because He is using it to make you a more valuable servant in His kingdom.

Having lived through some very disruptive moments of my own, I want to give you five principles to remember. They've helped me, and I trust they'll be just as valuable in your own travels down that long and winding road.

## Five Principles to Remember

### Principle #1: Disruptive Moments Are Often Divine Appointments

Second Corinthians 12 identifies Satan as the messenger sent to test and torment Paul. But the devil wasn't given free rein; he couldn't do anything to Paul that God wouldn't allow. Remember Job? Satan was allowed to test him, but only with the permission and conditions prescribed by God. Paul and Job always remembered that God was ultimately in control.

The Father is the One who disciplines His sons—Hebrews 12 makes that very clear. Every trial we face, difficult as it may be, comes from the hand of God, who loves us and wants us to grow. If we're wise enough, we will see that disruptive moments are really divine appointments.

That perspective will make all the difference for you. It will keep you from lashing out at God in despair. It will keep you from giving in to discouragement. You will say, "God, You are in control—You have a plan, and that's why You have allowed this to happen in my life."

Some years ago I was given a copy of a letter that I can imagine being written by God to someone going through a disruptive moment. It remains as poignant and pertinent now as it did then.

My child, I have a message for you today; let Me whisper it in your ear, that it may gild with glory any storm clouds which may arise, and smooth the rough places upon which you may have to tread. It is short—only five words—but let them sink into your inmost soul; use them as a pillow upon which to rest your weary head:

## THIS THING IS FROM ME

Have you ever thought of it, that all that concerns you, concerns Me, too? for "he that touches you, touches the apple of His eye" (Zechariah 2:8).

I would have you learn, when temptations assail you, and the "enemy comes in like a flood," that this thing is from Me; that your weakness needs My might, and your safety lies in letting Me fight for you.

You are very "precious in My sight" (Isaiah 43:4). Therefore it is My special delight to educate you.

Are you in money difficulties? Is it hard to make both ends meet? This thing is from Me, for I am your purse-bearer, and would have you draw from and depend upon Me. My supplies are limitless

(Philippians 4:19). I would have you prove My promises. Let it not be said of you, "you did not believe the LORD your God" (Deuteronomy 1:32).

Are you in difficult circumstances, surrounded by people who do not understand you, who never consult your taste, who put you in the background? This thing is from Me. I am the God of circumstances. You came not to this place by accident; it is the very place God meant for you. Have you not asked to be made humble? See, then, I have placed you in the very school where this lesson is taught; your surroundings and companions are only working out My will.

Are you passing through a night of sorrow? This thing is from Me. I am the "Man of Sorrows, and acquainted with grief." I have let earthly comforters fail you, that, by turning to Me, you may obtain everlasting consolation (2 Thessalonians 2:16, 17).

Has some friend disappointed you? One to whom you opened out your heart? This thing is from Me. I have allowed this disappointment to come, that you may learn.

I want to be your Confidant. Has someone repeated things about you that are untrue? Leave them to Me, and draw closer to Me, thy shelter out of reach of "the strife of tongues," for I "shall bring forth My righteousness as the light, and My judgment as the noonday" (Psalm 37:6).

Have your plans been upset? Are you bowed down and weary? This thing is from Me. You made your plans, then came asking Me to bless them; but I would have you let Me plan for you, and then I take the responsibility; for "this thing is too much for you, you are not able to perform it by yourself" (Exodus 18:18). You are only an instrument, not an agent.

Have you longed to do some great work for Me, and instead been laid aside on a bed of pain and weakness? This thing is from Me. I could not get your attention in your busy days, and I want to teach you some of My deepest lessons. "They also serve who only stand and wait." Some of My greatest workers are those shut out from active service, that they may learn to wield the weapon of prayer.

Are you suddenly called upon to occupy a difficult and responsible position? Launch out on Me. I am trusting you with the possession of difficulties. "For this thing the LORD your God will bless you in all your works and in all to which you put your hand" (Deuteronomy 15:10).

This day I place in your hands this pot of holy oil, make use of it freely, My child. Let every circumstance as it arises, every word that pains you, every interruption that would make you impatient, every revelation of your own weakness, be anointed with it! Remember, interruptions are divine instructions. The sting will go as you learn to see Me in all things.

Therefore "set your hearts on all the words which I testify among you today . . . for it is not a futile thing for you, because it is your life, and by this word you shall prolong your days in the land" (Deuteronomy 32:46, 47).[5]

The moment we accept the fact that our ordeal has been permitted, even intended by God, our perspective on disruptive moments will totally change. We will find ourselves saying, "God, You have allowed this in my life. I don't understand it, but I know that it couldn't have happened to me unless it was filtered through Your loving hands. So, this thing is from You."

*Principle #2: Progress without Pain Is Usually Not Possible*

We live in a skin-deep world. Our culture glorifies clothing, fashion, makeup, tummy tucks, and nose jobs. There may be nothing wrong with any of these, but in the end they are only cosmetic. Character and substance are shaped in the crucible of adversity. Show me someone who lives a carefree life with no problems or trials or dark nights of the soul, and I'll show you a shallow person.

Ron Mehl, another pastor who has battled cancer, summarizes this point succinctly: "[Disruptive moments] always leave us with a list of things to clean up and fix. They are times when God restores to us the things we lose through negligence, ignorance, rebellion, or sin. For the Christian, [disruptive moments] are no-lose propositions. They help us to see and acknowledge the loose shutters, missing shingles, and rotten fence posts in our lives while turning us back to the only One who can make the necessary repairs."6

Unless there is pain in the formula, we will never stop to listen carefully to what He is saying. We'll be moving along happily, thinking we're going somewhere—but in reality, we're only spinning our wheels. We're not making any progress at all toward the deeper things our Father longs to show us. Sometimes He must allow us to stumble along the everyday journey. We're wounded and filled with pain, yet our disaster is just the opposite of what it seems; it's the demonstration of God's "tough love"—His determination to teach us and to make us wiser and stronger.

Life, then, brings all of us disruptions. It's up to us to choose our response. It can make us bitter, or it can make us better.

If we choose to let the disruptive moment make us better, we will toughen up. We will face the bend in the road with courage. Listen again to Gordon MacDonald: "The spiritual masters have taught us . . . that the one who would get in touch with his soul must do so with diligence and determination. One must overcome feelings, fatigue, distractions, errant appetites, and popular opinion. One must not be afraid of silence, of stillness, or of entering the overpowering presence of divinity with a humble spirit."7

### Principle #3: The Promise of God Is the Provision of Grace

As we've delved into these two strategic biblical passages, we've seen one urgent theme that seems to stand out in bold letters. It is the voice of God saying to us over and over, "My grace is sufficient. My strength is made perfect in weakness. You are My son, and I will deal with you as My son." I'd like to direct you to one more snapshot from Scripture that completes the picture of God's provision in times of pain. You'll find it in John 15:1–8. In this passage, Jesus borrows a word picture from the plant kingdom. He explains that because He loves us, He must do some pruning in order for us to thrive and blossom. Do you understand how this principle works in gardening? Even with green things, God's concept of discipline holds true.

But the Gardener is loving and devoted. Someone has said, "The Father is never closer to the vine than when He is pruning it." That statement is right on the mark. You will find this truth consistently affirmed in the lives of wise, godly people who have faced disruptive moments. They will look at you and say without hesitation, "Never in all my life have I sensed the closeness and provision of God as I did when I came to the bend in the road. Never before have I been more fruitful than I've been since I came through the bend in the road."

*Principle #4: Disruptive Moments Produce Dynamic Growth*

We've looked at three Scripture passages together. They've yielded for us three specific products of adversity in the Christian life:

| | |
|---|---|
| 2 Corinthians 12:7–10 | More Power |
| Hebrews 12:5–11 | More Holiness |
| John 15:1–8 | More Fruit |

You can struggle against the disruptive moment, shake your fist at the heavens, and find yourself exhausted, defeated, and in despair—or you can accept the moment and let it train and strengthen you. The three passages above tell us that if you take the latter course, you'll discover on the other side more power, more holiness, and more fruit. Those are precious gifts that cannot be purchased with any coin other than tears. When you possess them, you'll comprehend with joy what God wanted so much for you to experience in your life.

God allows no pain without purpose. Instead, He uses pain to dispense power. His power can rest upon you only when you've abandoned the idea that you're big enough to go it alone. You're not big enough; you'll never make it without depending utterly upon Him and going in His strength. You're destined to fail without righteous-ness and holiness. And some pruning must take place, with sharpened shears, to cut away those things that would prevent righteousness and

---

*Those who navigate little streams and shallow creeks, know but little of the God of tempests; but those who "do business in great waters'" these see His "wonders in the deep." Among the huge Atlantic waves of bereavement, poverty, temptation, and reproach, we learn the power of Jehovah, because we feel the littleness of man.*

**—Charles Spurgeon**

---

holiness in your life. But how liberated you will be, how free to grow toward the heavens, after that pruning is accomplished!

Every plant, of course, must weather a storm every now and then. Ron Mehl has written, "Someone once told me that the times when plants grow the most are not necessarily during the warm, gentle rains or beautiful summer days. In fact, during fierce winds and raging storms come times of the most growth. Botanists tell us that if you were to take a cross-section of the earth during a vicious storm, you could literally observe the roots reaching further down into the soil."[8]

Can you feel it when the heavens open up and the wind and the rains thrash you? Can you feel your roots reaching ever deeper into His loving care?

*Principle #5: What We Receive from Disruptive Moments Depends upon How We Respond*

I remember so well the time when I came to my bend in the road. Everything God had given me to do was growing and thriving. The size of our church had doubled. The number of listeners to our *Turning Point* nationwide radio ministry had doubled. The books I had written were finding larger audiences. People were responding to our ministry. All of this was for the glory of God. And then, right in the midst of all these blessings came the disruptive moment. On the face of things, it seemed to make so little sense.

Have you had that kind of experience? Just when you had everything lined up in your life exactly as you wanted things to be, you experienced an unwelcome and unanticipated disaster that spoiled everything. And you asked many questions, all beginning with the word *why*.

"Why this, Lord?" you might ask. "Why now? Why not later? Why not someone else?"

We all ask the "why" questions. They're a natural part of being human. But we can ask better questions—we can ask "what" questions: "What, Lord? What would You have me do? What are You trying to teach me?"

I've faced pain, disappointment, doubt, and despair. In the midst of my trials, I've stopped asking the "why" questions and begun to focus on the "what" questions. I've told you the story of my terrifying medical diagnosis in 1994. But God wasn't through with me yet. I faced one more bend in the road; you'll read about it later in the book. In each of the following chapters, you'll hear from fellow strugglers and consider the deep message of hope that flows from the beautiful poetry of the psalms. You and I will share together the lessons the Lord offers so graciously to those who stumble and struggle.

I pray that the words of hope you'll find in this book will uplift and comfort you as they have me. And I hope my prayer becomes your prayer too:

> *Lord, what do You want to teach me to make me a better person? What are Your plans to make me more effective? Lead me and guide me through this process, O Lord. Be my teacher; show me Your ways. And don't let me miss any lesson You've prepared for me.*

# Psalm 71

1 In You, O LORD, I put my trust;
   Let me never be put to shame.
2 Deliver me in Your righteousness, and cause me to escape;
   Incline Your ear to me, and save me.
3 Be my strong habitation,
   To which I may resort continually;
   You have given the commandment to save me,
   For You are my rock and my fortress.
4 Deliver me, O my God, out of the hand of the wicked,
   Out of the hand of the unrighteous and cruel man.
5 For You are my hope, O Lord GOD;
   You are my trust from my youth.
6 By You I have been upheld from my birth;
   You are He who took me out of my mother's womb.
   My praise shall be continually of You.
7 I have become as a wonder to many,
   But You are my strong refuge.
8 Let my mouth be filled with Your praise
   And with Your glory all the day.
9 Do not cast me off in the time of old age;
   Do not forsake me when my strength fails.
10 For my enemies speak against me;
   And those who lie in wait for my life take counsel together,
11 Saying, "God has forsaken him;
   Pursue and take him, for there is none to deliver him."
12 O God, do not be far from me;
   O my God, make haste to help me!
13 Let them be confounded and consumed
   Who are adversaries of my life;

Let them be covered with reproach and dishonor
Who seek my hurt.

14 But I will hope continually,
And will praise You yet more and more.

15 My mouth shall tell of Your righteousness
And Your salvation all the day,
For I do not know their limits.

16 I will go in the strength of the Lord GOD;
I will make mention of Your righteousness, of Yours only.

17 O God, You have taught me from my youth;
And to this day I declare Your wondrous works.

18 Now also when I am old and grayheaded,
O God, do not forsake me,
Until I declare Your strength to this generation,
Your power to everyone who is to come.

19 Also Your righteousness, O God, is very high,
You who have done great things;
O God, who is like You?

20 You, who have shown me great and severe troubles,
Shall revive me again,
And bring me up again from the depths of the earth.

21 You shall increase my greatness,
And comfort me on every side.

22 Also with the lute I will praise you—
And Your faithfulness, O my God!
To You I will sing with the harp,
O Holy One of Israel.

23 My lips shall greatly rejoice when I sing to You,
And my soul, which You have redeemed.

24 My tongue also shall talk of Your righteousness all the day long;
For they are confounded,
For they are brought to shame
Who seek my hurt.

# 2
# Psalm for a Dark Night

Lord, Just today I read
That Paul and Silas were
Stripped and beaten
With wooden whips.
"Again and again the rods
Slashed across their bared backs"
But in their desolate dungeon
Their feet clamped in stocks
They prayed.
They sang.
They praised.
In this musty midnight of my life
Imprisoned in the dungeon of confusion
Bound by chains of anguish
Help me, please help me
To pray
To sing
To praise
Until the foundation shakes
Until the gates fling open
Until the chains fall off
Until I am free
To share the Good News
With other chain-bound prisoners.

—RUTH HARMS CALKIN,
 *TELL ME AGAIN, LORD, I FORGET*

Three o'clock in the morning.

At that darkest and most dismal of hours, there may be no silence deeper than the silence of a hospital corridor. During my stay at Green Hospital, I became closely acquainted with the time and the desolate feeling of it.

I also became acquainted with the feeling of morphine. When you reach a point at which you must be involved with such a terrifying medication, you are desperate indeed. My morphine drip was a distinctly uncomfortable all-day, all-night arrangement. Those of you who have experienced this medication know that morphine is a powerful and frightening narcotic, one that causes unpredictable reactions for different people.

My reaction to the drug was a waking nightmare of confusion and disorientation. I could only manage short periods of sleep punctuated by sudden, startled consciousness—like being shaken violently awake. After this jarring sensation, I would be unsure where I was, what day it might be, or what was happening to me. That was the pattern of my life: moments of sleep, moments of confusion. It lasted for about five days that all blurred together like an unpleasant dream.

The nights were worst, of course; they were long and dark and lonely. I remember waking abruptly one night, looking around with grogginess at the bed and the darkened room, and doing the best I could to get my bearings. There was nothing on my mind, with the exception of a Scripture passage that seemed to be lingering in wait for me. How had that biblical passage lodged in my mind?

I slowly began to remember. A friend had been talking to me about those verses. He had a sense of urgency about my need to read Psalm 71. "This is a psalm you've got to read, pastor!" he had said. And now, wide awake at 3:00 A.M., I decided this was a pretty good time to take his suggestion.

## A Light Shining in Darkness

Beneath the fluorescent light from my headboard, I reached for my Bible and turned to the psalm. Was this a good time to be reading the

Bible, with my mind addled by morphine? I knew in my heart it was indeed the right moment. I understood that God's power is greater than morphine, and He proved it once more in the stillness of a hospital ward. God's Spirit reached out to my soul through the inspired words of Psalm 71 and brought me comfort and assurance. Once again, like so many times before, His hand gathered me up through the Scriptures and pulled me into His powerful embrace. In the late-night loneliness and lack of a sound mind, I found blessed hope.

It doesn't matter how deep is the pit we've stumbled into—we can always grasp at that ray of heavenly hope. For example, consider the plight of Lawrence Hanratty. Here is how the media covered it:

> Jolted, jilted, hammered in a car crash and robbed, Lawrence Hanratty was named Friday as the unluckiest man in New York.
>
> Nearly electrocuted in a construction site accident in 1984 that put him in a coma for weeks, Hanratty lost the lawyers fighting for his liability claim—one was disbarred, two died—and his wife ran off with her lawyer.
>
> Hanratty, who spent years fighting heart and liver disease, had his car wrecked in a crash last year. When police left the scene of the accident, he was held up and robbed.
>
> "I say to myself, 'How much more am I going to be tested in life to see how much I can endure?'" Hanratty told the *New York Daily News* in a description of more than 10 years of agony.
>
> As if he hasn't tolerated enough hardship, 38-year-old Hanratty of Mt. Vernon, N.Y., said an insurance company now wants to cut off his worker's compensation benefits and his landlord has threatened to kick him out of his apartment.
>
> Depressed and suffering from agoraphobia, a fear of open spaces, Hanratty uses a canister of oxygen and takes 42 pills a day for his heart and liver ailments. But with help from neighbors and a New York state assemblyman, he is not giving up yet.
>
> "There's always hope," he said.[1]

"There's always hope," Mr. Hanratty was able to say, despite how little evidence life had given him to believe it. Have you ever been at the threshold of surrender? Have you been at the point of discarding your faith by the side of the road or requesting an extended sick leave from God's army? I've been there. And someone else has too. He recorded his feelings in Psalm 71.

Who wrote this psalm? We usually find the author's name inscribed at the top of the psalm. Turn to Psalm 23 and you'll read, "A Psalm of David." But Psalm 71 is interesting: The author has chosen to remain anonymous. All the same, I feel confident that it was written by David, who is giving us a kind of sequel to Psalm 70, the preceding one. These verses take up right where the previous ones leave off. And there's a fascinating and quite tragic story to be found in the background if we peek behind the curtains.

There was a time in King David's life when one of his sons, a young man named Adonijah, tried to usurp his father's throne. David had promised the title to another of his sons, Solomon. So political turmoil and family warfare were all entangled. Some scholars feel that David wrote these psalms during that heartrending time of family discord.

Can you imagine it? Here is elderly King David, nearing the end of his amazing life. He has brought the young nation of Israel to its greatest peak of power and stability. In the midst of building a dynasty, he has already survived a previous family insurrection. Absalom, his heir, had turned on his father and attempted to seize the throne. The cost to King David of his son's insurrection was horrendously heavy, including the life of Absalom and the unity of his people. Now his son Adonijah is attempting to steal what has been promised to Solomon. The whole nightmare seems to be coming to pass again. When you read about David's life, you realize you've only *thought* you had family turmoil.

David's aging heart was burdened with a deep grief you and I are probably incapable of beginning to comprehend. Had he served God so long for such a reward as this? David knew he'd made serious mistakes in his younger years, and he understood that his sin would bring consequences to be worked out in turmoil for both his family and his kingdom. Even so, this was a heavy price for a father who deeply loved his sons and the godly nation that had been entrusted to him. No pain exceeds that of an anguished and heartbroken parent, and David was suffering to the very core of his being.

Psalm 71 is an incredible jewel in the Scriptures. It's not lengthy—a mere twenty-four verses. And yet hidden within these double-dozen lines are at least fifty quotations or allusions to other psalms. The psalmist brought all of these references together in his troubled mind, considered them from the lens of a lifetime of godly wisdom, and pieced them all together in a mosaic masterpiece of heartfelt poetry. As you read it, you may begin to understand the amazing comfort and healing it brought to me at 3:00 A.M. in a silent hospital room. My mind began to take leave of my own troubles recalling the sorrows of an ancient king in a faraway land and the message of peace and liberation that came out of his despair.

## The Reality of Trials in the Believer's Life

There is a strange idea going around in churches today. Some Christians have the odd impression that being a believer will exempt them from all problems. Somehow they feel that, upon conversion, they're

---

*There is nothing, no circumstance, no trouble, no testing that can ever touch me until, first of all, it has come past God and past Christ, right through to me. If it has come that far, it has come with a great purpose.*

**—Alan Redpath**

---

issued the spiritual equivalent of ID cards that say, "This absolves the holder from any kind of pain or trouble while living on this planet."

It simply doesn't work that way. We Christians have no immunity whatsoever to pain or suffering. It matters not whether you're a new convert or a wise spiritual giant, you're still an imperfect human creature living in a fallen world, you struggle with all the blessings and burdens being a member of the family of man entails. When we become part of God's own family, what sets us apart is not any difference in the sin environment around us, but in how we deal with it.

Peter wrote, "Beloved, do not think it strange concerning the fiery trial which is to try you, as though some strange thing happened to you" (1 Pet. 4:12). In other words, don't be surprised if you give your life to Jesus Christ and you still stumble and take a fall the next day. You've gained no special right to bypass the human condition of suffering.

In Psalm 71 we find a poet who knew something about suffering. He saw his life as a pathway moving steeply uphill and filled with treacherous obstacles—a hill to be climbed in a lifetime of diligence and humility. He describes for us in passionate phrasing the view he sees as he looks upward to the horizon. Like any inspired poet, he compels us to look through his eyes, see that hill in every detail, and recognize it as our own. Then it becomes possible for us to begin to understand why we must climb that steep hill and why we face obstacles.

### Trials Because of Ungodly Foes

"Deliver me, O my God, out of the hand of *the wicked*, out of the hand of the *unrighteous and cruel man*" (v. 4; emphasis added).

David had some very dangerous enemies, and they were creating tremendous anxiety in his life. The word *cruel* comes from the same Hebrew word that is sometimes translated "leaven." It means this enemy was not only wicked, but he was also spreading his wickedness every way he could, as leaven spreads outward in the rising of bread dough. His evil was permeating the layers around itself like a contagion, infecting all that it touched.

This is a problem that is very simple: We have enemies to contend with. You may not have soldiers hunting you down, as David did, but someone may be angry with you at work. Perhaps he is angry with God, and because he knows about your faith, he focuses all the heat of his rage on you. You, as a believer, become the symbol of everything in life that has confused and infuriated him, so he tries to make your life miserable. I know Christians whose lives have been turned upside down because of another individual's unprovoked attack. It can happen, and it can happen to you.

## Trials Because of an Uncertain Future

"Do not cast me off in the time of old age; do not forsake me when my strength fails" (v. 9).

Sometimes the enemy is a bit more subtle. For example, could your enemy be a faceless foe such as aging? David answers in the affirmative in Psalm 71:9.

May I share something with you? At 3:00 A.M., all alone in my hospital room during a morphine drip, I did see aging as my enemy. I was reading this psalm, and I knew exactly what the psalmist meant. The very passage of time itself can become a trial to us. It seems as if the years have coldly discarded us by the side of the road while younger, stronger, and livelier feet sprint past us on the path. We hear the youthful laughter and feel the weight of our years. David pleads with God, "Do not cast me off in the time of old age; do not forsake me when my strength fails." That was my prayer, too, while hooked up to machines in a silent and lonely hospital wing.

Aging, of course, will bring illness, as much as we may choose to live in denial of the fact. I remember my self-satisfied feelings about my sunny health as I progressed through my physical examination in 1994. The last word I expected to hear was *cancer*. But as with any member of the human race, the more the aging process encroached on me, the greater became the possibilities I might encounter that disease. When the reality of it came to pass, I simply had to face it. I didn't vote for it; I didn't receive a notice in the mail from the surgeon general. Cancer is no respecter of persons. One of the facts about humanity is aging and all that comes with it. It's a trial we all must face.

### Trials Because of Unfaithful Friends

"For my *enemies* speak against me; and *those who lie in wait for my life* take counsel together, saying, 'God has forsaken him; pursue and take him, for there is none to deliver him.' O God, do not be far from me; O my God, make haste to help me! Let them be confounded and consumed who are *adversaries of my life;* let them be covered with reproach and dishonor *who seek my hurt*" (vv. 10–13; emphasis added).

Some trials come from those who aren't even enemies in the truest sense. We can be hurt by the very people who are closest to us. The coalition causing the trouble in this particular passage was not made up of Philistines or other foreign tribe. No, David's enemies were people within his own circle, from his own family. Among them were his sons, Absalom and Adonijah. These two beloved sons had each tried to usurp the throne. In this case, Adonijah sought to turn his own father's advancing years against him. He saw his elderly father as a ripe target for a power play. I urge you to think about that for a moment and to try to imagine how it must have broken a father's heart.

Sometimes the deepest cut is inflicted from the closest range. No wound is quite so painful as the one inflicted by someone we love and trust. Families are experiencing discord all over our country today. How tragic it is when people turn against their most basic social unit. My friends in the legal profession tell me that the bitterest and most painful scenes they ever encounter are in divorce courts. Men and women who were once bound to each other by vows of faithfulness and undying love have now become the fiercest of enemies intent on striking out at each other and inflicting pain.

A house divided against itself is a terrible trial indeed.


### Trials Because of an Unparalleled Heavenly Father

"Also Your righteousness, O God, is very high. You who have done great things; O God, who is like You? You . . . have shown me great and severe troubles" (vv. 19–20).

There is another way to look at trials, one that will require you to see them through a completely different lens. Trials can come through friends or enemies or aging, but they can also come from God Himself. Does that idea shock you?

Parents are less likely to be shocked. They can remember times when they had to allow their children to experience hardships they might easily have removed. Fathers and mothers are tempted to hover over a child, swooping in to deflect any temptation or threat that comes into the child's path. But something called love prevents them from doing that. Wise parents love their children enough to allow them to experience pain, for that shocking pain can teach things the wisest words of parents can't. As much as parents suffer when their children are hurting, they would suffer more if their children were never allowed to grow into all the wisdom and maturity intended for them.

Some things can't be learned through lectures; they must come at the cost of burned fingers or skinned knees. Parents know that, and they're able to comprehend the fact that God is another Parent—a perfect one—who must allow suffering in His own children to facilitate their growth. It's important to understand that God doesn't coldly stand aside during the trials we experience any more than you are aloof during your own children's episodes of poor decisions and unwanted consequences. Loving parents find themselves pacing the floor and praying intently as they watch the struggles of their children. They know deep in their hearts that their beloved children will come out of it wiser and more mature, but those parents hurt with their children just the same.

God sends trouble into our lives to strengthen us and to make us better children in His family. David recognizes this and, in essence, says, "God, You did it. You have shown me severe troubles." Doesn't that seem like a strange thing to thank God for?

No, because the psalmist realizes God loves us. As we saw in the last chapter, those whom the Lord loves, He chastens.

## The Result of Trials in the Believer's Life

We could imagine an infinite number of different kinds of trials. And the number of potential responses to these trials are also limitless. Anything can happen to us; many roads can be chosen by us. Our choices will determine what kind of people we turn out to be.

I've often been asked how it felt to learn I had cancer. "Were you afraid?" people ask. Absolutely! I was *desperately* afraid. There's no disputing that. Was I afraid to die? No. I'm not afraid to leave this life, although I'm not eager to do so either. A good bit of my fear focused on losing precious years with the people I love. Some of it was simply about pain. Some of it was about the unknown. How would you respond to the news that you were suffering from a possibly fatal disease? Imagine the thoughts and feelings that might flood your heart at such a time, and you'll know the same things I experienced.

Let's examine a few of those feelings:

### Vulnerability

Most of us live under the illusion of invulnerability; particularly when we're young; particularly, too, I think, when we're male. Men enjoy the delicious illusion of controlling their own destiny. We determine our own fate (or perceive we're doing so) by acting and taking things into our own hands. We feel we've got it all figured out, and everything is under control. Look us up fifty years from now—we'll be playing with our great-grandchildren. We'll live forever! We live in the illusion of invulnerability.

The first thing a serious crisis does is burst that pleasant bubble. Suddenly everything we've believed about life seems to be shattered. Our lives are in chaos just when everything seemed to be in such fine order.

Psalm 71:7 says it this way: "I have become as a wonder to many, but You are my strong refuge." What was David talking about?

David was a king. He knew that everyone was watching him to see what he'd do. If you happen to be a Christian leader, you know how absolutely true this is. When I announced that I had cancer, I knew exactly what people were saying: "David Jeremiah has been preaching all this 'faith in God' stuff for thirty years now. He's been 'talking the talk' just fine. But now he's living it out. How is he going to handle it? Can he 'walk the walk'?"

That's the position David found himself in. Everyone knew the awful details of his dysfunctional family. He was not only the king, but also the man who talked to everyone about God. Now he seemed to have feet of clay. What was he going to do?

David didn't know what to do, but he knew enough to watch God to find out what God would do. The king didn't have all the answers, but he knew Someone who did. He was wise enough to know the limits of his own wisdom.

If you're lacking in that ability, a sense of vulnerability will enhance it for you. You'll be painfully aware of your limitations. And you'll turn in abject humility to the only One in the entire universe who is indeed invulnerable.

### Insecurity

In Psalm 71:2, David cries out, "Deliver me in Your righteousness, and cause me to escape!"

Can you identify with that? It's the most basic cry the soul can release: *Lord, I want out!* Stop the world; I want to get off! Oh, how we'd love to simply wake up tomorrow morning and find that God has miraculously removed us from the crisis. Where do we go to reclaim the security and confidence we had so recently? We want things the way they were.

We've already heard David's words, "Do not cast me off in the time of old age; do not forsake me when my strength fails" (v. 9). Can you see the insecurity and loss expressed in those words? Remember the bold and courageous kind of man David was. But time and circumstances and failure have removed any illusions he had of being in control of his own destiny. He no longer buys into the illusion of invulnerability.

And that's not a bad thing. One commentator has called Psalm 71 "a psalm for a godly old man." I like the "godly" part, don't you? The "old man" part, well, that will have to grow on me. But this psalm does lay out a path for those who have traveled a great distance on the trail of life, progressed in years, and entered some of the wastelands. This psalm shows how to crown our mature years with godliness.

As we age, our natural defenses against life's injuries begin to erode. Perhaps we've retired and no longer have that cherished career to lean upon. Our income is no longer disposable. Our eyes are weaker, our joints are fragile, and our energy is fleeting. And we begin to see the names of our friends in the morning paper, no longer as the movers and shakers who dominate the business page, but in the section that gives the details of funeral services. What a humbling passage of life that is. Little by little, we're stripped of all the things in life that have lent us security. It's a season of slowly developing anxiety.

If we choose the right path, we find ourselves hurrying into the presence of God for true security and ultimate comfort. We've seen the worst of life. Now we're capable of understanding just how much we really depend on Him. We finally believe that indeed life is a vapor, as the Scriptures say. We have nothing to count on but our loving Father.

David wrote many psalms about hurrying into God's presence in fear and trembling. It's certainly one of the great themes of the psalms, and I've always found it interesting that he uses three key metaphors: "God, You are my strong *refuge* . . . You are my *rock* and my *fortress*" (emphasis added).

David was under attack from his own children. He had spent a lifetime building a strong and secure kingdom, and now he could feel it drifting out of his grasp. In the midst of his insecurity, he found that God was his refuge, his rock, and his fortress. And he fled into the comfort and safety of those walls.

Perhaps you've seen the film *Lawrence of Arabia*. The real T. E. Lawrence, who was a secret agent during the First World War, often engaged in desert guerrilla warfare against the Turks. The enemy forces who chased Lawrence constantly often felt they had him hemmed in and trapped. But he would ride to his hidden desert fortress. He was never too far away from it, and if worse came to worst, he could flee there, find safety, and strengthen himself on the ample provisions of food and water. Lawrence had a refuge, a rock, and a fortress in the dangers of the wilderness. But God provides a much better one for you and me.

In those times when we feel the hostile forces of the world pursuing us, we long for a strong refuge. As we feel suddenly exposed and vulnerable and our feet are unsteady in the shifting sands beneath us, we yearn for a rock and a fortress—the kind of security found only in God.

## Dependency

A powerful leader is invariably self-reliant and independent. It simply comes with the territory. He charts his own course and depends on his own resources. But sooner or later, he reaches his limit. Whether age or enemies overtake him, he finds he's not self-reliant after all. When trials come, the greatest leaders of all, the wisest ones, will then turn their eyes toward heaven. When their power hits its limit, they'll

---

*As I lift up my eyes to Him, and accept it as coming from the throne of God for some great purpose of blessing for my own heart, no sorrow will ever disturb me, no trial will ever disarm me, no circumstance will ever cause me to fret, for I shall rest in the joy of what my Lord is.*

**—Alan Redpath**

---

seek a power higher than themselves and begin to experience a feeling of dependency.

In that moment of transformation, we suddenly realize, "I don't control my world after all! I could become a victim, no matter how smart or sly or strong or elusive I may be. Lord, I have nowhere to turn. I have no more ideas and nowhere to run or hide. Dear God, if You don't stand firm and strong for me, then all is lost and I have no hope. Only You can rescue me."

Now you may be thinking, *This is true, but I've still got a ways to go. I'm fairly young. These are all things that don't need to concern me right now.* Think again. Your clock is ticking, and your time will come far more quickly than you ever felt possible. No one has ever said, "I thought I would never grow old. My youth seemed endless!" Every human clock ticks off the moments toward vulnerability, insecurity, and dependency.

*Emergency*

David says, "Make haste to help me!" (v. 12). In other words, "Lord, can You speed it up just a little bit? Yes, I've been told that You have Your own timetable, and I know that's reasonable, but can You scratch some things out and move my appointment up just a little bit? I promise not to ask again. This is an emergency!"

Isn't that the way we all feel when we make the heavenly 911 call?

I have a lot of reasons to love the psalms. I could spend eternity detailing them for you. Among the greatest of all my reasons is that they were written by genuine, historical people who faced trials no different from the ones you and I face. And these ordinary people expressed themselves accordingly. The psalmists made no attempt to put a spin on things. There were no editors with red pencils marking out the really tough expressions of emotions. They just told it like it was and let the words fly. Their tough, painful, and starkly honest words are there for you and me as part of God's Word.

David could certainly let the words fly when he felt a sense of urgency. He felt all the despair and panic of any man in pain. But he also leads us, time after time, to an understanding that completely changes our attitudes. This understanding is expressed in these questions: Are there truly such things as emergencies from the heavenly viewpoint? Is God ever taken by surprise? Is He ever alarmed? Does He panic? For each of these questions, the answer can only be an emphatic, "No!"

This is a tremendously difficult perspective for us to master and maintain: *We move in time, but God operates in eternity.* He sees the end from the beginning. He cannot be taken by surprise, for our past, present, and future are before Him and in His grip all at once. An emergency to you or me is an opportunity in the great mosaic of His purposes, a useful occasion for building our trust, stretching our faith, teaching us to hope, and nurturing our patience. As Paul wrote, "Hope that is seen is no hope at all. Who hopes for what he already has? But if we hope for what we do not yet have, we wait for it patiently" (Rom. 8:24–25 NIV). This is known as perspective, the lens through which you choose to look at the things that matter in life.

How will you choose to deal with your personal crisis—as an emergency or an opportunity? A stumbling block or a steppingstone? The moment you and I can begin to see things through the heavenly lens, the picture becomes bearable—and we find new strength.

We've discussed the reality of trials. We've explored their results. But where do we go from here? What should be our response to trials? We'll take on the implications of that question in the next few pages.

## The Response to Trials in the Believer's Life

Someone has said that Psalm 71 is filled with great praise and great complaining all at once. I'm not certain I would characterize this wonderful psalm in quite that way. I do know this: David brings us low then lifts us up. He takes us on a tour of the deep pit to which his own road has brought him then points us to the high road we should take when we come into those low places. As in so many of the psalms, David's pilgrimage embodies both human defeat and godly victory.

That's no insignificant footnote, for we tend to lack a theology of adversity in the church these days. A so-called prosperity gospel has so permeated our church life that we're constantly hearing a bit too much of the word *positive*. We're told to practice "positive thinking." We're assured that if we practice "positive confession," positive things will happen to us. Above all, we're exhorted to keep a positive attitude and look on the bright side.

*Positive* is a perfectly good word, and optimism is a fine thing. Unfortunately, life isn't always positive. Sometimes things go wrong. And if our minds are set on being relentlessly positive, the time will come when we may be living in fantasy. I like to be positive, and I count myself as a very positive thinker. But here's something I also believe: If you don't have a realistic view of adversity, the outcome won't be very positive when it's your turn to face it.

David wasn't much for fantasy worlds. When his life went wrong, he refused to ignore what was negative in his life. He was a realist, and he had a godly perspective. Let's follow David in his plan of operation.

### Remember the Character of God

When David saw the worst life had to dish out for him, he could still remember the perfection and faithfulness of God: "In You, O LORD, I put my trust; let me never be put to shame. Deliver me in Your righteousness, and cause me to escape; incline Your ear to me, and save me. Be my strong habitation, to which I may resort continually; You have given the commandment to save me, for You are my rock and my fortress" (vv. 1–3).

Whenever we face trials, we need to remember who God is. Sometimes we get so focused on our trials we forget to focus on Him. If you take your pen in hand and mark your Bible carefully as you go through this psalm, you'll see that throughout his prayer David made references to God's character:

- He remembers God's glory in verse 8.
- He acknowledges God's power and strength in verse 18.
- He remembers God's faithfulness in verse 22.

Five different times in Psalm 71—verses 2, 15, 16, 19, and 24—David mentions the righteousness of God. The reason is clear. David understood that there was one thing he must do when trials were swirling around his head, when his own children were not honoring him. *He must never forget that God is righteous and good, that He is a God who can be trusted.* Things may be bad, and they can always be worse, but God never changes. He is never any less in control. He never has a smaller portion of love for us, and His plan for us does not deviate in the tiniest detail. All else changes but God. As the poet said, He is the still point of the turning world. David knew that he must never allow these thoughts to leave his mind, so over and over again he spoke about the righteousness of God.

We're not dealing in naive, rosy sentiment, my friend. I've looked in the face of death, and you may have done the same. If you've made that dark journey, I've been there too, and I'm here to assure you that we have a God who is trustworthy. I may not fathom every twist and turn in my journey. Many things have happened for which I can't give a rational human explanation. I'm sure it's the same way for you. But I can lay it all at the feet of God and say with all my heart, "I don't know the meaning, but He does. He knows what He is doing. Our God makes no mistakes!"

When we go through hard times, everybody on the street has an opinion about why it is happening, where we should go for help, and what's going on. Isn't it confusing? People have told me about every alternative cancer therapy dreamed up within or outside the world of science. And yes, at first I wanted to read every word of every brochure placed in my hands by concerned friends. If there was any hope contained in any one of them, I was going to find out about it. If there was any way for me to take my healing into my own hands, I was ready to do anything and everything.

But after awhile, we reach a new mind-set in which we push aside all the dreams and schemes and contrivances, and we fall on our knees to say, "My Lord and my God, my hope is in *You.* All the rest is too much for my limited and distressed mind, and it amounts to little account anyway. I look to no one, and nothing, but You, and I await Your guidance."

*Review the Compassion of God*

David said, "Deliver me, O my God, out of the hand of the wicked, out of the hand of the unrighteous and cruel man. For You are my hope, O Lord GOD; You are my trust from my youth. By You I have been upheld from my birth; You are He who took me out of my mother's womb. My praise shall be continually of You" (vv. 4–6).

What did David do in his moment of despair? He simply went back into his memory and reviewed the many pieces of wisdom about God he had learned over time. He reminded himself that God had proved faithful to him throughout all his life. David had confronted a giant. He had faced a jealous king with murder on the mind and an army of assassins. He had faced the legions of challenging nations. Somehow Israel and its king had survived and prospered. In all these things, God had been faithful. The Lord had brought him through.

And what was true for that David has been true for me.

I can look back and say, "God, You have blessed me every day of my life in some new and surprising way. You have satisfied the deepest longings of my soul. You have guarded me and guided me through every crisis I've faced. You blessed me with godly parents. From the very moment I was born, I was nurtured on Your Word as if it were my mother's milk. And You delivered me out of the chaos of my troubled teenage years. You watched over me through college and through seminary. You sustained me through my early days of ministry when I could have become so discouraged that I might finally have just thrown in the towel and abandoned Your work. God, as I look back over the years and see the height and depth and breadth of Your great compassion, I can only say that indeed, great is Your faithfulness."

What about you? What is your testimony of God's grace and goodness? Even if you have walked with the Lord for only a few weeks, God has been good to you. And the faithfulness of God that has been extended to you up to this point is simply a reminder that God is good, that He is compassionate, and that He cares. He is not going to change in the middle of your life what He has been doing faithfully throughout all eternity.

*Rejoice in Celebration to God*

Here is where we find the central miracle at the heart of the psalm. This is when we know it's time to take off our shoes, for we're on holy ground. David is pouring out his heart to God over excruciating family troubles. He cries out to God because of the terrible pain he feels. This would be for you, for me, for nearly any member of the human race a time of deep self-pity and anger toward God. Yet somehow, in the midst of David's wounds and suffering, his prayer is filled with worship and praise. Knowing all that you do of the troubled world of King David, I challenge you to listen closely to his words and see if you can come away unmoved:

- "My praise shall be continually of You" (v. 6).
- "Let my mouth be filled with Your praise and with Your glory all the day" (v. 8).
- "But I will hope continually, and will praise You yet more and more. My mouth shall tell of Your righteousness and Your salvation all the day, for I do not know their limits" (vv. 14–15).
- "Also with the lute I will praise You—and Your faithfulness, O my God! To You I will sing with the harp, O Holy One of Israel. My lips shall greatly rejoice when I sing to You, and my soul, which You have redeemed. My tongue also shall talk of Your righteousness all the day long; for they are confounded, for they are brought to shame who seek my hurt" (vv. 22–24).

This is the mark of the truly godly: In the very midst of life's deepest misery, their voices are lifted in praise of God. In a shattered family, from the rubble of a ruined business career, out of the tragic loss of a loved one—in all of these places, a tear-choked voice lifts itself toward heaven in unrestrained worship. In the obscene cruelties of a prison camp, in a totalitarian nation where God's people are hunted and imprisoned, in a life of failed health in which death is the only certainty—there is somehow, against all odds, the sound of singing in the darkness. It occurs in the life of David. Perhaps it will occur in your life as well, in that moment in which your faith comes shining through its steepest challenge.

Such a response defies every expectation. How can we account for it without naming the name of Almighty God? Watch and wait, and you'll find it to be true. You'll be faced with a trial, and God will give you two gifts: a scripture for your mind and a song for your heart. And the song He gives you will burst forth in lovely melody in the midst of the darkest night. I don't apologize for the fact that in my hospital room, in the middle of the night and a morphine drip, I was in my uncomfortable bed praising God with my hands lifted up to the Lord. I was celebrating Him, thanking Him for life, for health, for family, for friends—all that He is and all that He does. It was the most joyful song that hospital ever heard.

Perhaps it sounds a little less than real to you. "I've suffered before," you say, "and I wasn't singing anything but the blues. The Bible was the last book I felt like reading, and the last thing I was in the mood for was worship."

You may have a point. In most cases, we don't *feel* like praising God in the oncology ward of a hospital. But it happens when we look deeply into His truth, when we step just far enough outside our own entrenched emotional defenses to take a good look at where God has been in the past and where we know Him to be in the present. We do it out of sheer obedience. And we also sing the song because perhaps we've had experience with praise. We've praised Him in the midst of the crisis then been astounded at what He did for us. Praise not only benefits God, but also the one who offers it.

When you're under attack by the armies of suffering, don't think you have no weapons to raise. Lift a song in worship and praise. They're powerful weapons in the hands of God's children.

*Renew Your Consecration to God*

Above every element of the psalm I read that night, this was the thought that stoked my fire. I was at a point where it was more than reasonable to wonder, "Is this the end of my ministry? Have I gotten to the end of my business here? Is God finished with me?"

This is what David says: "When I am old and gray-headed, O God, do not forsake me, *until I declare Your strength to this generation, Your power to everyone who is to come*" (v. 18; emphasis added). That sentence forestalls me from asking those questions. I take David's verse as my marching orders for the rest of my life, to declare God's strength to this generation. Never assume God is through with you. Gray hair means nothing. In God's way of doing things, the best is always yet to come!

He isn't finished with you or me. He never forgets or neglects us, though it does happen the other way around. It may be hard for you to believe, but God can be set aside and forgotten in church. We can go to church every Sunday and never hear anything about God. May I never enter the doors of God's house and neglect to tell people that He is strong and awesome. I want to praise His name and proclaim His power, not only to our generation, but also to our children, and to every generation that is to come.

### Reclaim Your Confidence in God and the Future

Have you found yourself taking a bleak view of things and giving in to cynicism? Have you gradually bought into a world-view based on Murphy's Law: Whatever can go wrong will go wrong? Psalm 71 takes you down a road that leads precisely in the opposite direction. Your cynicism is replaced by faith: Whatever can go wrong can—and will—be used by God. Instead of a future of good things constantly bent in the wrong direction, you see a godly future in which God bends the world's distorted hopes into His beautiful plan.

David has confidence in the future because he has confidence in the One holding it. He writes, "You shall increase my greatness, and comfort [encourage] me on every side" (v. 21). We need to understand the wording in this verse, particularly the word *greatness*. You and I have no greatness in ourselves for God to increase. David refers to his sphere of influence and his opportunity to make a difference.

Trials put us in place for that to happen. They are for our benefit, as unwelcome as they are at the time. They make us better men and women, which makes us more influential men and women who can make a difference for God's purposes. When you have walked through the fire, people begin to listen to you. When you have the wisdom

---

*"You must learn to live with the insecurities and the ambiguities of life. But know this: I am secure. I am certain. I am not ambiguous. In the storm, I am your Rock that cannot be moved. I am your God."*

---

borne of suffering, you begin to have the tools to accomplish something in the world.

Remember Peter, Jesus' disciple? He knew something about being tested. He wrote about the purpose of trials in 1 Peter 1:7: "That the genuineness of your faith, being much more precious than gold that perishes, though it is tested by fire, may be found to praise, honor, and glory at the revelation of Jesus Christ." Peter joins David in affirming that fire tempers the steel in your character. After it has burned its impression into you, you can burn your impression into the world.

The psalmist said in Psalm 119:67 and 71, "Before I was afflicted I went astray, but now I keep Your word. . . . It is good for me that I have been afflicted, that I may learn Your statutes." Testing makes you walk the straight path, while the untested go astray.

James, too, wants us to hear this same message. He says, "Consider it all joy, my brethren, when you encounter various trials, knowing that the testing of your faith produces endurance" (James 1:2–3 NASB). Testing gives you the fortitude to go the distance.

Peter leaves us with the blessing of those who will feel the heat of the oven and feel the grace of God in it: "But may the God of all grace, who called us to His eternal glory by Christ Jesus, after you have suffered a while, perfect, establish, strengthen, and settle you" (1 Pet. 5:10). There is the hope, my friends, of maturing, of strengthening, of settling after the fires of our crisis have burned out. We find ourselves wiser and better, and we can thank God for the worst we've been through.

Suffering and strength are two sides of the same coin. When I was younger, I heard that God doesn't greatly use someone until He crushes him. I never liked the sound of that, and I used to pray that I might be the exception. I used to say, "Lord, let me go straight to the heart of ministry without feeling the pain." But God doesn't make any exceptions.

You would be well advised to read a biography of the great preacher Charles Haddon Spurgeon. I always knew he was a great man, but when I looked more deeply into the details of his life, I learned that Spurgeon accomplished more in his one lifetime than most people could accomplish in two, even though he died at the age of fifty-seven. Spurgeon suffered with prolonged bouts of depression and anxiety, and his psychological and physical ailments were so crippling that he frequently was confined to bed for weeks.

Spurgeon came to see these problems as part of God's work in his life. His sufferings enabled him to comfort and encourage the many hurting people who were touched by his ministry. And he found a pattern to his life: His periods of depression invariably preceded seasons of God's special blessings on his ministry. He knew he did not suffer without reason.

The depression actually became, as Spurgeon described it, a sort of "John the Baptist" for him, heralding a new and mighty outpouring of God's Spirit. Here are his own words: "This depression comes over me whenever the Lord is preparing a larger blessing for my ministry; the cloud is black before it breaks. . . . The scouring of the vessel has fitted it for the Master's use. . . . Fasting gives an appetite for the banquet. . . . The Lord is revealed in the backside of the desert, while his servant keeps the sheep and waits in solitary."

Charles Haddon Spurgeon, this psychologically frail man, published more than 3,500 sermons, authored 135 books, and is still regarded today as the "Prince of Preachers."[2]

God is up to something when He sends difficulty our way.

Life is not going to be easy. But I do believe that it can be victorious. When you know Almighty God and His Son Jesus Christ, you can endure whatever is placed before you with strength that the world can't comprehend. If you don't know Christ, you must enter the battle without weapons or armor. You fight in your own strength, and you fall on your face.

Why? Because God is the only One who can help us when trials come into our lives. And He does more than help us. He is our rock, our fortress, our hope, and our confidence. As David wrote so many centuries ago, "Who, O God, is like You?" (Ps. 71:9 NIV).

The answer is, *no one*. God will send His rain on the just and the un-just, but His children, who recognize and embrace His ways, will know that the rain is cool, refreshing water from heaven. It makes us grow. It gives us joy. And it makes life—real life—possible in this dry and dusty world.

# Psalm 121

*A Song of Ascents.*

1 I will lift up my eyes to the hills—
From whence comes my help?
2 My help comes from the LORD,
Who made heaven and earth.
3 He will not allow your foot to be moved;
He who keeps you will not slumber.
4 Behold, He who keeps Israel
Shall neither slumber nor sleep.
5 The LORD is your keeper;
The LORD is your shade at your right hand.
6 The sun shall not strike you by day,
Nor the moon by night.
7 The LORD shall preserve you from all evil;
He shall preserve your soul.
8 The LORD shall preserve your going out and your coming in
From this time forth, and even forevermore.

# 3

# I Need Your Help, Lord

*Day by day and with each passing moment,*
*Strength I find to meet my trials here;*
*Trusting in my father's wise bestowment,*
*I've no cause for worry or for fear.*
*He whose heart is kind beyond all measure*
*Gives unto each day what he deems best—*
*Lovingly, its part of pain and pleasure,*
*Mingling toil with peace and rest.*

—CAROLINA SANDELL BERG

Many travelers, many roads.

For every pilgrim in this journey of life, the road will bend in a different direction. We can never know in advance which way it will turn, for the map doesn't display that kind of detail for us. We must walk on until we meet the bend or the dip or the steep, uphill climb that has been set in the path for each of us. And we look to God for the grace to meet that defining moment.

The bend in my road, of course, has been cancer. I can't say what yours will be or has been, but it will be equally challenging. And in time you'll want to tell others your story, just as I'm telling mine. That's a predictable quality of those of us who are survivors—we swap our war stories. My good friend Dr. John Hovey shared his narrative with me. In his case the foe wasn't cancer—but I'll let him tell you the story in his own words. Listen to the history of the bend in another traveler's road, and how it transformed forever the way he would see his God, himself, and those he loves.

—∽—

It was three years ago that my life took a fateful turn.

As a family, we love to take long walks on the California beaches. One particularly lovely day, we were taking such a walk and enjoying the sea and the wind and everything that goes with the beauty of the seashore. My wife, Mary, had noticed something that struck her as strange. It seemed to her that I wasn't swinging my left arm in a natural, fluid motion—and she was right. Now I'm a surgeon, as you know, and I began to notice a poor motor response as I transferred surgical instruments into and out of my left hand. You can imagine how such a thing would affect my work. In time, it influenced my surgical schedule, my suture technique, and my overall office practice as I increasingly struggled with simple manual dexterity.

During those weeks and months, I began to spend more and more time in reflection—crisis have that effect on us. I realized what the onslaught of this disability had begun to do to me. My surgical practice had become more and more demanding. And now, even the more simple activities of daily living became difficult. Getting ready for work in the morning took so much longer that even my quiet time began to be affected. Mary pointed out that my long, hard hours at the office not only kept me in a state of physical exhaustion, but they had been stealing more and more precious time way from the family who loved me.

All this work disruption and soul-searching culminated in a confrontation with reality. A few professional colleagues examined me, and their diagnosis was early Parkinson's disease. I had come to my own bend in the road.

I had put in twenty-five years of school and twenty-five years of exhausting and devoted work in the medical field; I had paid fifty years' worth of dues, the way I saw it. After all this time, I'd finally reached the peak years of my professional career. I was ready to enjoy the fruits of the harvest, but instead it seemed as if everything I had trained for was slipping away.

Every doctor loves the encouraging comments of his patients, especially those of us who do surgery. How would the loss of that affirmation affect me? Gradually, an important question surfaced: Was my identity as a doctor more important than my identity as His disciple?

As I read 1 Chronicles 29:11–12, the words seemed to leap from the page to cry out to me about my life and my concerns:

> For all that is in heaven and in earth is Yours; (*You own everything.*)
>
> Yours is the kingdom, O LORD, (*My practice is Yours.*)
>
> And You are exalted as head over all. (*Parkinson's is not a surprise to You.*)
>
> Both riches and honor come from You, (*not from my patients*)
>
> And You reign over all. (*You control my destiny.*)
>
> In Your hand is power and might; (*You are in control of my health.*)
>
> In Your hand it is to make great
> And to give strength to all. (*Do You have something else for me to do?*)

Since my retirement a year ago, the Lord has been more than faithful in showing me that His grace is sufficient. He has allowed me to identify with Jesus in the practical joy of being a carpenter and to develop a more disciplined study of His Word. He has allowed me to be available to assist the many people He puts in my path. He has given me the joy of increasing my participation in church activities and of giving more of the Lord's money back to Him.

This has been the bottom line for me: more time with the Lord, more time with His Word, and more time with my wife and family. Would you believe it if I told you that I've come to be truly thankful for Parkinson's disease? It's the truth.

No, I never expected this, and yes, it's been challenging to say the least—but it has allowed me to discover the unshakable truth that "God is my strength and power, and He makes my way perfect" (2 Sam. 22:33).

Can you appreciate the wisdom that has come from Dr. Hovey's bend in the road?

The late Charles Schulz's "Peanuts" comic strip always showed the characters sharing their philosophies of life. In one memorable strip, Lucy said, "Charlie Brown, life is like a deck chair. Some position the chair to see where they've been. Some position it to see where they are at the present."

Charlie Brown turned to her and replied in his usual melancholy way, "Lucy, I can't even get my deck chair unfolded."

I know a lot of people who feel that way about life. They don't know if it's all about looking back to see what life has meant, or looking forward to see what it will be, or simply sitting tight and trying not to think too much about it. They don't know how to get a grip on the meaning of things.

How can they get a good view from the deck chair when the ship is moving so fast? That's how one young businesswoman felt. She was approached by a real-estate agent who wanted to sell her a home. She said, "A home? We eat in restaurants, spend our mornings playing golf, and spend our afternoons playing bridge at the club. Every night we go to a movie. I don't need a home—I need a garage."

It's a common feeling, isn't it? Life is moving by too quickly; the pace is too frantic. How can we stop long enough to consider the

---

*Give your entire attention to what God is doing right now,*
*and don't get worked up about what may or may not happen*
*tomorrow. God will help you deal with whatever*
*hard things come up when the time comes.*

**—Matthew 6:34 (MSG)**

---

deep meanings of life? The questions are tough ones in any case. Even to those of us who follow Christ, the topics of pain and suffering and ultimate meaning are complex and confusing. How can we cope with them?

One thing is certain—just as we begin to ponder all these questions and start to take ourselves seriously, we're humbled by the words of Scripture. After all, the Bible tells us that life is like a vapor that appears for a little while and then vanishes. It's like grass that grows for a season only to be cut down and scattered by the winds.

As we struggle to confront the meaning of life, it's natural for us to fall back on these word pictures, the little parables that give us a handle for dealing with great concepts. Vapors, grass—and, of course, roads. By this time in the book it's clear to you that I love the word picture of the pilgrim on a journey through a foreign land. John Bunyan paints a masterpiece from that image in his classic book *Pilgrim's Progress*. Life is a journey, and we must all walk the path. In the words of the old spiritual, "This world is not my own, I'm just a-passing through."

So many of the psalms are written for pilgrims on the path. As we read Psalm 121, we can hear the psalmist crying out, "Lord, I need guidance for my journey. I've lost my way. Can't You show me the right way to go?"

In this beautiful psalm of just eight verses, we're encouraged to trust God even when life gives us what we haven't asked for. The confidence expressed in Psalm 121 is rooted in the grandeur of the psalmist's vision of God—the Maker of heaven and earth, the Lord who can be trusted to help us at every point along the journey, through the sunny passages as well as the darker trek through forests of night. The psalmist lifts his eyes to the hills above and sees the One who is not only the destination of the journey, but also the strength for every step of it.

In spite of all the perils we encounter, the mountainous crags and the desert wastelands, *we can trust the Lord*. Yes, He is awesome and we feel small and insignificant, but the psalmist assures us that God bridges the gap. He is never too great to care; we are never too small for His caring. The psalm reflects on a God who soothes us in our anxiety and watches over us as a shepherd with his sheep.

As you hold your Bible open to this wonderful chapter, you find these important words in superscription: "A Song of Ascents." What does that mean?

There are fifteen of these special psalms, the first of them being Psalm 120. In those ancient days, the Israelites would travel to Jerusalem for feast days at the temple. Coming from whatever distant town they called home, the pilgrims would make the long journey by foot, walking with their families and friends and enjoying their holiday travel. They were eager for good times in the Holy City, seeing friends again over the feast and making sacrifices to God. Scholars believe the songs of ascents were written to sing along the road from the lowlands of Palestine up to Jerusalem.

As the travelers walked up that natural incline, the uphill trek to Jerusalem, they'd sing another of these joyful psalms at each new level. In fact, if you read them in order, you can almost see the stages of the journey, moving onward and upward toward the temple where the people would arrive for the worship of God. Has your family ever enjoyed a sing-along during a vacation journey in the car? Have you sung on the way to church, preparing your hearts for worship? I hope you have. These psalms are the music of the uphill journey.

In Psalm 42:4 we catch a glimpse of this: "When I remember these things, I pour out my soul within me. For I used to go with the multitude; I went with them to the house of God, with the voice of joy and praise, with a multitude that kept a pilgrim feast." They were songs for the happy throng—though it's interesting that these songs were also sung by the captives of Jerusalem upon their return from Babylonian exile. That was an uphill journey from the pits of despair.

We've seen something of the historical context. But of course these psalms are alive, not limited to ancient history. For us today, the pilgrimage songs become metaphors for our own spiritual journey. Though we don't often attend sacred feasts in Jerusalem, the road we walk takes us from the lowlands of our present circumstances to the higher place to which God has called us. The songs of ascents contain essential truths for our journey through this life, as we make our way to be with God for eternity. We can quickly grasp their symbolism and find deep encouragement in these little songs.

The Bible never lies to us by claiming that life is easy. Christianity is no free pass; there are no shortcuts to bypass the essential human experience. But somehow people get that mistaken idea, and when they eventually face trouble—as they always do—they come to the irrational conclusion that the presence of trouble implies the absence of God. A greater mistake cannot be imagined.

God's Word reminds us that we are pilgrims and strangers in a foreign land whose roads are filled with hazards. The road is long, weary, and dangerous. It winds through veils of tears and Bunyan's Slough of Despond, but the long and winding road finally comes to the City of God, the place of joy and feasting. Simply stated, that's the biblical view of life in the world.

So where can we go to find traveler's assistance?

## The Possibilities for Help on Our Journey

### We Can Look Around for Help

The psalmist says, "I will lift up mine eyes to the hills" (v. 1). He has prepared for his journey through the mountains to Jerusalem. As he enters the road, he takes a moment to gaze up to the horizon. He thinks of the miles ahead, the twists and turns and surprises, the old friends and new ones whose acquaintances he will make. He thinks of the dust and the heat, the darkness and the thirsty miles. He admires the graceful line where the mountains embrace the sky.

I've always been intrigued by the prominence of mountains in the Bible. Many great things happened on mountaintops: the sacrifice of Isaac on Mount Moriah, the giving of the Law on Mount Sinai, the Transfiguration of Christ, the message on Mount Olivet, Elijah's prophetic showdown on Mount Carmel (more on that one later)—and, of course, all of history turns on a crucifixion one dark Friday on Mount Calvary. Climactic moments in the biblical narrative always seem to seek higher ground.

You may not live anywhere near the mountains, and you may even prefer the beach as a vacation destination. I must confess that I'm a "mountain man" at heart. I boast with pride to all my friends around the country that I'm twenty minutes away from the mountains and twenty minutes away from the ocean. On a couple of occasions, as I'm quick to point out, I've partaken of sea and slope in the same day! Some of us like to show off, you see. I know people who water-ski and snow ski on the same day, just for bragging purposes to impress their friends back east.

But there's something grand and majestic about mountains. They set the landscape and the people in context. Nothing calms my spirit

---

*Blessed are those whose strength is in you,*
*who have set their hearts on pilgrimage.*

**—Psalm 84:5 (NIV)**

---

or helps me to get things in perspective more effectively than a visit to the highest hills. I drive up into the Laguna Mountains and find a special place where I can survey the natural grandeur and reflect on my Creator. If I've lost Him in the confinement of the city, I can find Him in the immensity of the peaks. Something about the majesty of mountains invokes the majesty of God.

That happens in the Scriptures too. Listen to Isaiah 55:12: "For you shall go out with joy, and be led out with peace; the mountains and the hills shall break forth into singing before you."

Psalm 125:1–2 captures the same idea: "Those who trust in the LORD are like Mount Zion, which cannot be moved, but abides forever. As the mountains surround Jerusalem, so the LORD surrounds His people from this time forth and forever."

There are many passages in the Old Testament that describe the mountains as a place of blessing, but we know all too well that mountains can also be a place of danger. Rarely does a winter go by that we don't hear of someone being lost in the mountain terrain. The snow cover cuts off the navigation of outdoorsmen, who cannot retrace their steps out of the wilderness.

In ancient times, mountains were sites of danger and hardship. Their rocks and caves hid wild animals and bloodthirsty bandits. Pagan cultures built their temples in the mountains. Godly pilgrims found a sense of majesty in the high country, but they also found a sense of danger and a fear of the unknown. It was a place of fear and of hope, of danger and salvation. The Lord God could be sought there, but pagan gods were enshrined as well.

The psalmist must have thought of these things, reflecting on the many meanings of mountains. He gazed upward at the outset of the journey and said, "I will look to the hills."

## We Can Look Within for Help

I must confess to falling victim to a widespread misconception about this psalm. Maybe you've experienced it too. We were raised with the traditional King James Version and its time-honored punctuation. It can be misleading in this particular instance.

Take a good look at the first verse of Psalm 121. The psalmist says, "I will lift up my eyes to the hills—from whence comes my help?" The New King James Version, which we use in this book, has corrected the punctuation, but I used to misread the two phrases as one: "I will lift up my eyes unto the hills from whence cometh my help." I used to conclude that we look for help from the mountains.

But that's not what the psalm says at all. The writer makes a statement: "I will lift up my eyes to the hills." He breaks off and asks a question: "From whence comes my help?" What a difference a dash makes! The traveler looks to the hills, then he looks inward. And as he looks inward, he asks himself the question, "Where am I going to find help?" He feels all the hesitancy and concern many of us do before we set out on a long journey. Traveling has a measure of insecurity about it, because we're out of our comfort zones. *What if something terrible happens while I'm out of town? Who can I turn to?*

This is what writers call an "internal monologue"—and what you and I call "talking to ourselves." Is that a healthy thing to do? Well, the fact is we do it all the time. Our Psalm 121 traveler is talking to himself. He feels a little anxiety about getting through the high hills to arrive at his faraway destination of Jerusalem. And he naturally thinks, *Will anyone help me if I get sick or I'm attacked or I run out of money?*

He looks around.

Then he looks within.

Finally, he looks above.

### We Can Look Above for Help

In the second verse, we find the solid foundation of this psalm: "My help comes from the LORD, who made heaven and earth." At last the psalmist comes to the point that provides the essence of his song. He is telling himself, "I've looked up to the mountains, and I find no help. I've looked within, and I find no guidance. But finally I've looked up, and I've realized the source of my help. It comes from no one but God."

What a lesson for life's travelers on this earth: *My help comes from the Lord.*

The Lord is described here as the God who made heaven and earth. Do you think these words are window dressing, perhaps a flowery poetic device? Not at all. These words are chosen quite deliberately. The idea of being loved by a Creator who hung the stars in space and set the earth upon its course is a powerful source of encouragement. If He can guide the planets, surely He can guide our little steps. That's why we find this phrase so frequently used in blessings the Hebrews granted each other. Look at the following examples (emphasis added):

- "May you be blessed by the LORD, *who made heaven and earth*" (Ps. 115:15).
- "The LORD *who made heaven and earth* bless you from Zion!" (Ps. 134:3).

- "Happy is he who has the God of Jacob for his help,
  whose hope is in the LORD his God, *who made heaven and earth*"
  (Ps. 146:5–6).

The power of this statement is wrapped up in the idea that since God is the Creator of all things, and since all things are His handiwork, His power is not to be questioned. The Creator has made everything we can see or touch or imagine; when we cast our hopes on Him, we're not only coming to a God who *cares*, but a God who *can*.

God is not merely the Creator of all things, but He is the Sustainer of all things as well. In writing to the Colossians, Paul writes: "By Him all things are created." And he goes on to say, "He is before all things, and in Him all things consist" (Col. 1:16–17). This is very important, for at some times during history God has been characterized by philosophers as a "cosmic watchmaker" who has created the world and then abandoned it to its own devices to tick away the moments until it runs out of time. That's not the God of the Bible. After creation, He is intimately involved with the work of His hands, holding it all together. If, even for a moment, He were to remove His hand from this universe, it wouldn't tick happily away like a watch in the grass; it would all fly apart into oblivion. But our God doesn't do that. Instead, He continues to sustain us. He creates and He sustains.

On that day when your journey brings you to a bend in the road, you'll be filled with an unaccustomed sense of helplessness. You'll cry out, "Lord, I need help!" In your moment of deep anxiety, remember this: The One to whom you are praying is the One who made heaven and earth. He is the Creator God. I don't know what kind of problem you may be facing—in the weariness of the journey, I'm certain it can seem all but insurmountable. But take a deep breath and a new look, in the perspective of the One who created and sustains every atom of the universe. He's up to the challenge, don't you think?

That thought renews our strength to carry on.

## The Promises of Help on Our Journey

We notice something slightly odd as we come to the third verse of this psalm. If we're reading through it quickly, we may not even notice. The writer's perspective changes from first person ("I") to second person ("you"). This may seem like so much grammatical wrangling to you, and you may be tempted to leave this one to your high-school English teacher to worry about. But it's actually a rather significant point. For example, some have made the case that an entirely new character has walked onstage and begins to speak in this verse. They suggest that in the first couple of verses, the psalmist asked the questions; now someone else, perhaps a priest, has come along to provide the answers.

I don't buy into that particular interpretation. I believe what we have here is an internal dialogue in the heart of the psalmist—if you'll remember, we detected an internal monologue in the opening of the psalm; now a dialogue is suggested as the traveler frames answers to his own questions. He has chosen to write it all down, of course, so the "you" really refers to himself and ourselves as well. "Who will help me?" he asks. He concludes, "Here is what God will do for you and for me."

In the process of answering his question for our benefit, the psalmist uses eight small verses to make three immense points invaluable to our journey toward those hills. You'll stand, as he did, looking down that road and up those mountains. Your heart will cry out to God, and here is what you'll need to remember.

### The Lord Perceives You

We can't see God, but you need to know that He sees you—*always*. He knows you. Aren't you glad that God knows who you are? Isn't it unbelievable? The God who made heaven and earth knows you by name!

He knows the very hairs on your head *by number*. Jesus assured us of that (see Matt. 10:30). That's a very intimate kind of knowledge. Believe me, I've been up close and personal with the issue of hair quantity. Chemotherapy, as you know, is involved with cancer treatment, and hair loss is inevitable with chemotherapy. I had to brace myself for the loss of my silvery locks! I had the pleasure of looking in the mirror every day and remembering that He numbers the hairs on my head. I was glad Someone was keeping inventory. I numbered those hairs myself, sadly watching them fall out. But He knew the exact number. He knows us intimately.

If God numbers the hairs on your head, don't you think He's up-to-date on the larger issues of your life? Don't you think He knows exactly how you feel—and cares deeply? When you say, "God, I need Your help," you need to know that He knows you. He perceives you.

Notice what the text says next: "He will not allow your foot to be moved; He who keeps you will not slumber. Behold, He who keeps Israel shall neither slumber nor sleep" (vv. 3–4).

Lloyd John Ogilvie tells a story about Bishop Quayle, who was a leader in the Methodist church years ago. One night, the bishop worked into the early morning hours trying to finish his work and solve his various problems. It happened that the Bible on his desk was open to Psalm 121. At a moment of intense pressure, Quayle was feeling tired and frustrated and annoyed. Suddenly his eye fell on the startling words that told him God never slumbers, that our Lord watches over us on a twenty-four-hour vigil.

Here was Bishop Quayle burning the midnight oil, worrying over so many things—and God watching over him as he worried. Here was Bishop Quayle working for God rather than allowing God to work through him. It came home to the minister, with great impact, that such a life was exhausting and ultimately a losing battle.

In his inner being he heard the Lord say, "Quayle, there's no need for both of us to stay up all night. I'm going to stay up anyway. You go to bed and get a good sleep."[1]

Have you ever paced the floor at night because of your kids, a financial problem for which you didn't know the answer, a sickness, or other problem in your life? If you're like me, you worry and wonder who is taking care of things. Then you read in the Bible that the God in whom you have trusted, the One you ask for help, never sleeps. He never takes a day off, and He's never out of town. You don't even need a secret cell phone number or e-mail address. God is right there, watching you, so close to you that you don't even need to call out to Him. He's watching over you, even as you sleep, because He loves you.

My friend Ron Mehl has written a book entitled *God Works the Night Shift*. That's one of the best titles I've heard in a long time. Isn't it a great thought? God is always there, no matter when it is that you need Him. In the loneliest, darkest hour of the night, He is there because He doesn't slumber or sleep.

I have always loved the story of Elijah, the Old Testament prophet. Maybe it's because he's another mountain man. He called that great showdown with the prophets of Baal on Mount Carmel, as recorded in 1 Kings 18:1–40. On one side were all the prophets of the false god, Baal; on the other side was Elijah, all by himself, representing the God of Abraham, Isaac, and Jacob. It was a contest to determine who the real God was, and Elijah threw down the gauntlet. He said, "Here's how we'll play. You put a sacrifice on your altar, and I'll put one on mine. We'll each call on our respective gods to consume our sacrifice with fire. May the best God win."

God versus Baal—the sacrifice of the century! Elijah let the other side go first. From morning until noon, the prophets of Baal cried out to their god to send the fire—but the heavens were silent. How embarrassing for these prophets when their god was a no-show! You can imagine the increasing panic in their voices. They cried aloud, leaped about, wept, rolled on the ground, and even cut themselves to let the blood flow. Nothing helped.

Just about noon, the prophets were about to run out of time. It was a shutout, bottom of the ninth, and things were looking bleak for all the Baal believers. That's when Elijah did something that no preacher should ever do.

Sarcasm, to be sure, is a quality I don't admire; I've always said there's no place for it in the life of a godly man or woman. But to be honest,

Elijah had an unmistakable little mean streak in him. He was looking at all those leaping, wailing Baal prophets with their unlit sacrifice, and he simply couldn't resist: "Elijah mocked them and said, 'Cry aloud, for

---

*Go in where thou wilt, He sees thee: light thy lamp, He sees thee; quench its light, He sees thee. Fear Him who ever beholds thee.*

**—Saint Augustine**

---

he is a god; either he is meditating, or he is busy, or he is on a journey, or perhaps he is sleeping and must be awakened.'"

Can you hear the taunting? Elijah was clearly enjoying the failure of his corrupt, pagan competitors. But he had to be confident to take that approach, for now it was *his* turn to demonstrate the power of his God. The rest, as they say, is history—as well as more proof that our Creator never goes to sleep. He is never too busy. Our Lord is attentive to all our needs, and Elijah put an exclamation point on that statement before the king, the Baal backers, and the entire crowd who had flocked to Mount Carmel to take in the show. Elijah prayed, and God answered him in no uncertain terms by sending fire to consume his sacrifice.

Alexander the Great was once asked how he could sleep so soundly while constantly surrounded with danger. He replied that he lost no sleep at all: Parmenio, his faithful guard, kept watch so he could rest. If a general can sleep because a mere man is watching over him by night, how much more should we sleep, knowing our eternal God is keeping watch? He never slumbers. He never sleeps. He perceives you, and I hope your sleep is deep and refreshing in the knowledge of it.

## The Lord Protects You

"The LORD is your keeper; the LORD is your shade at your right hand. The sun shall not strike you by day, nor the moon by night" (vv. 5–6).

Now we come to another promise, and we remember the traveler whose eyes have looked up toward the horizon before his dangerous journey. He feels reassurance that God is keeping watch over him by night and shading him during the noon heat. Can you imagine a more devoted Master than that?

God is the pilgrim's shade on his right hand. The word *shade* is very important. Travelers along the ancient roads in this part of the world felt deep anxiety about the desert heat. Sunstroke was a serious issue. If you've ever visited Israel and traveled up the long road to Masada, you know how stifling the heat can be—dry and oppressive enough to drain away every ounce of your vitality.

"The LORD is your shade at your right hand," and again it's worth taking a close look at the particular phrase chosen to drive home the point. The phrase "right hand" suggests a wonderful truth about the place we hold in the heart of God. Psalm 98:1 says, "Oh sing to the LORD a new song! For He has done marvelous things. His right hand and His holy arm have gained Him the victory." The Scriptures consistently speak of the right hand of the Lord as indicative of His power. He has given you shade in His right hand, we're told. He protects you around the clock, with mighty power. That should bolster your courage.

He protects us by day. "The sun shall not strike you by day," the traveler proclaims. The forceful words *beat* or *hit* or *smite* or *kill* help us fully appreciate the deadly assault of the Mediterranean sun and the safety of the shade available only in our loving God.

Then, when the day is over, He will protect us by night. Verse 6 continues, "Nor the moon by night." Have you ever heard of being "moonstruck"? In the period of time when this psalm was written, there were all kinds of superstitions circulating concerning the moon. In fact, Matthew 17:15 records a story about a man who begged Jesus to heal his son. He described his deranged son in these terms: "For he is an epileptic and suffers severely; for he often falls into the fire and often into the water." And if you dig just a bit deeper into the background of this word *epileptic*, you'll discover that in most translations the word is actually *moonstruck*. People believed that the moonlight brought dangers, and the moon could be as deadly as the sun. You could be "struck" by both.

Needless to say, we're a bit beyond primitive lunar superstition. We don't lose any sleep over the prospect of being struck by the moon. And far be it from our sophisticated culture to fall prey to that kind of craziness—right? Not so fast: Such ideas about the moon linger on. When we say somebody is crazy, we call him or her a *lunatic*. Craziness is *lunacy*. Both these words come from the word *lunar*, or *moon*. Maybe we aren't as sophisticated as we think.

In any case, many people suffer from night fears. Nearly every child has begged for a night-light. Aging people often come to fear the night as well. The darkness and loneliness of it hold special terrors for them. Some suffer from insomnia and the long, dark night becomes even longer—a difficult time for them to endure.

For all of us who have struggled or been struck by fear, whether of the sun or the moon or anything else on the horizon, the message is this: *God is great. He will provide safety for you in the heat of the day, and in the terrors of the night He will never leave your side.*

### The Lord Preserves You

"The LORD shall preserve you from all evil; He shall preserve your soul. The LORD shall preserve your going out and your coming in from this time forth, and even forevermore" (vv. 7–8).

This wonderful promise contains four precious truths.

**1. The Lord preserves us from evil.** God will help us make it through when evil and danger rear their heads. Think about the worst that can happen, the most evil thing that could befall you. Nothing is outside His control. Think about every kind of disaster that terrifies humanity. Every one you can name is subject to the God who preserves. Bad things do happen, but they happen within His supervision and long-term purposes. It's foolish to believe things have gotten out of His control; it simply cannot happen.

**2. The Lord preserves our existence.** "He shall preserve your soul," says the seventh verse. As our pilgrim narrator reassures us that God will keep our souls from all harm, he uses a particular word for *soul*. Hebrew writings usually reach for this word when the meaning is *life.* In other words, God is going to *keep your life.* It doesn't end when you breathe your last breath. There is much more to the idea of life than the womb-to-tomb understanding to which we limit ourselves.

As we grieve at a funeral, we know we've come to a punctuation mark in someone's life. And that's what it is—but that mark is not a period, as we assume, but merely a comma. We need put no question mark on that one! You are an eternal creature. And He is the keeper of your existence, guarding your soul through earthly life and eternity as well.

The traveler looks at the long road before him, the hills above him, and reminds himself that this is one short journey in the world, set within a joyful journey in God's eternal world. That context lifts his spirits.

**3. The Lord preserves us every day.** I love this phrase: "The LORD shall preserve your going out and your coming in" (v. 8).

Sometimes when I rise in the morning and take a good look at the schedule blaring at me from my daily planner, I sigh deeply and feel like a slave to the world's demands. Do you ever feel that way? Go out, come in; go out, come in. The days begin to look alike as they entangle themselves into urgent appointments—this meeting, then the next one. Yet God promises to preserve us even as we go out and come in—which is, by the way, a wonderful Old Testament idiom that expresses the regular routines of life.

This promise extends even deeper into the world of everyday responsibilities. Maybe you have small children at home. You look at the day and think, *Boy, this is just like yesterday. And yesterday was like the day before. All I do is get up in the morning, take care of kids, wash clothes, clean up their messes, prepare them for school, run errands all over town, come home, make dinner, and fall in bed too tired even to sleep. Then I get up the next morning and start all over again.* In your darker moments you begin to wonder, *Is God involved in all of this? Does He care at all about the endless treadmill of my life?*

Let me assure you that He does care. He watches over you and preserves you in your going out and in your coming in. This is a promise that God's Word repeats over and over, so that there may be no question about it. He cares.

In his commentary on the Gospel of Luke, William Barclay quotes a little poem about the routines of life that was obviously written by a woman who was working at home:

> Lord of all pots and pans and things,
> Since I have no time to be
> A saint by doing lovely things
> Or watching late with Thee,
> Or dreaming in the dawnlight,
> Or storming heaven's gates,
> Make me a saint by getting meals
> And washing up the plates.[2]

God uses the kitchen filled with pots and pans, or the desk filled with business memos, as laboratories for sainthood. He watches over the routines of life. He watches our going out and our coming in.

**4. The Lord preserves us eternally.** The psalmist proclaims that the Lord will preserve us "from this time forth, and even forevermore" (v. 8).

God's care extends not only to every place and to every setting, but it also spans all of time and eternity. Time plays tricks on us, doesn't it? For the child anticipating Christmas morning, it moves like molasses, and a week might as well be a year. For an adult, the years seem to fly, and we can't believe how quickly each succeeding one whirls by us.

We begin to see time as our enemy. Its accelerating pace frightens and discourages us. If time is cold and uncaring, we think, then God must be too—but don't ever think such a terrible thought, for it's not so. God cares for us in time and eternity. Time is only His tool to bring us wisdom and perspective.

## The Keeper of Our Lives

A pious Jew in today's world keeps certain elements in his home in keeping with the traditions of his faith. If you were to visit such a man, you'd come to his door and notice a small metal container on the outside doorway and also on the inside. He calls this little metal container a *mezuzah*. It enshrines for him, in a physical way, the words of Deuteronomy chapters 6 and 11, which tell us that we are to train up our children in the way they should go and that we are to teach them as they go out and as they come in.

So there at the doorway is the *mezuzah*. As the pious Jew leaves his home to travel to his place of work, he touches this little metal box with his right hand and repeats aloud a few of the words contained within it, asking God to preserve him as he goes out and comes in. His final words will always be, "The Lord keep you both now and forevermore."

Whether we "go out" to travel around the block or around the world, the Lord is our keeper. Eugene Peterson writes about God's watchful care over us:

> The Christian life is not a quiet escape to a garden where we can walk and talk uninterruptedly with our Lord; nor a fantasy trip to a heavenly city where we can compare blue ribbons and gold medals with others who have made it to the winners' circle. . . . The Christian life is going to God. In going to God, Christians travel the same ground that everyone else walks on, breathe the same air, drink the same water, shop in the same stores, read the same newspapers, are citizens under the same governments, pay the same prices for groceries and gasoline, fear the same dangers, are subject to the same pressures, get the same distresses, are buried in the same ground.
>
> The difference is that each step we walk, each breath we breathe, we know we are preserved by God, we know we are accompanied by God, we know we are ruled by God; and therefore, no matter what doubts we endure or what accidents we experience, the Lord will preserve us from evil, he will keep our life.[3]

I must return to my dear friend Dr. John Hovey, who has shared with you the bend in his road—a diagnosis of Parkinson's disease. I'm happy to give Dr. Hovey the last word on this topic. He says, "My family, like so many others, enjoys a fabulous turkey dinner on Thanksgiving Day. We enjoy the delicious feast set before us, and then we indulge in a family tradition that has become an established

---

*Thou hast granted me many blessings;*
*Now let me accept tribulation from Thy hand.*
*Thou wilt not lay on me more than I can bear.*
*Thou makest all things work together*
*for good for Thy children.*

**—Dietrich Bonhoeffer**

---

part of our celebration over the years. And I'm certain many other families do something similar. We take turns around the table sharing aloud what we're thankful for this particular year."

Dr. Hovey continues, "We always seem to have guests at our Thanksgiving feast, and they don't know what to expect. So I usually go first to break the ice. On the year I've told you about, the year of my diagnosis, I began by saying I was eternally grateful that God chose me as His child. I expressed how deeply thankful I was to have a loving family. Then I went on to say I was thankful for Parkinson's disease.

"Why? Because God used Parkinson's disease to bring me closer to Himself, to His Word, and to my family."

When the bend in the road seems treacherous, as it did for Dr. Hovey, we can smile and look right past it. We can lift our eyes above that bend and take in the beautiful hills outlined against the horizon. Then we can cast our gaze beyond even those, past the horizon and into the face of our Father. We know He loves us and watches over us, over the entire journey here and in the next world.

No matter what the future holds, no matter what may lie around the next corner, our help comes from the Lord who loves us. Nothing can keep us from His love. Parkinson's disease can't do it. Cancer can't do it. No matter what it is you're facing, whichever way your road bends—whatever obstacle looms before you in your road, that obstacle can't do it either.

> For I am persuaded that neither death nor life,
> nor angels nor principalities nor powers,
> nor things present nor things to come,
> nor height nor depth, nor any other created thing,
> shall be able to separate us from the love of God
> which is in Christ Jesus our Lord.
> —Romans 8:38–39

# Psalm 13

*To the chief musician. A Psalm of David.*

1 How long, O LORD? Will You forget me forever?
  How long will You hide Your face from me?
2 How long shall I take counsel in my soul,
  Having sorrow in my heart daily?
  How long will my enemy be exalted over me?
3 Consider and hear me, O LORD my God;
  Enlighten my eyes, lest I sleep the sleep of death;
4 Lest my enemy say,
  "I have prevailed against him";
  Lest those who trouble me rejoice when I am moved.
5 But I have trusted in Your mercy;
  My heart shall rejoice in Your salvation.
6 I will sing to the LORD,
  Because He has dealt bountifully with me.

# 4

# When God Delays

*When peace like a river attendeth my way,*
*When sorrows like sea billows roll—*
*Whatever my lot, Thou hast taught me to say*
*It is well, it is well with my soul.*

—HORATIO G. SPAFFORD,
"IT IS WELL WITH MY SOUL"

You and I live in an aging society. Of course, that's a statement that would be true of any time and place, wouldn't it? I know of no "land that time forgot." Everyone everywhere is a day older each morning they rise from bed.

But there's a particular crisis of aging in our culture. People who belong to that huge segment of society born between the end of the Second World War and the mid-1960s are finding their hair turning gray. They are worrying about being replaced by younger workers. The Pepsi Generation is quickly becoming the Geritol Gang. Many among us are coping for the first time with chronic illness, relentless pain, daily medication, and an exhausting and demoralizing battle against the time limits of the human frame.

Some of the illnesses have newly coined titles; others are old and familiar. Perhaps none is more heartbreaking than mental illness. Like any illness, the struggle against mental illness is difficult and depressing. But in the case of fighting against the loss of the human mind itself, there are unique and particularly devastating sorrows. Sharon Paul, a family friend, gives us an accurate idea of living and coping with a challenge of that magnitude in the following passage.

———

You can't judge a book by its cover—nor can you tell what's inside someone by his or her outside appearance.

If you could see me, you'd agree that my appearance is fairly ordinary. I've been married for eighteen years, about one or two of which could be described by the word *normal*—at least as the world defines that concept. As the medical world defines things, I am mentally ill.

By the time such an official diagnosis could be made, it was actually something of a relief. Does that statement shock you? You see, I'd been told I had demons inside of me. A formal medical diagnosis was very helpful; it made it possible for me to be treated properly and to better understand the many facets of my condition.

I was hospitalized for many years. That period is over, but even now I must spend time in hospitals when I face a crisis. Sometimes people want to know how I can be a Christian and still have these conditions, particularly conditions that could lead people like me to harm themselves. But they don't understand the reality of depression as I do. I feel better about all of it when I think about people of great faith who faced depression like mine—people such as Jeremiah, David, and Elijah.

There were times in our country when people like me would have been put away somewhere, out of sight and out of mind. But we've made progress since then, and I can find freedom in talking about my depression and even reaching out to others who are coping with what I've been through.

On my good days, you're likely to find me chatty, loving, caring, and serving others. I can take responsibility for myself. I pray, read the Bible, and try to work through the darker memories from my past.

On my bad days, I can simply be thankful for those loving people who care enough to reach out to me. My world becomes black and unmanageable, and I become unwilling to look in the mirror or eat. I spend my time terrified, crying, hearing voices that I know aren't there, and longing to lose myself in the darkness or to embrace the final release of death.

I have days when I get lost and can't find my way home. This often makes me afraid to go out the front door or into the backyard. I have other days when I weep for hours for no apparent reason. Sometimes the stimulus of the world is so overwhelming that I can't cope, and my only response is either to flee to the safety of a stronger individual or simply to the comfort of darkness.

Those are simply the everyday details of life when you cope with depression.

For me to function on a daily basis, I need the help of my husband, my Christian therapist, my psychiatrist, my close friends, my medication, and my Lord Jesus.

That's the nature of the life I live.

And yet, I must tell you that even on my darkest days—even when life is a deep tunnel with no light visible to me—I can still say I've seen Jesus. I've seen Him with the eyes of my spirit, even if the eyes of my mind and heart are blinded. I can feel His presence, even if I can't feel anything else but pain and panic. I'm so grateful that He is my Savior, for without Him, I'm very certain I would be dead.

In every life, at some time, a person finds himself in that dark tunnel where no light is visible. You weep and you cry out in frustration and you plead, "Lord, I can't take any more! I have no more patience and no more strength to hold out; I must hear from You *today*. If You don't resolve this issue, I don't know what I am going to do. Can't You see that I'm desperate? *Why don't You help me?*"

Most of us have been there. How about you? It may have been because of a long, drawn-out sickness. It may have been a long-term financial problem. It may have been a struggle with grief. It may have been an alcoholic spouse or an unsaved loved one or a dysfunction in the family. Or perhaps you've suffered through a problem at work: a demanding, unreasonable boss or a jealous, spiteful fellow worker whom you have to cope with every day, with no resolution in sight. Or maybe, like Sharon Paul, you've spent a lifetime sparring with mental illness.

Before you know it, you find yourself in David's shoes and can understand his heartfelt words and emotions. This man is a hero and a man of God—the favorite son and sweet singer of Israel. He is a man after God's own heart, yet he is a man of anguish and suffering, one given to depths of depression who cries out to God, "How long?"

David's boyhood had been that of a shepherd boy, just one of several sons in a large family. But what a fateful turn that life had taken. From the moment David killed the giant Goliath, he himself became a hunted man. One moment he was the toast of the nation; the next he was a young man hiding out in caves. The king, the insecure and temperamental Saul, was bitterly jealous. His stock had plummeted as that of the shepherd boy had skyrocketed. The women of Israel celebrated the victory of David over Goliath by singing a song which is recorded for us in 1 Samuel 18:7: "Saul has slain his thousands, and David his ten thousands." If you were the king, would you like to hear such a melody echoing through your streets?

It was an intolerable situation for a jealous and egotistical monarch. In 1 Samuel 18:8–9 we read his predictable response: "Saul was very angry, and the saying displeased him; and he said, 'They have ascribed to David ten thousands, and to me they have ascribed but thousands. Now what more can he have but the kingdom?' So Saul eyed David from that day forward."

He *eyed* him. Have you got a good mental image of that? Have you ever gotten that kind of treatment from a coworker or a fellow student or even a member of your church? Saul gave David the evil eye. He saw him through the blurry green lens of jealousy, which had become an obsession. First Samuel 18:29 tells us that Saul made an enemy out of the young man because he feared him. Fear is often the root of our great mistakes in life.

That is a story you may already be quite familiar with. But we often forget that David was a fugitive for eight or nine years. We forget that he lived a life on the run in the very country where he was a national hero. Furthermore, his life and plight were complicated by all kinds of personal entanglements. For instance, Saul, David's ultimate enemy, the same ruthless king whose life was dedicated to hunting him down and murdering him, was also the father of a son who was David's dear-

---

*There are some favors that the Almighty does not grant either the first, or the second, or the third time you ask Him, because He wishes you to pray for a long time and often He wills this delay to keep you in a state of humility—and to make you realize the value of His grace.*

**—Jean Eudes**

---

est friend and a daughter who had stolen David's heart. Can you imagine a more complicated personal scenario than that?

During these eight or nine years, David had to remain constantly on the move. He lived in the fields and in the forests, in the caves and in the deserts. Finally he was chased out of the land of Israel and into the very midst of the Philistines, the enemies whose hero he had slain. David ended up in a city called Gath, but the locals identified him quickly. The only way he could think of to escape was to act as if he'd lost his mind. The Scripture says that in order to get away from Achish, the king of Gath, David dribbled in his beard, scratched his hands on the doors, and gave the most convincing impression he could of insanity.

Later, David had the protection of six hundred of his faithful men. He settled in a place called Ziklag, where he managed to live peaceably for sixteen months. But one day he left on a military mission. When he returned home, the city of Ziklag had been burned to the ground. All the wives and the children whom the soldiers had left behind had been carried away—including David's own family.

David's men were not merely grief-stricken, but filled with fury. They turned their anger on David and threatened to stone him to death. It was all David's fault—that's the way they saw it. As far as

they were concerned, David, their leader, had cost them their wives
and their children. First Samuel 30 tells of David's deep distress. He
had lost his own family and was blamed for the loss of hundreds of
other women and children. And now he faced death by stoning.

He had killed a giant and become a hero—but he had to live a life
of a fugitive. He was an anointed king—but he had to live like a beast
of the fields. Now he faced a violent death at the hands of the men he
trusted. David was desperate. Out of the pain in his heart, he cried out
to the Lord. And out of that furnace of his desperation came the incredible words of Psalm 13:

> How long, O LORD? Will You forget me forever? How long will You
> hide Your face from me? How long shall I take counsel in my soul, hav-
> ing sorrow in my heart daily? How long will my enemy be exalted over
> me? Consider and hear me, O LORD my God; enlighten my eyes, lest I
> sleep the sleep of death; lest my enemy say, 'I have prevailed against
> him'; lest those who trouble me rejoice when I am moved. But I have
> trusted in Your mercy; my heart shall rejoice in Your salvation. I will
> sing to the LORD, because He has dealt bountifully with me.

F. B. Meyer, one of the great writers of biblical commentaries, said,
"Saul's persecutions lasted for eight or nine years; and no hope of ter-
mination appeared. David was a man who spends five hundred days
passing through a forest. The tangled over-growth hides the sun; and
he begins to despair of ever emerging."[1]

David wrote this psalm when he was physically exhausted and
emotionally depressed. His troubles with King Saul had gone on year
after year, and he was dispirited and discouraged. This psalm was
wrung out of the extremity of his soul. He simply could not go on, not
for another day, not for another hour, not even for another minute.[2]

As we relate to God, we're so much like small children. You have a
better perspective for appreciating this fact if you've ever been a parent. You're driving your family to a vacation at the beach far away.
Those little voices come from the backseat, saying over and over,
"How much longer? How much farther?" And of course, "Are we there

yet?" You've said it as a child yourself or heard it as a parent. And from the backseat of life, we call out the same questions to God: "How much longer, Lord? How much farther? Are we there yet?"

We can see and feel that impatience and desperation in the words of David. I'm glad he put his deepest feelings into writing. It reassures me to know that someone we hold as a spiritual hero, someone whom God has honored, had the courage to say the kinds of things that we often feel ashamed of saying. In so many ways, David is one more child in the backseat of a long, hot journey. Aren't we all?

## Our Struggle When God Delays

On those occasions when you struggle with God's timing, it's good to know these feelings didn't originate with you. Not only did David express the feelings you've had, but he did so repeatedly. Read through the psalms, and you'll find a number of them like the one we're exploring in this chapter. So many of them begin with a sigh and end with a song. But in life, you can't take in the song without letting out the sigh.

Just as a song has a refrain, this psalm's sigh has one—a recurring phrase that always comes back around. This time, the chorus or refrain is repeated four times: *How long?* That's right, David is singing the blues. He's overwhelmed with a sense of the permanence of trouble. Trouble springs up when we want it least, seems to have no solution, seems to mock our most diligent efforts to lead a happy and peaceful life, and finally consumes our last ounce of patience. And David, much like you, finally lifts his eyes to heaven in exasperation and says, "How much longer, O God? How much longer?" It's David's blues chorus.

Aren't you grateful for the psalms that are such remarkable illustrations of honest prayer? I don't always pray with total honesty, and allow me to venture a guess that you don't, either. Your friend at work brushes by you at the copy machine. "How's it going?" he smiles. And you say, "I'm doing fine," or you might even say, "Couldn't be better."

But wait a minute! Didn't you have an argument with your spouse this morning? Didn't you just now catch a lecture from your boss? So you just told your friend a whopper, and you don't even think about it. How many times have you and I both done that?

Well, doing that causes little damage to relationships with your friends, because they have no idea what is really going on in your life. But we have much less success posturing before God. He is with you during the argument with your spouse; He is saddened by the confrontation with your boss. And when you force a smile into your prayers and say, "I couldn't be better, Lord!" He is again saddened. He knows what you're going through, and He has been looking forward to talking it over with you. He'd be much happier with an exasperated "How long, Lord!" than with your forced smile.

### When God Delays, We Feel Forgotten

You will come to the point of believing God has forgotten you. Don't worry—it's a common experience. We all pass through a dark stage of feeling that God either isn't there at all, or at the very least, He has forgotten us. Perhaps our problems aren't important to Him, we imagine. The psalmist encounters just those very doubts. In Psalm 10:1 he

---

*It is not under the sharpest, but the longest trials,*
*that we are most in danger of fainting.*

**—Andrew Fuller**

---

cries out, "Why do You stand afar off, O LORD? Why do You hide yourself in times of trouble?"

Maybe these cynical words have slithered through your mind: "God is always around when I don't need Him. But just wait until trouble comes around, when I go looking for Him. Just try to find Him then—He goes into hiding." If we stop and think about it, we haven't been too eager to find God when things were going well or when the smaller problems came up. Even the larger trials can be handled up to a point. We can take a certain amount with our faith intact. But the longer we go without God's peace and perspective in the midst of bad times, the more our faith begins to weaken.

Consider Job, the wise and godly man of the Old Testament. He lost his children, his animals, and his servants—virtually everything he had—all in one mind-bending period of tragedy. These were great losses, not garden-variety trials. But Job handled them all with patience and deep inner strength. Times did not improve for him. The devil extended his lease on Job's life, and the suffering servant of God began to realize that he was in for a long-term battle. That's when he began to come apart at the seams.

Everyone has a point somewhere in the geography of their souls marking the limits of their faith. It is the point at which faith begins to unravel. For younger Christians, that point may be just around the corner; seasoned believers can travel much farther before reaching it. Only we ourselves know where the point lies, and we find out during a season of testing. A trial will build to a crescendo in your life. You attempt to handle it, and you pray about it. But life will not cooperate. As the days turn to weeks, then weeks to months, and even months to years, you reach that personal point, somewhere in the scheme of your suffering, when you begin to give up on God.

What you believe is that He has given up on you. You may even be feeling that way right now. If so, please allow me to remind you that what you're contemplating is a simple impossibility. God never gives up on you; He never ceases to care about you, and He will not abandon His work on you—of which your trial is a part. I love the poignant words in Isaiah 49:15–16: "Can a woman forget her nursing child, and not have compassion on the son of her womb? Surely they may forget, yet I will not forget you. See, I have inscribed you on the palms of My hands; your walls are continually before Me."

The word picture is a revealing one, isn't it? Try to suggest a relationship more intimate than that between a mother and her nursing child. God wants us to realize that even if that woman could somehow forget the precious child at her breast, He would never forget you. He even says, "Your name is written on the palms of My hands." That image instantly snaps into focus in your mind—your very name tattooed on the palms of His hands. That means it is engraved there; it cannot be removed.

Such is God's concern for you. He cannot forget you. No matter what storm you're weathering now, you have never left God's mind or heart.

### When God Delays, We Feel Forsaken

"How long will You hide Your face from me?" (v. 1). We can feel the frustration and despair in David's words. It seems as if God has forgotten him, yes, but even worse: It feels as if God has purposely averted His eyes from David, so as not to be bothered by the troubles of His suffering child. Perhaps he knows better, but David feels as if God simply doesn't care. David feels forsaken.

*Forgotten* is one thing, but *forsaken* is another matter entirely. We very innocently forget people—people we love and care about. That can happen in the hectic pace of things. But the act of forsaking is very intentional—*premeditated forgetfulness.* David said to himself, "Here I am at this place in my lifelong relationship with God, a relationship I was given to believe was a very special one; I've spent my days fleeing for my life, hiding, fighting battles, and losing families, finding myself farther than ever from that throne I was promised so long ago; and I cannot get beyond the conviction that God has forgotten and even forsaken me. He has led me through all these trials to abandon me."

That is how David feels; that is how you have felt: *My God, why have You forsaken me?*

You might recognize those words. Jesus said them in His anguish on the cross. Do you know where Jesus got those words? He pulled them from Psalm 22. If you study that psalm, you'll find that the same man, David, has repeated Psalm 13 almost exactly: "My God, My God, why have You forsaken Me? Why are You so far from helping

Me, and from the words of My groaning? O My God, I cry in the day-time, but You do not hear; and in the night season, and am not silent" (Ps. 22:1–2).

Here is the surprise that an in-depth study of the psalms will offer you. Psalm 22 has no historic place in the life of David as other ones do. This is what scholars call a Messianic psalm, looking ahead to Is-rael's long-promised hero and deliverer. It foretells the crucifixion of the Lord Jesus Christ, giving details of the torture and excruciating pain of crucifixion centuries before that method of execution was even invented. Old Testament people could read this psalm and look through a window to see the climactic event of the New Testament, as seen through the eyes of Christ.

And it all came full circle. In time, when the prophetic event came to pass, the Lord Jesus hung suffering on the cross and quoted the very words of Psalm 22 creating a window into the Old Testament. We read that "about the ninth hour Jesus cried out with a loud voice, saying, *'Eli, Eli, lama sabachthani?'* that is, 'My God, My God, why have You forsaken Me?'" (Matt. 27:46).

It's helpful to know that David suffered and felt forsaken. But it's life-changing to realize that even Jesus Himself—the Lord of heaven and earth, enclosed in flesh—experienced the same emotions. Please take in the full import of these words: The Lord Jesus Christ not only felt forsaken, *He was forsaken*. The Father turned His back on Jesus be-cause He was a holy and just God who could not look upon the sin that Jesus carried to the cross—your sin and mine. The next time you feel forsaken and lift up your voice to pray to Almighty God, do this—go to a private place and spend significant time reflecting on the incredible truth that the One who hears your prayers has been there too. He knows exactly how you feel. He knows what it means to be forsaken.

"My God, My God," He cried out, "why have You forsaken Me?" He was forsaken indeed—but we are never forsaken. Here is the truth you must fully comprehend and stake your life upon if you remember no other words from this chapter: *He turned His back upon His Son so that He would never have to turn His back on you.* That was the excruciating price

He paid because He loves you that much. He lived and died and suffered on this earth so you wouldn't have to be forsaken.

When we cry out to Him in the midst of our trials, even when we can't sense it, God hears us. He'll never forsake us. That idea is pounded home in the clearest words possible in Hebrews 13:5: "For He himself has said, 'I will never leave you nor forsake you.'"

But that doesn't mean we'll never *feel* forsaken. Emotions will bring us to that point, and we can feel free to express our honest, naked feelings to God when that comes to pass.

## When God Delays, We Feel Frustrated

Have you felt frustrated with God? If we're honest, we've all had times when we've said, or at least felt like saying, "God, I'm really upset. I've been praying about this for years, for months. It doesn't seem as if You're there." Listen to the words of the psalmist in the second verse of Psalm 13: "How long shall I take counsel in my soul, having sorrow in my heart daily? How long will my enemy be exalted over me?"

David is frustrated for two reasons.

1. **He's frustrated because of his own emotions.** He says, "Every day I go through this. Every day I must deal with this." Someone said that the problem with life is that it's so *daily*. Each morning we must rise and face our challenges—and the same ones are there every day, rain or shine, summer, winter, spring, or fall. Whatever we have to deal with, when we get up and "reboot" our minds, all the same crises take up right where they left off.

James Montgomery Boice, who has written a wonderful commentary on the Book of Psalms, says, "The third time David asks, 'How long?' he refers to a combination of what we would call dark thoughts and uncontrollable emotions. When we no longer sense that God is blessing us, we tend to ruminate on our failures and get into an emotional funk. And when our emotions take over it is always hard to get back onto a level course. That is because the best means of doing this—calm reflection and a review of past blessings—are being swept away. We discover that we cannot settle ourselves long enough to complete this exercise."[3] The problem begins to take over in our lives.

Have you ever experienced the frustration of something painful or negative or sad becoming your constant and daily companion? Of course, you know what to do—you've been taught to read your Bible, to pray, and to spend time with God's people. But you're no longer

---

*David was talking about that knot in the stomach, the lead weight in the breast that makes the thought of food nauseating. . . . We can't sleep, can't eat, can't settle to anything. Every time we try to get our mind on something else, back it comes—that gnawing ache inside.*

**—John Phillips**

---

dealing with a problem; the problem is dealing with *you*. It has taken over. It has gotten you into such an emotional bind that no matter how hard you try, you know you can't do the things you should do. It happened to David. He was frustrated by his emotions.

2. **He was frustrated because of his enemy.** David cried, "How long will my enemy be exalted over me?" (v. 2).

Try to take in this scenario. Imagine being told, early in life, that you would be the president of the United States, or perhaps that you would become the most powerful and successful business leader in the nation. And you were actually given that position, sworn in as president or appointed as CEO. Then, every possible harrowing event came to pass in your life. Imagine your frustration: You had visions of sitting in the Oval Office, or in an executive suite at the top of a towering skyscraper, changing the course of world events. Instead, you're running for your life and your friends have turned against you. The promises seem always to be deferred to some unspecified future time.

This was David's plight. He was the king in waiting; David had already been anointed by Samuel as the king of Israel, back in his days as a shepherd. Do you know how much time passed between David's anointing and the moment he actually became king? Fifteen years.

Jesse, David's father, had brought the boy to the prophet Samuel. Samuel had poured oil over David's head and had given him the wonderful news that he was the heir to the throne of Israel. Then David had gone back to the fields. He had slain a giant, and that's where all the plans seemed to go awry.

What was the meaning of all this? David shook his fist at the sky above him and cried out, "How long, Lord, is my enemy going to be exalted over me?" The king-in-perpetual-waiting evaluated his own resources (not too impressive as a desperate fugitive), and he evaluated the resources of Saul, a jealous, murderous, ungodly king. This bloodthirsty monarch had once sent thirty thousand men after the shepherd boy. Whose side was God on? If the answer was "David's," you could have fooled the young man. God seemed to give Saul everything and David nothing.

David, taking a stand with six hundred men against a kingdom, said, "Lord, what do You want from me? The monster in pursuit of me has a kingdom, and I have a cave. What on earth do You expect me to do?"

In his depression, it may well be that David decided God had taken on more than He could handle. Perhaps God had begun with all the best intentions for David. He had helped him kill the giant but wasn't prepared for all the chaos that followed. In other words, God had just gotten in over His head. So why should David keep resisting? He couldn't fight an evil empire. He had nothing but God, and God wasn't talking.

I doubt you'll ever face a hostile army or have a king put a price on your head. All the same, we have an enemy worse than any number of kings or assassins or regiments. The Bible tells us in 1 Peter 5:8 that we are to "be sober, be vigilant; because your adversary the devil walks about like a roaring lion, seeking whom he may devour."

I don't know if the enemy has ever pursued you, but he is relentless. You wonder, "Lord, how am I ever going to get victory over this sin, this problem, this addiction? I'm doing everything I know how to do, but it's just too much for me." David felt that way; he was frustrated and overwhelmed by his enemy to the point of giving in. Look carefully at the text, and you'll see how honestly he describes his feelings about being a fugitive and fleeing from the most powerful man on earth.

This is all very understandable and human. It's a comfort to know David had the kind of black days we do. But aren't you glad the psalm doesn't stop there? David may have thought he didn't have a prayer, but in fact, he was just where God wanted him.

## Our Supplication When God Delays

Despite the desolation of his emotional state, at least David prayed. And what kind of prayer did he offer?

There is no textbook for genuine prayer. There is no professor who can teach it, no pastor who can make it happen for you. True prayer is a spontaneous outpouring of honesty and need from the soul's foundation. In calm times, we say a prayer. In desperate times, we truly *pray*.

"Lord," you cry, "I'm lost and helpless. I have nowhere else to turn." So, having come to the end of your own limited resources, you are desperate enough to try your last resort: You go to the Creator of the universe who loves you and made you and holds all the answers in His hand. That's when you pray.

### The Foundation of Our Prayer

David repeats one little word three times in his prayer of desperation: the word *lest*. This is the kind of small, inconspicuous word on which the entire meaning of a Scripture passage can hinge. *Lest* is a conditional word. First, David says, "Lest I sleep the sleep of death." David was so worn out physically and emotionally that he fully expected to die. He seemed to have come to the last page, and since the book of his life story was about to close, it seemed like an appropriate time to pray.

Not only did he fear his own death, but he also feared his own defeat. He said, "Lest my enemy say, 'I have prevailed against him.'"

There is the word *lest* again. David is certain that Saul will come out the winner. David is preparing to surrender as a prisoner, and it seems like an appropriate time to pray.

Perhaps worst of all, David feared his own disgrace: "Lest those who trouble me rejoice when I am moved" (v. 4). Everyone in Israel knew that David was being pursued by Saul. When the enemy caught him, David would be humiliated, a subject of mockery. And the terrible thought of that for one who had been promised a kingdom made it seem like an appropriate time to pray.

Three great fears moved David to his knees. Quite frankly, he was not motivated to pray because he was a godly man, although we know that he was a man after God's own heart. David prayed in Psalm 13 because he was desperate. Through the years, I've often observed how God steers us into that emotional cul-de-sac. He likes to corral us into a corner where the only way out is up. We have nowhere else to turn, and that's when we get serious about praying.

If you're going through a time of trouble right now, as so many of us are, don't rail against God for what He has done to bring you to this place. Instead, ask Him how you can learn to be His trusting child and how you can hang on to the desperation that brings about sincere, heartfelt prayer. "O Lord God, I can't get through one day without You. I can't make it through these next hours without You."

When we become desperate, we cry out, "O Lord, help me!" And He always does.

### The Form of Our Prayer

In his desperation, David prayed three prayers in verse 3. First He said, "Lord, consider me." The words actually mean, "Look on me." What he wanted to say was, "Lord, don't turn Your back on me anymore. Turn around and look at me and see me!"

His second prayer is, "Lord, hear me." David is pleading with God to answer his questions. "Lord, please hear what I'm saying."

And then there's a very interesting third request. He says, "Lord, enlighten my eyes." My first interpretation of that phrase was, "Lord, show me what You're doing." But that's not the meaning of the phrase. It really means, "Lord, put the light back in my eyes." Isn't that a fascinating thing to put in our prayers? *Put the light back in my eyes.*

You can easily spot a person suffering through depression. His face gives him away. Depression transforms one's countenance into a mask, empty and rigid. Most of all, the light in the person's eyes has been extinguished. David says, "O Lord, I have no hope. Please *see* me and *hear* me—and put the light back in my eyes." What a moving prayer this is.

But we come to a surprising place in David's prayer. If you read the chapter thoughtfully, you can't help but think, *Doesn't this portion belong somewhere else?* For we've heard the cries of a tortured man. We've heard his pleading and fears, and we've seen just how low a man can sink. And there in the depths of his despair come two verses in which despair is replaced by triumph. David is no longer the bitter, hopeless man who feels God can't or won't help him. He's suddenly a man filled with praise and a sense of victory, a man who has regained the light in his eyes.

## The Focus of Our Prayer

David worked honestly through his darkest, most hopeless feelings. Then he turned his eyes away from his troubles and fixed his gaze on God. The focus of his prayer became "O Lord, my God." David called upon God; he called upon the power of God. In the midst of his prayer, in bringing his desperate plea to God, he began to look away from his problems and to see the One whom he had been addressing. He is suddenly conscious of an exalted and holy God, the Lord of the universe sitting enthroned in heaven. He addresses his Lord as *Jehovah Elohim.*

*Jehovah* reflects God's promises; *Elohim* reflects God's power. David says, "O God of power and promise, I appeal to You." In this moment of transformation, I believe David's mind must have gone back to the promise that was given him, the promise that he should ascend to the throne. I believe he had a resurgence of faith that he would sit on Israel's throne. God had promised him something, despite all that had transpired, and that meant something. It had to, he suddenly realized. David's heart suddenly returned to the conviction that the God who promises is the God who is powerful, who can stand behind His promises. David's faith rebounds and reasserts itself.

I always turn with joy to Jeremiah 20:11 when I'm facing difficulty: "The LORD is with me as a mighty, awesome one. Therefore my persecutors will stumble, and will not prevail. They will be greatly ashamed, for they will not prosper. Their everlasting confusion will never be forgotten."

A similar promise is found in Psalm 138:7–8: "Though I walk in the midst of trouble, You will revive me; You will stretch out Your hand against the wrath of my enemies, and Your right hand will save me. The LORD will perfect that which concerns me; Your mercy, O LORD, endures forever; do not forsake the works of Your hands."

We can find tremendous hope of victory in the midst of the deepest pits life can drop us into. But it's no simple process. There isn't a handy, guaranteed formula for hope in the midst of suffering. It takes absolute, fall-on-your-face humility and genuine, gut-wrenchingly honest prayer. We must come to the point where we hear ourselves saying, "Lord God, my life is devastated. I've been victimized by my emotions and overwhelmed by my problems. Life has thrown all it can at me, and I've caved in. I've experienced none of the victory; I haven't honored You. I am at the point of surrender. But O Lord God, in the midst of all of this, help me to see and know my Mighty Awesome One, *Jehovah Elohim*."

Only in the abject humility of such a prayer can we begin to catch the briefest glimmer of Him, and only then will our plummeting fortunes begin to reverse themselves.

There is a threefold progression in this psalm moving from tears to triumph. Right in the center lies the ultimate truth that makes the difference. That truth is that *Jehovah Elohim*—Almighty God—is in charge. No wonder David breaks into joyful song.

## Our Song When God Delays

*Our Song Is a Song of Triumph*
"But I have trusted in Your mercy; my heart shall rejoice in Your salvation. I will sing to the LORD, because He has dealt bountifully with me" (vv. 5–6).

David's song is a song of triumph. And how did he reach that point? He began to see God.

Our troubles can cause us to avoid the places where we're most likely to see Him. I'm always puzzled when troubled people fall away from the church. They may be strong pillars of the local fellowship, but when trouble comes along, they disappear. Have you ever noticed that?

"We've missed you in church."

"Well, the truth is that we're having trouble in our marriage."

If that's true, get up early and go to both services! You need all the church you can get in such a time. Our faith isn't a luxury intended for periods of smooth sailing—neither is our fellowship. When trouble

---

*The steadfast love of the LORD never ceases,*

*his mercies never come to an end;*

*they are new every morning;*

*great is your faithfulness.*

**—Lamentations 3:22 (NRSV)**

---

comes along, that's when it's wonderful to be part of a faithful, Bible-believing body of people who will rally around you. They'll pray for you, support you with their resources, encourage you, and counsel you in the tough decisions. The devil is the only one whose opinion is that you should take a sabbatical from church in the hard times.

David says, "I have trusted in Your mercy; my heart shall rejoice in Your salvation." What does that word *salvation* mean to you? I hope you realize that it means more than being saved from judgment; it can also be about salvation from predicaments that occur in the here and now. God saves us in the big picture, but the Bible assures us that He saves us in the small ones too—when we ask Him.

You might question that conclusion, because you think about poor, beleaguered David. How exactly has God saved him in this situation? Saul is still coming after him. The armies are still on the march. Things look as hopeless as ever, on the face of things. What has really changed?

Nothing—except David's memory. He has recalled, as the spirit of prayer took hold of him and God counseled his hurting soul, that nothing has changed about *God*. Our Lord is changeless. He has been mighty in the past, and that has not changed. He has been loving and full of blessing, and that has not changed. He has had a plan for David, and that has not changed either. David has remembered these things, and he sings with joy, in words that simultaneously reflect past promises and future fulfillment: "God, You have delivered me!"

Has David been delivered from his plight? No, but in his heart and mind he has seen blessed deliverance, and he has claimed the promise of God. He proclaims—in advance, with the conviction of things hoped for and the evidence of things not seen—that "God has delivered me." David, the future king, has such faith in the future that he speaks of it in the past tense.

### Our Song Is a Song of Thanksgiving

David writes, "I will sing to the LORD, because He has dealt bountifully with me" (v. 6). If you want to stay healthy as a Christian, you need to go back and remember what God has done for you in the past. You need to polish the monuments to the great victories in your life. That's among the wonderful reasons for keeping a journal. David consults the journal in his mind of his dealings with his Lord, and he realizes, "God has dealt bountifully with me."

How often David must have, in his quieter moments, thought back to that tumultuous day in the field, that day when he tried on the king's armor and couldn't fit into it. He must have recalled the intimidating size and fearsome demeanor of that giant whom he faced with only a sling and five smooth stones. God had dealt bountifully with him then, and that was an understatement. David must have reviewed it often.

David took out that nine-foot-six-inch giant with a single shot and, in doing so, preserved Israel. There was no way to experience such a thing and not realize it was God's work. David must have thought back even farther, to a time when God gave him incredible, super-human strength and adrenaline to challenge wild animals that were threatening his flock of sheep. Why, a boy of his age couldn't have prevailed against a bear and a lion without God's presence. God clearly had a special purpose for him.

And it was undeniable that there had been times when Saul had been closing in for the kill. The game had seemed to be up. He was right in the very grasp of Saul and his sword, yet a miracle had always arrived.

We know from the psalms that David called upon his memory often to nurture and refresh his faith. When anxiety for the future built up—and it did time and again—David faced it with the testimony of the past. His life may not have been what he might have chosen, but it was a life that could never have lasted this long without God's intervention.

What a terrible danger it is for us to become trapped in the claustrophobia of the present during a crisis. That's our first impulse. The clear and present danger is so huge, so imposing, that it blocks our view behind us and ahead of us. We desperately need perspective. We can't change the future until it arrives, but we can gain wisdom from the past. It should hold for us an absolute conviction on the question of who God is and what He's done for us previously.

Make your list, and check it twice. Just what has God done for you? You lost your job, and you thought the world would end. What did God do? Your marriage was in terrible trouble, or perhaps you even faced the devastation of a divorce. What did God do? How about when one of your children broke your heart? Do you remember God's love for you then? Make a detailed inventory of His faithfulness in your life, and you'll be surprised at the length of it.

"I waited patiently for the LORD; and He inclined to me, and heard my cry. He also brought me up out of a horrible pit, out of the miry clay, and set my feet upon a rock, and established my steps. He has put a new song in my mouth—praise to our God; many will see it and fear, and will trust in the LORD" (Ps. 40:1–3).

Psalm 28:7 says it this way: "The LORD is my strength and my shield; my heart trusted in Him, and I am helped; therefore my heart greatly rejoices, and with my song I will praise Him."

Does it seem strange to you that Psalm 13, so filled with misery, builds to a final note of triumph, trust, and praise to the Almighty One? There's nothing strange about it. That's the way faith should work. We come to God honestly, pour our hearts out to Him, and experience renewed faith as He prods our memories and reaffirms His love.

In the Old Testament, there is a story of a prophet by the name of Habakkuk who lived at a time when the people of God lived in rebellion against His holy principles. Habakkuk was the prophet called to confront them in their wickedness, so he stood in their midst and cried out, "God, what are You going to do about this?"

The second verse of that prophet's book reminds us of Psalm 13. Habakkuk says, "O LORD, how long shall I cry, and You will not hear? Even cry out to You, 'Violence!' and You will not save."

God finally responded to Habakkuk's question in a veiled way. And once the prophet had worked over that answer and begun to grasp what it implied, he was shocked. It was the last answer he'd ever have imagined. For instance, in that same chapter, the Lord says to Habakkuk, "Look among the nations and watch—be utterly astounded! For I will work a work in your days which you would not believe, though it were told you'" (Hab. 1:5).

What kind of an answer is that? *What are You up to, Lord?* God is saying, "Take a good look around you and figure it out. If I tried to tell you, you wouldn't believe Me anyway."

God was absolutely right, I need not tell you. Habakkuk couldn't believe it. God had a plan to use the Chaldeans, a nation that was many times more evil and wicked than the people of Israel, to judge the people of Israel. I can just see this prophet of God putting his hands over his head and wailing, "O, Lord! The problem was terrible, and the answer is even worse!"

Habakkuk can't make any sense out of it at all. Why would God use those more evil than Israel as a means of punishing them? Where is justice or logic in such a thing? It made no sense. And the only sort of conclusion the prophet could ever come to in his perplexity was that God is God, and His ways are not our ways.

And yet Habakkuk finally does come to another conclusion: "Though the fig tree may not blossom, nor fruit be on the vines; though the labor of the olive may fail, and the fields yield no food; though the flock be cut off from the fold, and there be no herd in the stalls—yet I will rejoice in the LORD, I will joy in the God of my salvation. The LORD God is my strength; He will make my feet like deer's feet, and He will make me walk on my high hills" (Hab. 3:17–19).

Habakkuk, you see, made a choice. His country was in turmoil; his God had no answers that made sense. When there was no explanation for things that he could wrap his mind around, the prophet said, "I do have one option: I can praise God. The world around me may be in turmoil, yet though all of it falls apart, I will rejoice in the God of my salvation."

That same choice faces you. You can demand all the answers, neatly gift-wrapped. You can insist that God quickly resolve every trial and injustice in your life. You can hold out for the world, and your life within it, to become suddenly fair and rational, though they've never been so in the first place.

Or you can choose to lift up your eyes to the heavens, pour out your tears and grief and anger, and say in the very midst of them, "God, I have no clue what this turmoil is all about or where it is leading, but this is my resolution: I will put my trust in You, and I will praise You with all of my heart, unconditionally!"

The same God who has been there for you in the past is the God who is going to be there for you in the future. He will bring resolution in His own time, according to His own purposes. We become pre-occupied with our circumstances; God is preoccupied with our char-acter. He will allow the tough times for the higher good of our character until He is finished with the great work that is invisible to our earthly eyes.

And yet, you can be encouraged. God never waits too long. He is never late, nor does He lose control. He makes no misjudgments or mistakes. Next time you're in that ceaseless tunnel, and there seems to be no light to lead you on, think of Sharon Paul's words: "Even on my darkest days, I can still say I've seen Jesus. I've seen Him with the eyes of my spirit, even if the eyes of my mind and heart are blinded. I'm so grateful that He is my Savior."

The writer of Psalm 13 concluded, "I will sing to the LORD, for he has been good to me" (NIV). I hope you've learned the joy of singing when God delays.

# Psalm 138

*A Psalm of David.*

1  I will praise You with my whole heart;
   Before the gods I will sing praises to You.
2  I will worship toward Your holy temple,
   And praise Your name
   For Your lovingkindness and Your truth;
   For You have magnified Your word above all Your name.
3  In the day when I cried out, You answered me,
   And made me bold with strength in my soul.
4  All the kings of the earth shall praise You, O LORD,
   When they hear the words of Your mouth.
5  Yes, they shall sing of the ways of the LORD,
   For great is the glory of the LORD.
6  Though the LORD is on high,
   Yet He regards the lowly;
   But the proud He knows from afar.
7  Though I walk in the midst of trouble, You will revive me;
   You will stretch out Your hand
   Against the wrath of my enemies,
   And Your right hand will save me.
8  The LORD will perfect that which concerns me;
   Your mercy, O LORD, endures forever;
   Do not forsake the works of Your hands.

# 5

# Worship in Times of Trouble

*I found a Friend when life seemed not worth living*
*I found a Friend so tender and forgiving*
*I can't conceive how such a thing could be,*
*That Jesus cares for even me.*
*Each day, each year, my faith in Him is growing*
*He's ever near, His love is overflowing.*
*I have no fear, my worldly cares are few*
*I can depend on Him to see me through.*
*I found a Friend and He is your friend too.*

—BARCLAY (RON) ALLEN

Carole Carlson was a good friend and a gifted writer. We collaborated on several projects before her death in late 1999, and her talents always shone brightly. Carole was a woman of character who understood bends in the road because she had made the trip herself. She knew what it was like to have a peaceful life suddenly disrupted by tragedy. A few years before she went home to be with her Lord, she sat down and wrote me a poignant account of her journey. She shared with me the nightmare she'd encountered and come to terms with. I felt the heart-wrenching emotions of her experiences, as I'm certain you will.

I believe Carole would have appreciated the topic of this book, and it pleases me that she can "collaborate" with me on it through these thoughts from her insightful pen. Her words live on and minister to you today, though Carole herself is no longer with us. Here is what she wrote:

———

Kent left the house that Thursday with a smile and a bear hug from his mom. At eighteen, life for him was wonderful. He had graduated from high school with honors and had a good job working in a toy factory, and college was in his sights. The night before, he had gone to church and heard a message from two verses: "All things work together for good" (Rom. 8:28) and "In everything give thanks" (1 Thess. 5:18).

Kent was in a thankful mood, especially grateful for the airplane he and his dad had just purchased. His dream was to become a missionary pilot; the future gleamed with promise.

On Thursday night he called home and said, "Mom, I'm just going to go out and practice a few 'touch and goes.' Hold supper for me—I'll be home by nine."

Kent never came home.

In a clump of trees at the edge of a little country airport lay the crashed plane and the bodies of Kent and his buddy Rick. One moment in time changed our lives. On that warm June night, God chose to take one of our precious children.

How does a parent continue to *exist* beyond that moment? Will the knots in our insides ever leave?

In the weeks and months to follow, I learned more about God's love than I had in all my years of being a Christian. I learned that His Word speaks to our needs. "My grace is sufficient for you, for My strength is made perfect in weakness" (2 Cor. 12:9).

When I felt helpless to do even the small tasks of the day, I'd repeat, "I can do all things through Christ who strengthens me" (Phil. 4:13). Every time I saw a good-looking blond kid on the street and thought my heart would break, I remembered the verse Kent had underlined in his Bible: "But I do not want you to be ignorant, brethren, concerning those who have fallen asleep, lest you sorrow as others who have no hope" (1 Thess. 4:13).

When I began to indulge in self-pity, I'd embrace my husband, Ward, who was suffering as intensely as I was, and remember that God said, "Therefore comfort each other and edify one another, just as you also are doing" (1 Thess. 5:11).

In fact, we found strength in encouraging others. Kent's little brother didn't understand why his buddy didn't come home. His big sister had lost her pal and confidant. The friends in the youth group at church questioned God and the kids at school asked, "Why?" "Why?" "Why?"

The grace of God gave us comfort, but it also pierced us with the urgency to reach out to others. Ward and I grew closer together as we tried to console other parents who had suffered a loss. We developed an uncommon boldness to minister to those who were hurting.

I wish for no one the experience of losing a child. But a far greater tragedy is to lose the opportunity to know Jesus Christ intimately. How grateful we are that our children know and love Him. Life has meaning for us simply because we have the assurance, when this life is over, that we will all be reunited.

---

Life comes crashing down.

It happens for every one of us—not always with planes or automobiles or loss of family members or failed marriages. Somehow, all the same, life comes crashing down. The loss of one's own child may well be the most excruciating blow a loving parent can endure, but you can be certain that every other tragedy life dispenses offers its own unique form of suffering.

You're never prepared. That's the essence of the pain. Possibly for the first time in your life, you wonder whether there's any purpose in going on. For the first time, you wonder whether the gift of life on this earth—for *you*—is really a gift. For the first time, you seem to lack the strength even to rise from bed and perform the little rituals and have the little conversations that give daily life its color and rhythm. With a heart smashed in ten thousand pieces, you have no clue where to turn.

How wonderful, then, is that moment when you discover you can run into the arms of a Father who loves you and weeps with you. What an incredible moment when you fully comprehend that healing is possible. In Psalm 138:7, David wrote, "Though I walk in the midst of trouble, You will revive me."

He is ever faithful; He is ever present and attentive. One of the things we discover in the psalms is that we not only have a Lord God and a Savior when we face tragedy—even incomparable pain like the loss of a young, beloved child—but we have a wonderful Friend in the bargain.

Again and again, the psalms return to this beautiful, melodious theme. They burst out in song—for what other form than music could this book have ever taken?—over the amazing news that the high and holy God of creation is our Friend. They remind us that He knows every need we feel, every craving we experience. They assure us He is not a God who dwells in some distant, unapproachable realm, who paid a short call on this planet centuries ago—but that He is an always-present Father, who is totally immersed in the smallest details of our lives.

And when we come to Him in the midst of trouble, He hears us; He knows us. He loves us as we love our own children.

## In Times of Present Trouble, the Lord Is to Be Worshiped

In Psalm 138, we find the song of "a man after God's own heart" who had traveled a long journey down the road of spiritual wisdom. He understood many deep truths about his relationship with God—one of which is brought home with clarity and passion here. David came to see that in times of trouble, the most clearly marked path to God is not the way of struggle and desperation. It is, instead, the path of worship. Psalm 138 speaks to us about worship in times of trouble.

## Let Us Worship the Lord Thankfully

David opens this psalm by saying, "I will praise You." Who is the object of his praise? He doesn't say in the beginning, but he will go on to use the name of the Lord six times. The personal pronoun that refers to His name is found ten times in the first stanza. The words *You* and *Your* are everywhere. David is caught up in the majesty and presence of God.

As he writes, "I will praise You," the word he uses for "praise" deserves our attention. It gives a meaning to the sentence that might better be expressed as, "I will give thanks to You." Praise and thanksgiving are closely related. For David, this is a time of worship in a time of trouble, and he launches it by giving thanks to God. It takes a certain degree of wisdom and maturity for you and I to reach such a level. When difficulties burden us, we must struggle to remember our reasons for gratitude to God. This won't happen if we imprison ourselves within self-pity and preoccupation with loss. It requires the fortitude to open our eyes and see that, whatever seems to have been taken from us, we have received so much more that should move us toward gratitude.

In a spirit of thanksgiving, David has found the starting line that makes the difference. Scripture tells us elsewhere that we are to "come before His presence with thanksgiving" (Ps. 95:2).

Psalm 100:4 offers the same strategy. We are to "enter into His gates with thanksgiving, and into His courts with praise. Be thankful to Him, and bless His name." Gratitude is a doorway that admits us into the courts of godliness. Focusing inward on our misery traps us in our own private dungeon, and we lock ourselves away from those richer interiors that provide the healing and wisdom we need.

Gratitude is the key. You and I too often enter the Lord's courts driving a truck, don't we? We back it up to the courtyard, pull the lever, and unload everything we've been carrying. During the long nights, those supplies of tears and resentment and self-absorption have been building up. We can't enter into His presence without dumping all of it all over the steps of His holy courts. There is certainly a time for casting all our burdens upon the Lord—but perhaps not right there at the front gate. The psalms challenge us to come into His presence with thanksgiving. We worship the Lord God with a grateful heart in times of pain and crisis.

Is that a difficult lesson to learn? The next one is even tougher!

## Let Us Worship the Lord Wholeheartedly

As you work through the life and writings of David over a lifetime, you'll come to this conclusion about him: Notwithstanding the blemishes and failings of his humanity, David was a man who offered himself wholeheartedly to God. Notice how he begins this psalm with the words: "I will praise You . . . I will sing praises to You" (v. 1); "I will worship . . . and praise Your name" (v. 2). These are variations on a theme—his heart formulates and reformulates new expressions for the worship and praise that is spontaneously flowing from him.

Worship for David, you see, was no matter for pews and passivity. He threw his entire heart and soul and mind into the praise of God! What pursuits in your life claim your all?

Here is how God would answer that question: *you.* He gave His all for *you.*

The Lord God Almighty has taken note of us. He became one of us, and then He gave up His life out of love for us. That's no mild commitment. He gave Himself wholeheartedly for us, and He allows us to enter into His very presence. Meanwhile, we sit in our pews harboring the great fear that we might slip up and let our emotions show in our worship. What would those people in the pew behind us think?

As long as those people sitting behind us are claiming any part of our concern, we're not giving ourselves wholeheartedly to the worship of the Lord God. It's worth stopping to examine which owns the greater portion of our heart: God or our public image. The answer could be a disturbing one.

Psalm 119 is the Bible's longest chapter. It's devoted to the power and glory and study of the Word of God. Read that psalm in its entirety sometime. What you'll find is that salted all through those verses, again and again, are the phrases "wholehearted" and "with a whole heart."

- "Blessed are those who keep His testimonies, who seek Him with the whole heart!" (v. 2).
- "With my whole heart I have sought You; oh, let me not wander from Your commandments!" (v. 10).
- "Give me understanding, and I shall keep Your law; indeed, I shall observe it with my whole heart" (v. 34).
- "I entreated Your favor with my whole heart" (v. 58).

The message could be no clearer. When you approach God, you must do so with an undivided heart. How do you come to the Lord with your worship? How do you approach Him in times of trouble? In times of blessing? Perhaps you're like me; in terms of approaching

---

*We know not what the future holds*
*But take each day as it unfolds*
*The bitter with the sweet God blends.*
*We wisely take what 'ere He sends.*
*His dealings are in wisdom made,*
*The warming sun or chilling shade.*
*On mountain top in the dell*
*Our Father doeth all things well.*

**—David B. Stewart**

---

God wholeheartedly, I've found it's often easier in times of need than times of abundance. When life is smooth and calm, that's when I'm tempted to hold back a part of my heart. I tend to relax, as if I have everything under control. But I won't be relaxing for too long. God sends the storm to force us to look for Christ walking on the waves. The thunder gets our attention, and when we're humbled in fear, we're far more likely to approach Him with our entire being.

## Let Us Worship the Lord Courageously

David is determined that nothing should come between him and the worship of God.

In the opening refrain of Psalm 138, he writes, "Before the gods I will sing praises to You" (v. 1). The word *gods* refers to the pagan deities and leaders of the nations surrounding Judah. Our modern world is filled with false gods, and so was David's. He is showing a bit of godly arrogance here. In effect, he is saying, "Some people I know will fall silent while they're surrounded by pagan statues. But I intend to walk right up and worship You in the very midst of them all! I'm not ashamed of my Lord and my God." He didn't care what others thought. As for him and his house, they would serve the Lord.

Do you feel cultural pressure? The heat is rising for Christians in our society. There is more and more outright hostility for those who would claim Christian allegiances. I can remember when it was much more common to see families in restaurants joining hands around the table to thank and praise God before eating. Our family still does this—how about yours? It's wonderful to sit in a restaurant and see a family boldly praying together at another table. I try to encourage such families as I see them. We all need that encouragement in a world that ridicules us for trusting and obeying our Lord.

David said, "I couldn't care less what they think! I plan to praise my God in front of the pagan gods. I plan to speak of my God even to those who deny Him." David praised God *courageously*—with his heart, his soul, and his mind.

## Let Us Worship the Lord Intelligently

Sometimes we come to the worship of God and don't know where to begin. What do we say? How can we praise? Anything we do with excellence must be done with intelligence, and there are intelligent ways to worship God. Here is how to praise Him:

**Praise Him for His mercy and truth**. David said he would praise

God's name for His lovingkindness and truth (v. 2). The word *lov-ingkindness* is the Hebrew word *hessed*, which is actually the word for *mercy*. Have you ever noticed how often mercy and truth are found to-gether in the same passage? These two traits are twins in the Old Tes-tament. In the psalms especially, we repeatedly see mercy and truth wedded together in the same text. For instance, Psalm 25:10 says, "All the paths of the LORD are *mercy and truth*." In Psalm 57:3 we read, "God shall send forth His *mercy and His truth*." And Psalm 85:10 says, "*Mercy and truth* have met together" (emphasis added on all).

Here's the big question: Why would the two qualities of mercy and truth be consistently paired together in Scripture? To find the answer, we need only take one good look in the mirror and another good look at the people around us. It's interesting to see that there are some people who are gifted in mercy and others who place a high premium on truth—but they're not often the same people. The high-on-mercy, low-on-truth advocate ends up practicing injustice. He issues mercy as a free pass without accountability or standards. And you know this person's opposite: The high-on-truth, low-on-mercy fellow is a self-righteous, modern-day Pharisee who will use the truth as a blunt weapon to injure people.

But our Lord perfectly balances mercy and truth. His mercy is poured out in the light of absolute truth, and His truth is saturated by infinite mercy. Neither is compromised in any way. When you come before Him in trouble, you know that He hears the very deepest cry of your heart even as He deals with you according to His divine stan-dard. And because He is both merciful and truthful, when He gives you His Word, you can count on its being fulfilled.

Jesus embodied perfect truth and perfect mercy, and He is our model for doing the same.

**Praise Him for His magnified Word.** There are ideas and concepts I accept without completely understanding them. One of these is that God values His integrity so much that He has elevated it higher than His own name. Let me explain what I mean. When you study the Word of God, you can know He'll be with you—and why He has ele-vated His Word higher than anything in the universe. The Word of

God carries an authority matching that of the very name of God. Now, that's no insignificant item; it means that we can absolutely, fundamentally place our trust in the integrity of God. His Word is trustworthy, for He is trustworthy. He will always balance mercy and truth, and He can be relied upon to keep His Word—and to provide for us.

**Praise Him for His mighty provision.** Think about these words: "In the day when I cried out, You answered me, and made me bold with strength in my soul" (v. 3). I love this psalm! Why? Because every word is important. First of all, God doesn't delay in answering us when we come to Him. We may think He delays because we have our own timetable in mind, but God hears us the instant we cry out.

God will always be there when we're in trouble. Whatever He chooses to do about our circumstances, and whenever He chooses to do it, He will strengthen us for the battle. When David cried out to

---

*When trouble comes . . .*

*Sometimes God takes us through it,*

*Sometimes He helps us in it,*

*Sometimes He keeps us from it.*

---

the Lord, he always received an infusion of renewed vitality to face the problems ahead of him. "O Lord God," David often cries out in victory, "I called for Your help and You gave me power to stand in the midst of my enemies and my crises."

Let me be very clear that I'm not putting in a request for any more trouble in my life. I've had all I need for a while. Just the same, I can say that my darkest days have almost been worthwhile just for the experience of seeing God keep His promise to provide strength and endurance. I predict that I may be speaking for you too.

## In Times of Future Triumph, the Lord Is to Be Worshiped

Crisis psalms nearly always lead to visible transformation. We see the psalmist in his pain, desperation, and supplication—then we see God transform him and fill him with renewed faith and resolution. In the fourth verse of this psalm, David forgets his crisis and gazes prophetically into the future. He says, in effect, "When it seems as if my life is caving in, I can still choose to praise God. But how humble are my troubled words of worship compared to the praise that will echo and resound around the world one day—the day His name is lifted up! The world will be joined together in praise and exaltation of His glories."

Thus David becomes a prophet. Would you like to hear about the future world he sees?

### All Kings of the Earth Will Praise the Lord

Every knee shall bow; that will be the scenario.

Every king, president, premier, and prime minister across the expanse of the globe will bow before King Jesus and give Him the glory. The Bible tells us that "the kingdoms of this world have become the kingdoms of our Lord and of His Christ, and He shall reign forever and ever!" (Rev. 11:15). All people groups and all cultures will acknowledge that Jesus Christ is Lord. And Paul adds that "at the name of Jesus every knee should bow, of those in heaven, and of those on earth, and of those under the earth, and that every tongue should confess that Jesus Christ is Lord, to the glory of God the Father" (Phil. 2:10–11). So we can see that John caught a glimpse of that breathtaking new world, and Paul was allowed a hint of it too.

Before either of them lived, God revealed the same future vision to David. "All the kings of the earth shall praise You, O LORD," he wrote. And God gave him this glimpse in the midst of his worldly problems. "Now I praise You in my solitary suffering," he said. "Someday we will all be praising You in Your glory."

There was a commercial on television that used the catchline, "You can pay me now or pay me later." I don't remember what the product was, but I remember the line: *Pay me now or pay me later.* David's words in the psalm bring that commercial back to my mind, for God is saying, "Praise Me now or praise Me later. But you will praise Me someday, for every knee will bow and every tongue will confess that Christ is Lord."

Kings and commoners alike will worship God. The lofty will bow low, as the lowly are lifted up.

### All Kinds of People Will Be Acknowledged by the Lord

God doesn't make distinctions about our place on earth. David divides people into two groups—the lofty and the lowly—but God seeks love and reconciliation with them all.

The Lord has always sided with the lowly. I think about this as I visit New York's inner city and see the people living in filth and poverty. No matter what devastating circumstances these people have experienced, no matter how low their lives have sunk or how far they've been pushed away from God, I sense a special relationship between God and the lowly. Jesus exemplified God's heart for the poor. They reach out to Him too. He relates in a special way to the victims of life—people who have been brought so low they can hardly lift their heads.

Isaiah 57:15 says, "Thus says the High and Lofty One who inhabits eternity, whose name is Holy: 'I dwell in the high and holy place, with him who has a contrite and humble spirit, to revive the spirit of the humble, and to revive the heart of the contrite ones.'" Some have suggested that God thinks the most highly of people who don't think highly of themselves. He hears their prayers and reaches out to them.

The church is the body of Christ who made Himself lowly. The church is not characterized by the high and lofty for the most part. Christian prosperity is the exception more than the rule. The church has historically been composed of people who wander together in their lowliness and their need for a Savior. We have been people who would be of little account in the world, but who understand that God is no respecter of persons, and that the ground is level at the foot of the cross. The church is a celebration party for people too lowly for parties—the broken and needy and contrite. They're God's people.

God has another kind of relationship with the lofty—those proud and arrogant enough to have declared independence from God. What is this relationship? David says the Lord resists the lofty. "The proud He knows from afar" (Ps. 138:6). Remember that God always reverses the human equation so that the first in worldly values become last, and the last become first. For the humble, who with hearts of desperation come with heads bowed seeking God's forgiveness, He shelters. He puts robes around their shoulders and rings on their fingers. For the proud and independent, He continues to wait by the side of the road. He knows them from afar.

The Bible tells us we must bow in humble recognition of who we are and who God is. And if we can't do that, there's no hope for us. In His presence, there is no proud and distinguished individual. The wealthiest ruler in the history of this planet stands as a beggar in rags in the presence of an omnipotent, glorious Creator. Those distinctions we set among ourselves mean absolutely nothing in the context of His majesty. So we can only kneel to acknowledge the truth of our condition. If we cannot see ourselves as heaven sees us, we cannot see ourselves.

## In Times of Uncertainty, the Lord Is to Be Worshiped

David writes in verse 7, "Though I walk in the midst of trouble, You will revive me; You will stretch out Your hand against the wrath of my enemies, and Your right hand will save me."

It's one thing to be in trouble. You can have trouble on a nice day. You can have trouble with your children or your coworkers, but these are usually little troubles you know you can rise above. It's another thing to be *in the midst of trouble*. The appropriate word would be *stuck*. You find yourself in a crisis with no immediate resolution. You know this thing isn't going away. You know that when you wake up tomorrow morning, and the morning after that, this matter will leap to the forefront of your mind as soon as you wipe the sleep from your eyes. Some problem has risen up like a great tidal wave from the depths, and it dominates your landscape.

But if you're like David, there is something behind that wave—or perhaps it is between you and the wave—and that thing is called *hope*.

## The Lord Continues to Protect Us

If such a thing as an honorary doctorate in Crises and Catastrophes had existed, David would have been awarded one. Although he was a man after God's own heart, his life was one long procession of problems. As we've seen, he spent years fleeing the wrath of a king—living as a fugitive, hiding, and sleeping in caves. When he finally did become king, he immediately had to deal with geopolitical crises on every front. His nation of Israel was at war with everyone in sight.

David coped. He calmed the waters the best he could, and when everything had settled down on the political front, that's when the domestic front exploded. He was like a man whose career finally begins to look promising, who gets the big promotion—and suddenly he has marital trouble and his sons get into trouble with the police. David's own sons were in open rebellion against him. The house of David was crumbling; there were cracks in the foundation.

Would you agree that David walked in the midst of trouble? If you're having a problem in your family or on the job, I challenge you to read the life of David. Maybe you'll feel a little better. David walked in the midst of trouble—he made terrible, fateful mistakes—yet he always remained one of God's favorite children.

God had promised to protect His child, and neither party to that promise ever forgot it. Think about nearly everyone's favorite chapter of Scripture, Psalm 23. When David so movingly paints us a picture of the Good Shepherd watching over His sheep, we see again David's faith and trust in a protecting God. David sang, "He restores my soul; He leads me in the paths of righteousness for His name's sake. Yea, though I walk through the valley of the shadow of death, I will fear no evil; for You are with me; Your rod and Your staff, they comfort me" (Ps. 23:3–4).

*When you pass through the waters, I will be with you;*
*And through the rivers, they shall not overflow you.*
*When you walk through the fire, you shall not be burned,*
*Nor shall the flame scorch you,*
*For I am the LORD your God,*
*The Holy One of Israel, your Savior.*
*—Isaiah 43:2–3*

Every believer knows that when we walk through the valley of tears, God walks beside us; when we pass through the fire, He draws close to deflect the flames; when we wade through the flood, He is nearby to keep our heads up. In the storm or in the earthquake or in the midst of any disaster threatening to engulf us—that's the time we feel the presence of the Lord as we've never felt Him before. Other so-called friends may disappear. Their words may falter and their support may vanish. But God is closest in the crises, surrounding us with His presence. He promised us He would do it, and our Lord is always as good as His word.

David, recipient of the honorary degree in Crises and Catastrophes, bears testimony to that fact. His acceptance speech for such a degree would sound much like one of these psalms: thanks and praise to God Almighty, who keeps His promises. But at the end of the speech, David would add one more startling idea. He would assure you that the Lord will not only protect you, but *He will perfect you.*

## The Lord Continues to Perfect Us

He is perfecting us. That means He is bringing to completion everything in the world that surrounds and defines us.

What happens when we go through troubles and lose our perspective? We begin to think that God has forgotten us. He must have discarded that plan He had for this life; He must have scratched us from His divine daily planner. It's a terrible feeling to have the sense that God has put you aside.

And of course, it's never true. When we navigate troubled waters, God is the Master of not only the waves, but also the ship. He never abandons His plans or His people. He will see the voyage through to its final destination.

But we're stubborn creatures who struggle to learn. And we learn the least when the sun is shining and the winds are crisp and life feels good. Peace and prosperity have never provided effective classrooms. Crisis and catastrophe, on the other hand, offer master's degrees. By the way, that accreditation makes you a Master of Disaster.

The truth etches itself into your mind and heart when you find yourself forced into a one-on-one relationship of dependency upon God. It's the "school of hard knocks," to be certain, but there's one momentous consolation: All the while, even while the bruises ache and the scars are fresh, He is still working all things together for our good and for His. It's essential that we cling to His promise of continuous perfection. He is our only hope, our only asset, our only possibility, and as we look into His eyes, we realize that from the very beginning life has always been like that. We just wouldn't learn it, for we're stubborn creatures.

During the difficult days, what is He doing? I call Psalm 138:8 the "Philippians 1:6 of the Old Testament." Sometimes there are church members or radio friends who ask me to sign my name in their Bibles. I often jot "Philippians 1:6" beside my name, because it says this: "Being confident of this very thing, that He who has begun a good work in you will complete it until the day of Jesus Christ."

No matter what, you must never forget that when you're deep in the midst of trouble, God is still busy at work in you, though He may be doing so out of your sight. Street workers are out of sight too. As you walk through a busy city avenue, you'll see an open manhole marked by a sign that says "Men at Work." You can't see them, but you can be sure they labor on in the dark underside of the city. Just mentally place a "God at Work" sign into that scar where your troubles have taken their toll. He's involved in very expensive renovation. You may be paying the bill right now, but you're going to like the beautiful new design and furnishings of your life.

He is perfecting you. He's working on the new design. It's true that you don't remember signing the papers for the design. Our God, the Landlord of our lives, doesn't ask our permission. But He is eager to show us how well He can protect us, so that He might demonstrate in the process how wonderfully He can perfect us. Then, when the noise and the dust of it all are gone, the dross will have been burned off. What is left will be all the gold of a lifetime of God's ongoing project of perfection in us.

What a wonderful God! When we begin to look at our difficulties from the perspective of the psalms, our depression fades. Our hope increases. Our love for God is intensified.

### David's Final Appeal: "Do Not Forsake the Work of Your Hands!"

David asks the Lord to keep up the good work. "Do not forsake the works of Your hands," he says (v. 8). This is a man who has become aware of the work of the Sculptor who has been chipping away the raw stone of his life for years. He finally comprehends that at the end of all the painful chiseling, something smoother and elegant—a finer work of art—truly emerges.

*The works of Your hands.* David has felt the expert work of those skilled fingers, and he knows those hands hold his life in their secure grip. He is saying, "Lord, You started this work on me. Your art project began a lifetime ago with a small shepherd boy. It was inaugurated when Samuel poured the oil over my head to establish a new identity for me—a royal identity. He poured the oil, but You've poured on the wisdom, like burning oil, in the course of a lifetime. And You've continued to bring the king from the stone. Continue what You've begun, O Lord. Pour it on!"

Have you ever imagined yourself literally in the hands of the Lord? It's a wonderful thought. Those hands that created the universe, that hurled the stars out into space and crafted the mountains and seashores, and then molded Adam from the dust of the earth; those hands that took the nails and reached out in pain across the wooden beams to embrace all of humanity—*those* hands now hold and caress you with gentle love.

You and I stand beside David to say, "Lord, lift me up in those powerful hands. And let them continue their work, even when it causes the pain of authentic discipline."

### Learning to Walk

Ron Mehl lives the life of a leukemia victim—not that it stops him from being a popular and productive pastor. He goes about his daily work in the Northwest, serving his congregation and preaching his sermons, always in the knowledge that he'll never truly be free of his disease. He even manages to travel across the country, preaching triumphantly and radiating the love of Christ, because Ron Mehl is a champion.

Ron had a friend who had recently become a grandfather for the first time. He invited Ron to come to his home for dinner and see his precious new granddaughter. She was learning to walk, and Ron's friend couldn't wait to show off his precocious little grandchild. He was like any new grandparent—bursting with pride he couldn't contain.

"Bumpa" was his designated grandparent name. Bumpa lifted the little girl and placed her beside the sofa so she could lean against it for balance. But it was clear to Ron that her chubby little legs were very tentative and unsteady. Even leaning against the sofa, she seemed certain to fall. But the proud grandfather was determined that the little girl would show her stuff. He walked across the room and sat in his chair. "Come on, little darling!" he called. "Come see ol' Bumpa."

The little girl really wanted to go to ol' Bumpa. Her heart was in it, and her spirit was game. She stepped out in a faith that exceeded her wobbly legs and collapsed in a little pile on the soft carpet. Ron teased his friend. He said, "Maybe she's just had a hard day."

But ol' Bumpa was determined his granddaughter could make the journey across the living room. So again she was propped up, and again she was exhorted to move forward. And one more time there was a heap of a ten-month-old little girl on the floor. Perhaps she landed a bit harder this time, or perhaps she was frustrated by the weakness of her young legs. In any case, she began to cry.

Then Ron's friend did a wonderful thing.

He could have allowed the little girl to crawl away in whimpering defeat, but instead he reached down with his big, work-hardened hands and took hold of her chubby little fingers. He lifted her up, turned her around, and set her tiny feet on top of his own. As he lifted his left foot, hers lifted with it. When he lifted his right foot, she took a step too.

And so Bumpa and his granddaughter walked across the floor. A huge smile chased the tears off her face, because, after all, she was walking!

"That was a sight I never forgot," Ron said. Ron knows what it's like to live in the limitations of a body that can't measure up to the heart's aspirations; he knows what it's like to have great hands reach down to bolster him and propel him forward.

How often have you tried to move forward in your own feeble power and ended up in a heap on the floor? You think you can do it, and God allows you to try. Proving to yourself and everybody around that you're simply not up to the task, you give up or give in. And just then, He reaches down with those loving hands and lifts you up to walk you through the barriers of your life—in His limitless strength.

That's the promise. He gave it to you and to me, and He stands behind His Word.

He stands behind *you* too. He may allow you to fall, but He'll never allow you to be defeated. That's an idea to set securely into your heart. Don't let life's commotion shake it away from you, because it carries hope. Whatever you may be facing today, don't give up or give in. Wait for those marvelous, loving hands to cover your own—and be ready to laugh with delight as He walks you, in His power, to places you never thought you could reach.

# Psalm 63

*A Psalm of David when he was in the wilderness of Judah.*

1 O God, You are my God;
   Early will I seek You;
   My soul thirsts for You;
   My flesh longs for You
   In a dry and thirsty land
   Where there is no water.
2 So I have looked for You in the sanctuary,
   To see Your power and Your glory.
3 Because Your lovingkindness is better than life,
   My lips shall praise You.
4 Thus I will bless You while I live;
   I will lift up my hands in Your name.
5 My soul shall be satisfied as with marrow and fatness,
   And my mouth shall praise You with joyful lips.
6 When I remember You on my bed,
   I meditate on You in the night watches.
7 Because You have been my help,
   Therefore in the shadow of Your wings I will rejoice.
8 My soul follows close behind You;
   Your right hand upholds me.
9 But those who seek my life, to destroy it,
   Shall go into the lower parts of the earth.
10 They shall fall by the sword;
   They shall be a portion for jackals.
11 But the king shall rejoice in God;
   Everyone who swears by Him shall glory;
   But the mouth of those who speak lies shall be stopped.

# 6

# A Desert Psalm

Listen carefully to the story of Steve Garrison. But before you listen, know that he was a thriving real-estate developer in California—among the best in the nation in his line of work. His prospects were soaring, and there seemed to be nothing but blue sky ahead of him.

Know also that he was a dedicated leader in his church and his local Christian Businessmen's Fellowship. Materially and spiritually, the path of Steve's life was a journey of joy—until the day his world fell apart. Here is how Steve tells the story.

———

My company was doing well. Sure, America was mired in a recession, but for a while we were hopeful of missing the worst of it in Southern California. We were invincible—at least that's how it seemed. The way we were building, selling, and profiting, why should we have worried?

But as you know, we didn't quite make it through. When the recession made it to the West Coast, its impact was that of a sledgehammer.

The slowdown in commercial real estate began late in 1990. By the end of the next financial quarter, construction was at a standstill; buildings sat half-finished, suspended in time, just like our careers. Boom times were over.

During the two previous years, my company had built thirty-six buildings to sell or lease in five industrial parks. We had accumulated some resources. But now it was early in 1991, and I was left with nine new commercial and industrial buildings on my hands. They stood tenantless with no buyers in sight. We'd kept our hands busy while the California sun was shining, and all our assets were tied up in the properties; the cash reserves vanished like water-mirages on a desert highway. My wife and I reluctantly cashed in our IRAs to meet our financial obligations, and in April of 1991, I had to release my last few employees. The doors to Garrison Development were shut and locked for the last time.

I was extremely fortunate to find employment as a commercial real-estate consultant. But even that drifted out of my grasp—within six months, the recession had cut me off and left me unemployed once again. All of this happened within a year. I'd owned my own company, with a career seemingly blessed by God; then I'd lost that and the job that followed.

I knew where I stood: My faith was going to be tested. It had been eighteen years since I had accepted Christ as my Lord and Savior, and I had trusted Him with my life and my family and all my prospects. I knew that I worshiped a sovereign God who is absolutely in control of everything. I knew I shouldn't keep my eyes on my unpleasant circumstances, but on His guidance. I knew I had to keep on trusting and obeying, hard times or not. So I kept my faith in Him—I had no other choice.

I'd come to my bend in the road. And just around my bend I found myself in a spiritual desert, arid and dry. I began to see that my walk with Him had gradually eroded during years of fruitfulness. With the blinders removed from my eyes, I was seeing myself in an unattractive new light; God was showing me hard truths about myself that I didn't want to see. Such things as my reputation, the esteem of my colleagues, and my net worth and assets had become pagan idols in my life. I'd had no idea that I'd lifted those things to such a level.

I saw my relationships honestly too. I hadn't always dispensed grace to those who worked with me. I'd been critical and impatient with my employees, rather than letting my relationship with Christ soak into that part of my life.

These things all came as a shock, because I'd thought I had it all together. God was "lovingly beating me up," as I've described it since then. These were difficult lessons to learn, but I sat at His feet and listened to His Word. And in the midst of the discipline, I came to love Him more than I had in the past—much more.

But there was still my livelihood to worry about. I stayed on the lookout for opportunities to make a new start in business life. In time, God led me to launch my own real-estate consulting business. That was the right move, because the Lord is the One who established it. Today I work with companies that are either relocating or expanding their facilities. The California economy has recovered and rebounded, though it has never matched the heyday of the late 1980s. My business has matched that trend—it's not as lucrative as it was in the "good old days," but I think my work life is just where God wants it to be.

These years have built my faith like nothing else could have done. I've learned the incredible power of praising God in the midst of adversity. I've discovered how to step back and look at my life and concerns from an eternal perspective, and it's been wonderful to find how many anxieties simply fade away when I do that.

———

Steve Garrison's story is repeated a thousand times every day somewhere in our world. The details may vary, but the path is the same. But I'm not telling you anything you don't already know. Nobody expects to sail through life without a little rain and a few choppy waves. We expect the poor weather, but we have certain ideas about how the storm front will move in.

We expect we'll run into an occasional setback at appropriate times.

There's naturally going to be an inconvenience during our time in school, or a misadventure in the raising of a family. We have our mental calendars marked for the occasional midlife crisis or the messy business decision. As we figure it, we'll dispense with these inconveniences without losing more than a step or two along the path of life. We expect bumps, more than bends, in our roads—after which we can settle in and enjoy health, wealth, and happiness until the sun sets. Most of us envision an early retirement in that dream house, with the dream grandchildren and the dream retirement pension to allow us to see the world and partake of the American Dream.

That's the plan, anyway.

But the best laid plans often come to naught. Just ask Steve Garrison if his life moved in precisely the spiral he had charted in his mind. We never know what lies in the road ahead, and we never know when our world will fall apart. It may be when the journey has barely begun. It may come in the active middle years. Or perhaps in the quiet of those mature years, when we long to rest and enjoy the fruits of a lifetime, a terrible surprise will disrupt all we've hoped and arranged.

King David faced this variety of bitter disappointment—not that his life had been easy and carefree up to this point. We've seen the physical, personal, and political dangers he faced from the time the prophet Samuel came to visit his family when David was a young man. But the "man after God's own heart" had passed every grueling test. He had prevailed; Israel had thrived. The kingdom had grown to unprecedented heights of power and respectability. David looked toward a time when a temple might be built to house the ark of the covenant and enshrine God's law for generations.

But things didn't work out that way. His family was ripped by tragedy, bloodshed, and bitterness. It would have been enough to break the heart of many a middle-aged man less sensitive than David.

In an earlier chapter, we mentioned David's strained relationship with his son Absalom. We know this about Absalom: He was a physically handsome man, one of the few whose outward appearance is described in the Bible. And he must have had impressive charisma, because he succeeded in building a personal power base among the people of Israel. Right under the nose of his father, the king, Absalom convinced a strong coalition of citizens that the son should take the place of the father in the palace of Jerusalem. Absalom had set his heart on taking that place of power—by whatever means necessary.

He was very shrewd in public relations, understanding the importance of "grass-roots" politics. Absalom spent much of his time at the city gates, where the streets were filled with people entering and leaving the city. As they gathered, he worked the crowd. He made friends, listened to problems, and told how he thought they should be solved. David's boy was drawing crowds. The whispers inevitably began circulating: "We could use a change—here's the kind of fresh leadership we need." "The old man has lost a step—he ought to step aside and let the boy have his turn."

Absalom did something else: He nurtured and encouraged bitterness. The Scriptures tell us that as the citizens of Israel were bringing lawsuits to the king to settle, Absalom intercepted them and said, "It's a shame there's no one in the palace interested in settling this legal dispute you have here. I'm afraid we simply don't have a king in place to care about you—the one we have isn't interested in your problems. I know if I were king, I'd be right on top of a lawsuit such as this one, and I'd certainly get results—you can count on that. But of course, I'm not the king, am I?" And the Bible tells us that Absalom even began to hug the people there at the gate, reaching out, touching, embracing. He did everything we see politicians do today during campaign season. He was working the crowd in the best political tradition. As the Scriptures summarize it, "Absalom stole the hearts of the men of Israel" (2 Sam. 15:6).

The crowd at the gate began to evolve from a group of casual passersby to something like a political bloc. And quicker than you can say "insurgent," King David was receiving the startling news that a coup d'état was underway within his own court.

Keep in mind that we're talking about David, the people's choice—king by popular demand as well as divine appointment. This was the hero who had slain the giant, outlasted the tyrant, and multiplied the kingdom! The very idea of a coup was in itself unthinkable, a poison-tipped sword to his heart. But this rumor that the source of a coup was his own precious son—well, that was enough to send a father to an early death by broken heart. He loved Absalom deeply. And Absalom was set on destroying everything that David had fought and survived and perspired to build.

That wasn't all; things were even worse. Ahithophel, his favorite counselor and friend, was identified as one of the conspirators. Amasa, his nephew, was also in on the plot. How had the house become divided against itself? David must have been tortured by recriminating doubts. Maybe his son was right; maybe he'd "lost a step." At this moment of decision, with the fate of a nation in the balance, the king hesitated. In the midst of a no-win proposition, the king couldn't decide how to act, and every moment of delay solidified the strength of Absalom's battalion.

Absalom set up his bureaucracy, establishing headquarters in Hebron, which was a few miles from Jerusalem. And he spread the word throughout the kingdom that at the sound of the trumpet, everyone who cared about a new government for Jerusalem should rally to the side of the "new sheriff in town."

David heard this too, of course. And he knew he had missed his opportunity to put down the rebellion. The price of delay was that his life—along with those of his loyal circle—was seriously in danger. There was no recourse but flight from the palace and even from the city. What a tragic moment for a leader of historic significance! The man who need not fear stepping into the very presence of God had to flee for fear of his own son, his own flesh and blood.

As always, a few were courageous enough to stand firm with David even when his prospects were low. He took these followers and retreated from Jerusalem across the Kidron Valley and into the desert of Judah. He only hoped for a safe refuge where he could sort out the terrible mess he had somehow allowed his kingdom to slip into.

What goes through the mind of a seasoned and deeply spiritual king at such a moment? We know the answer, because David opened the pages of his blood-smeared, tear-drenched old journal and inscribed the immortal words of Psalm 63. Thousands of years later, we can look over his sad, sagging shoulders and peer into his journal and into his very soul.

How can we identify with an extraordinary life like that of David? You've probably never lived a life on the run because of an angry king, but an angry boss may have kept you on the run. You may never have been the object of a political coup, but you may have felt the pinch of younger coworkers pushing you off the corporate ladder. You may never have fled your home to protect yourself from your own child, but you may have felt the heartbreak of children who failed to honor their father and mother as they grew older.

In moments like those, you've found yourself in deserts that had no sand, deserts of personal desolation, spiritual despondency, and emotional depression. And as Steve Garrison discovered, when that moment of ordeal arrives, we're almost never prepared in body, mind, or spirit.

## David's Hunger for God

Psalm 63 begins with its narrator, David, isolated in the desert. His first impulse is to call out for God to come and comfort him. The king in exile feels a gaping hole in his heart that only God can fill. His family has deserted him, his subjects have rejected him, and he has come to a place where his only refuge, his sole consolation, is his Creator.

One commentator, evoking the image of David in the desert, offers this observation: "We may imagine the psalmist in the wilderness. It is night, and he stands at his tent door. The light of moon and stars sprawls on a sandy waste, stretching into dimness and mystery. He is lonely and sad, and the emptiness all around and the memory of better times breeds this great longing in his soul."[1]

You and I get the picture. We know what it's like to feel emotionally bankrupt. There in the desert, David looks across the parched wasteland and sees it as a mirror of his own soul. And what can he offer in such a situation other than the response of any child who has stumbled and injured himself? David cries out to his Father to come, pick him up, and care for his hurts.

First of all, we see his desire for God. The first phrase in verse 1 is interesting. The original words of the Hebrew language are *Elohim Eli.* In our language it reads, "O Creator God, my God." The barrenness of his personal desert of the soul is swallowing him up. He cries out to the Creator of deserts and oases, "O Creator God, You are my God." The Lord of the desert is also the Lord of deliverance from it; David reaches for the comfort of that connection.

Then he uses three expressions to describe his hunger and thirst for intimacy with his God. The first phrase is, "Early will I seek You." Don't brush by those words too quickly! Come, let us reason together about what it really means to "seek God."

### Seeking for God

The expression "to seek," in the Hebrew, is related to the Hebrew word for *dawn*. Do you find that curious? Here's the connection: Nothing can precede dawn in a day. As David awakes, he is seeking God. Nothing can come before that. It's the dawn of his daily life.

This phrase "early will I seek You" has such an impact upon this psalm that the Armenian and Greek Orthodox churches often refer to this chapter as the "Morning Psalm." In their liturgy they sing, "Early will I seek You."

### Thirsting for God

David surveys the foreboding landscape around him: nothing but sand and heat, and no wells of cool, life-giving water. It strikes him that his life is little different. He thirsts for water to drink, but he also thirsts for the kind of spiritual water only God can provide. "Blessed are those who hunger and thirst for righteousness," Jesus says to us in Matthew 5:6. David himself has already sung in Psalm 42:2, "My soul thirsts for God, for the living God." Thirst is identified all through the Scriptures as the best metaphor to understand the deep spiritual yearning that each of us finds implanted within us.

But what has intensified David's thirst? This is a man who has sought after God all his life, but the great heartbreaks of life have

---

*Say to those who are fearful-hearted,*
*"Be strong, do not fear!*
*Behold, your God will come with vengeance,*
*With the recompense of God;*
*He will come and save you."*
*Then the eyes of the blind shall be opened,*
*And the ears of the deaf shall be unstopped.*
*Then the lame shall leap like a deer,*
*And the tongue of the dumb sing.*
*For waters shall burst forth in the wilderness,*
*And streams in the desert.*

*—Isaiah 35:4–6*

---

always driven him to seek God with a deeper thirst, a more powerful sorrow, and a more desperate knowledge of the terrible, hopeless plight of trying to live without his Master.


## Longing for God

The words are so powerful, so evocative, and so passionate: "My flesh longs for You in a dry and thirsty land where there is no water" (Ps. 63:1).

When David speaks of longing, he uses words that are actually connected to fainting. The idea he has in mind is that of *weakness*. He is saying, "O Lord God, I've collapsed in every way! The strength has drained out of my body, and I've fainted. I'm desperate to be revived in the way only You can restore me to life and breath."

David points us to the fact that body, mind, and spirit are inter-dependent. When the spirit is ill, the body will be affected. His long-ing for refreshment and revival and recovery are physical and spiritual. David speaks of body and soul almost interchangeably in the psalms. He feels the pain of spiritual and emotional distress in every ligament and nerve of his body, and that pain seeks a spiritual solu-tion—it drives him to long for God in his soul.

### Desiring, Deciding, Delighting in God

C. S. Lewis gave us a wonderful book called *Reflections on the Psalms*. If you enjoy reading the psalms, you'll be delighted with his book. Lewis wrote about the psalms more eloquently than anyone else I know. For example, listen to Lewis on the topic of David's hunger for God: "The poets in David's day knew far less reason than we do for loving God. They did not know that He offered them eternal joy. Still less that He would die to win it for them. Yet they express a longing for God, for His mere presence, which comes only to Christians in their best mo-ments."[2]

How right he is! We have so much more reason to seek God. We can know Him so much better. Yet how seldom we exhibit the ur-gency and desperation of the psalmist. But when the road bends into the dry desert of life and we find ourselves in arid desolation, our cry for God becomes the very focus of our existence.

What a vivid picture the psalmist paints for us in the early verses of Psalm 63. The dry and thirsty land that surrounds him physically is the picture of his soul without God. He realizes that the world itself can be a desert; indeed, the most luxurious palaces of kings can be dry and desolate wastelands. Only God can bring refreshment and rejuve-nated life. We can be surrounded by those things we've identified as pleasures and yet find no joy in them.

Someone has said that Satan knows nothing at all about pleasure;

his specialty is amusement. Only God knows genuine pleasure. About fifteen years ago, author Neil Postman wrote an indicting study of our modern culture; he called his book *Amusing Ourselves to Death*. That title nicely captures the danger of chasing after pleasure, as our culture

---

*You will show me the path of life;*
*In Your presence is fullness of joy;*
*At Your right hand are pleasures forevermore.*

**—Psalm 16:11**

---

does, and capturing it, only to find it empty and joyless. We've actually found nothing more than amusement, at great cost to our souls. Genuine pleasure is ordained by God and intended for our deep joy and delight. It can only be captured by knowing God, realizing He knows us, and being at rest in His presence.

Verse 2 brings us to an interesting decision by David regarding God's presence. But we can't truly appreciate this verse without filling in the blank—that is, learning a little more about what the author was thinking as he fled from the treachery of his son. Here is the background.

David was leaving the city. There was a group of loyal priests who were evacuating the city with the royal delegation. Two of these were Abiathar—David's personal chaplain—and the priest who served by his side, Zadok. David wasn't aware that these two men, before leaving the city of Jerusalem, had crept back into the sanctuary where the ark of the covenant was kept. The ark had always been carried by the use of two iron bars, which fit through rings on the side of the great structure. Priests would then lift and carry the ark by these bars. Abiathar and Zadok inserted the bars and raised the ark of the covenant to their shoulders. Then they carried this sacred shrine of the Law outside the city. They had forgotten one crucial factor—they hadn't asked for David's approval.

As they left Jerusalem and crossed the Kidron Valley, David discovered what the two men had done. They had brought the holy ark of

the covenant into the peril of the open country where David and his
followers had fled. The ark symbolized the visible, practically tan-
gible presence of God among the people of Israel. It was the most sacred material object in existence. The temple would be built one
generation later for no other reason than to provide a worthy vessel to
house it. The ark of the covenant was the physical symbol of God's
presence. You or I might have been eager to carry it along to represent
the spirit of God among those fleeing for their lives. But David didn't
feel that way at all.

We read in 2 Samuel 15:24–25 that "there was Zadok also, and all
the Levites with him, bearing the ark of the covenant of God. And
they set down the ark of God, and Abiathar went up until all the people had finished crossing over from the city. Then the king said to
Zadok, 'Carry the ark of God back into the city. If I find favor in the
eyes of the LORD, He will bring me back and show me both it and His
habitation.'" Pick up the story four verses later: "Therefore Zadok and
Abiathar carried the ark of God back to Jerusalem. And they remained
there."

We simply must conclude that David didn't think and act in the
way you or I might have. He sent the ark back to the city. In his view,
the sacred vessel belonged there, period, case closed. More impor-
tantly, David needed something more than a *symbol* of God's presence;
he needed the *reality* of God's presence. This was the thinking behind
his words to the two priests: "This isn't about the ark of the covenant
and the work of priests. This is about *the very presence and guidance* of
Almighty God Himself. If He goes with me, I'll see Jerusalem and my
home once again, and the ark will be waiting for me there. If God has
rejected me, all of the holy vessels in the world will do me no good."

David wasn't interested in relics and symbols of divinity. He insisted on the authentic presence of God Himself. There could be no
substitutes. Now we understand David's words in the second verse:
"So I have looked for You in the sanctuary, to see Your power and Your
glory."

David *desired* the true God; he *decided* based on the true God. Finally,
we can see in the third verse how he *delighted* in God. He said, "Because

Your lovingkindness is better than life, my lips shall praise You." His life was hanging in the balance, yet he realized that true life can only be found in the true God. He is saying an amazing thing. In essence he says, "Lord God, the way that You love me is more precious to me than life itself."

You'd better believe life is precious! The only alternative I can think of is death. So why is God's lovingkindness better than life? The answer is simple: God's love is eternal. Earthly life is not. As Paul wrote to the Corinthians, nearly everything else passes away, but the love of God, like His Word, is one of those things that resounds beyond the confines of this brief life in this bounded space. His love is greater than life!

## Worshiping with God's People

The view inside David's heart always makes for a fascinating picture. He was by no means, from any perspective, a perfect man. His failures are as legendary as his accomplishments. He was a great leader who happened to be a member of that struggling, stumbling band known as the human race. Yet the final record of his life testifies to a consistent pattern—when the heat and pressure were ratcheted up a few levels, he seized hold of his relationship with God, gripping it with both hands and every ounce of his strength and every beat of his heart. David wasn't mouthing words of piety as an act of last-resort desperation. He sincerely, urgently yearned to be in God's presence. He craved the unique experience of worshiping with the people of God.

During my illness there were certain "frequently asked questions" I became accustomed to hearing. One of these was, "Are you afraid?" Here is my answer to that question: *Afraid, no. I am scared to death!*

Another question: "Have you cried?" My impulsive answer: *None of your business!* I didn't say this, of course; it's not a godly response to loving, concerned friends. For an extended period of time, the true answer was: *No, I have not.* I knew what was set out before me, and God prepared me for it. But the day came when the tears were shaken loose. I wept deeply. Please understand this is a difficult subject for me—as I remarked above, my first impulse is to be very private with my tears. But there's a significant point I wish to share with you, and that point requires transparency on my part.

It was Easter Sunday. Donna and I were in a hotel in Del Mar, California, near the outpatient stem cell transplant program at Scripps Clinic. The nightmarish adventure of the cancer experience had reached its blackest point in our lives. Our spirits were as low as they could possibly have been. And yet it was Easter Sunday; I rose early and made my way out to the hotel room's little living area. My thought was to escape the awful mood that had come over me. I would turn on the television set and find something to give me hope, something to set my mind on things eternal.

I may have been misguided in my efforts. There are better places to seek encouragement than Sunday morning television. But I had little spirit for any other endeavor, so I channel-surfed. I made the rounds of all the stations on the hotel television until I came across a broadcast from a large church. I found Easter music, church pageantry, and worship—just what I was looking for. I sat back and soaked in all the trappings of the people gathered for praise, and I lost myself for a few moments. I lowered my guard. And without any clue to what was about to happen, I suddenly began to sob convulsively. I completely lost my composure and nearly flooded the sofa and the living area with sloppy tears.

I was so embarrassed.

Donna rounded the corner, hurrying from the next room. Her eyes were great ovals. "Are you all right?" she asked.

"No, I'm not," I replied. "I want to be in church. I don't want to be here; I don't belong here. *I belong in church.*" It was a startling moment of discovery for me—realizing just how deep was my craving to be among the people of God on His day. There was no place else on earth for me to be but within the walls of the special kind of place set apart for the worship and magnification of God—a place happily filled with my brothers and sisters in faith.

I know you're smiling, nodding, and saying, "Of course, Pastor Jeremiah! You're the preacher—that's where preachers like to be!"

But it runs a bit deeper than that. It's not about preaching, but the experience of genuine, godly worship in the context of the living, celebrating body of Christ. Can you experience God outside the bricks and mortar of a steeple-topped building? Absolutely. But, dear reader, there's something holy and essential and irreplaceable about the Spirit of God manifest among His people, *especially* on Easter Sunday. In that lonely hotel room I suddenly felt a deep, burning exile from the only place where I can live and thrive and breathe the cool air of true fellowship.

I made a deep, serious vow in my heart that I *would* improve. I would be among my brothers and my sisters again, praising God.

And I meant business.

If you can understand what I felt, you can understand what David was feeling in his exile in the desert. There he stood, looking back across the barren desert sands to the horizon beyond which Jerusalem, the city of God, sat without him. There the people of God went about their lives and worshiped God together. He remembered the great feast days with their singing and pageantry. As he squinted at the horizon and felt so keenly his separation from God's people, he cried out in the pain of the gaping empty place in his heart. David ached for communion with God and the community of God.

In the next few verses, David helps us understand what we can expect when our path leads us through the desert's open, merciless spaces. He shows us how, when we feel we're walking alone through life's wasteland, we can make the journey in the comforting presence of our Lord.

## What David Did

Do you associate praise with discipline? Most of us think of praise as positive and spontaneous, while we think of discipline as negative and forced. But that's the crucial point of this section of David's psalm.

There are those times when we walk through the desert, and our throats fill with dry dust. We feel thirsty, but the last thing we would think of to do would be to lift our voices and sing a song of victory.

---

*Discipline is the act of inducing pain and stress*
*in one's life in order to grow into greater toughness, capacity,*
*endurance, or strength. So spiritual discipline is that effort of pressing*
*the soul so that it will enlarge its capacity to hear God speak and,*
*as a result, to generate inner force that will guide*
*and empower one's mind and outer life.*

**—Gordon MacDonald**

---

But that's exactly the thing that will give us strength and endurance. In the hard times, praise is an act of obedience and discipline. It may not be spontaneous, but when we manage to praise God in the midst of pain, the results can be dramatic.

**David praised God.** We find ourselves in deserts or dungeons. Our friends would give us all kinds of advice, but the last thing they might counsel us to do would be to praise God. When Job lay suffering with every earthly pleasure stripped away, his wife advised him to "curse God and die." But such an attitude is in itself a form of death. It's spiritual suicide.

Genuine praise, offered stubbornly in the face of adversity, makes no sense by any worldly calculation. That's fine. There are deeper truths that don't "make sense" on the surface of things. The great Christian mathematician Blaise Pascal once said that "the heart has its reasons which the reason does not know." God's rules fly in the face of our logic. When we begin to praise God, not in response to prosperity, but in defiance of misfortune, we align ourselves with the deepest truths of the universe, the place where God dispenses deep wisdom and spiritual maturity. We unleash His victorious power in the world of pain and suffering. We create the environment where miracles occur.

And the first miracle occurs inside the mind of the afflicted.

Psalm 63 from first to last is a psalm about David praising God. It's not a psalm about being happy or about changing circumstances. We almost feel, in reading between the lines, that David anticipates the end of his life approaching. We can almost hear him saying, "Lord, I don't know how many days You have allotted for me. There could be seven remaining, or seven thousand. And I cannot know what those days might hold, joy or sorrow. But I do know I intend to spend them exalting Your blessed name."

Listen to the echoes of this sentiment in Psalm 104:33: "I will sing to the LORD as long as I live; I will sing praise to my God while I have my being." *Whatever breath You give me, Lord, easy or labored, I will give back to You in singing praise.*

As we move through this psalm, we find a variety of ways to praise the Lord. The first six verses of Psalm 63 offer seven different approaches, and each one is a precious jewel. Let's take in each facet of the psalm's diamond:

- *We praise Him with our lips.* "My lips shall praise You" (v. 3).
- *We praise Him with our tongues.* "Thus I will bless You" (v. 4).
- *We praise Him with our hands.* "I will lift up my hands in Your name" (v. 4).
- *We praise Him with our wills.* "My soul shall be satisfied" (v. 5).
- *We praise Him with our mouths.* "My mouth shall praise You" (v. 5).
- *We praise Him with our memories.* "When I remember You on my bed" (v. 6).
- *We praise Him with our intellects.* " I meditate on You in the night watches" (v. 6).

Think of that—praising God with your lips, your tongue, your hands, your will, your mouth, your memory, and your intellect. Our Father has issued us a full armory of weapons for use in the world. We fill them with the wrong ammunition. When the enemy closes in, we'll never defeat him using his own weapons. Instead, we load the weapons of our lips, our tongues, our hands, our wills, our mouths, our memories, and our intellects with the most powerful gunpowder that has ever been discharged on earth—worship and praise.

In the midst of the lonely desert road, what are you to do? Praise God with every part of your body, mind, and spirit. Learn to praise God regardless of your personal circumstances, and you'll see miracles occur. Your heart and mind will be renewed. Your perspective will widen panoramically. And your attitude toward God will never be the same.

**David pictured God.** Yes, David praised God, though his entire life was unraveling. He praised God in the desert. But he didn't stop there. His wise move is found in verses 6 and 7: He began to *picture* God.

Please don't misunderstand—this isn't about the trendy, New Age version of visualization. Take a close look at David's words in verses 6 and 7: "When I remember You on my bed, I meditate on You in the night watches. Because You have been my help, therefore in the shadow of Your wings I will rejoice."

David was not the kind of man to toss and turn in the night, fretting over circumstances beyond his control. He was in a mess, to be sure. But when insomnia cut him off from the sleep his body needed, he had one certain remedy—he meditated upon the Person of God.

We've all lost sleep over our anxieties. Maybe your child has left your home after a heated dispute or your financial health is in jeopardy. Maybe the future of your employment is no more than a question mark. Or perhaps your marriage is on the rocks. As for me, it was personal illness; I don't believe I ever lost a night of sleep until my health took a disastrous turn.

David tossed and turned in his bed too. But he had a prescription for sleeplessness, and it didn't involve the pills that too often grow into dependencies for people today. When David found himself sleepless, his thoughts drifted heavenward. He found God in the night watches. What a liberating lesson for those who labor miserably under insomnia! Our response is often to give in to increasing

desperation, which, needless to say, pushes the goal of sleep even farther away. Our thoughts entangle themselves in negative emotions.

Instead, we can find a placid spirit by turning the wheels of our
minds to the things of God. What has He done in your life? What is
He up to at the present? Why not spend time counting those blessings—naming them one by one—and offering praise to the King?
Sleep will come softly to a contented mind, and it will be deep and refreshing. That's a promise.

Lewis Smedes has written a wonderful book about hope that includes this striking insight: "A person who has the habit of hope also
has the habit of remembering. Hope needs memories the way a
writer needs notes. This is partly because hope depends so much on
imagination. Our images of the future are sweepings from our re-
membrances of things past. If we expect to keep hope alive, we need
to keep memory alive. Happy memories of good things we hoped
for that were fulfilled, and grateful memories of bad things we survived."[3]

When treading through life's desert, it helps to remember God's
help in ages past. We gain a wise perspective by realizing that nothing
that can be happening now is a surprise to Him. Our memories are
spiritual investments; they reap dividends when we consult them and
discover once again the perpetual faithfulness of God.

As I've studied the life of David, I've thought about the great king of
Israel tossing and turning in his bedchamber. I can imagine the loom-
ing giant of despair haunting him in the night and keeping him from
sleep, and I know how David responded. He thought of another
giant, one who loomed before him so many years ago. Here was a
nine-foot-six warrior, facing off with a young man with no weapon in
reach but a slingshot and five smooth stones—four more stones than
he actually needed. The world would not have given promising odds
to the challenger in that match. But David knew that if God is for us,
it's simply irrelevant who is against us. Height measurements are beside the point. Jesus said that invisible faith comparable in size to a
nearly microscopic mustard seed will prevail against a mountain, for
the faith is aligned with the will of a sovereign God.

David knew that—as a young shepherd and as a seasoned monarch. Nearly any anxiety can cast a long and menacing shadow during the night watch. Any minor worry can become Goliath when lights are low. But in the shining light of God's presence, the details of this life find their true size. "I am the Lord," we hear Him say. "Is there anything too great for Me?" David may have reflected that at one time a giant seemed invincible for an unarmored shepherd boy; surely there was no reason to give in to fear now, after so many years of the Father's faithfulness.

The shadows of the night were deep and mysterious. But David found refuge in more comforting shadows; he said to his Lord, "Because You have been my help, therefore in the shadow of Your wings I will rejoice" (v. 7).

**David prayed to God.** What did David do? He praised God to dispel the darkness; he pictured God to find encouragement. And finally, he prayed to his God. He wrote, "My soul follows close behind You; Your right hand upholds me" (v. 8).

Here is the closest translation of that first phrase: "My soul clings to You, God." That's something we do quite naturally in a crisis if our emotional wiring is functioning—we reach for God and hang on tight. We don't know what else to do. Sometimes a trauma is required to draw us as close to God as we should have been all along.

I'd like to share with you an experience that might clarify this point.

## Fear of Fireworks

I'm afraid we committed a serious miscalculation with our grandson not too long ago. We took him to a San Diego Padres baseball game the night of a huge fireworks display. The idea was mine. I envisioned our little family group, with my grandson David Todd at the center, taking in the thrill of a nighttime sky canvas splashed with the breathtaking colors of summer fireworks. It was such an innocent notion. It never occurred to me that the thundering explosions of such a show were capable of terrifying a small boy.

I took the family to the game with smiling anticipation. David Todd sat on Poppy's lap (that's me), and his eyes were wide as he interacted with all the wonderful new sights and sounds as the major lea-

---

*Helplessness is the real secret and the impelling power of prayer . . .*
*For it is only when we are helpless that we open our hearts to Jesus*
*and let Him help us in our distress, according to His grace and mercy.*

**—O. H. Hallesby**

---

guers played their nine innings. We were having great fun. But then came the fireworks—and that was the end of the party.

When the explosions suddenly jolted the stadium, little David Todd scrambled out of my lap and into his daddy's arms. You've never seen a child move so fast. And as I watched with alarm and crashing disappointment, I'll never forget what I saw. The little boy buried his head deeply in his daddy's shoulder and clung to him for dear life, with every terrified bit of strength he had. And I noticed that his dad had a mutually tight grip on his child.

King David's calm and fruitful life had also suddenly given way to deafening explosions. He scrambled from the comforts of the throne into the arms of his true Father, and he desperately buried his head in the Lord's loving shoulder. That's what you and I do so reflexively and so spontaneously, and it's absolutely the right response. How many times have you heard it from a friend or a relative? "It was such a terrible, frightening experience, but I never sensed the presence of God more than I did during those dark days."

Needless to say, God calmed the troubled waters of David's soul. He dealt with his enemies and gave His child a victory. And even while David endured his exile, he knew God would not fail him. You'll see this in the psalms: a kind of godly premonition He offers David— and He offers you and me—that things are going to be all right; the storm is going to pass. You feel some small light glimmer in your heart, and it pulses with a tiny but undeniable hope: *God will not fail me.*

David received that from God. And history confirms his assurance: One day, the armies of Absalom ventured forth to face the armies of David, and the forces of the father prevailed against those of the son. Have you heard the denouement? It features the indelible image of the handsome young Absalom, riding a mule toward his destiny as his great head of hair danced in the breeze. Passing beneath a terebinth tree, his hair caught in the branches. The Scriptures tell us rather ironically that "he was left hanging between heaven and earth" (2 Sam. 18:9). There he hung until Joab, David's general, came along and took Absalom's life—against the wishes of Absalom's grieving father. The political crisis was dispelled. David was left with a broken heart, but he was free to return to the throne of Israel with impunity. His shortcomings as a father had exacted the price of a son, but God had brought him through and preserved him just the same.

David had made his desert journey, just as all of us must travel that same road. Steve Garrison made the journey. I did. How about you?

I may not know you by name, but I'm certain that if you're not treading through the dust of despair at this very moment, the time is certain to come. But when that day arrives, you will not face it unarmed. The Bible, sharper than any two-edged sword, stands ready for combat. It contains desert psalms that can become your battle plans. The ammunition of praise is ready for discharge. And close by your side will be a faithful, powerful God filled with lovingkindness and plans for you, plans that lead to spiritual victory and personal fulfillment.

When your day comes, you'll no doubt be surprised. Just remember that nothing surprises God. He has prepared every detail for the disciplinary adventure that will lead to your wisdom, strength, and maturity. He knows that the quietness of the desert is a place for you to get to know Him better, with so much more depth and fulfillment. He doesn't exult in your pain, but He delights in your tighter embrace. He has so much to show you and share with you.

And He knows the way through the wilderness to the hills of joy and laughter. Take His hand, little one, and follow.

# Psalm 30

*A Psalm. A Song at the dedication of the house of David.*

1 I will extol You, O LORD, for You have lifted me up,
And have not let my foes rejoice over me.
2 O LORD my God, I cried out to You,
And You have healed me.
3 O LORD, You have brought my soul up from the grave;
You have kept me alive, that I should not go down to the pit.
4 Sing praise to the LORD, You saints of His,
And give thanks at the remembrance of His holy name.
5 For His anger is but for a moment,
His favor is for life;
Weeping may endure for a night,
But joy comes in the morning.
6 Now in my prosperity I said,
"I shall never be moved."
7 LORD, by Your favor You have made my mountain stand strong;
You hid Your face, and I was troubled.
8 I cried out to You, O LORD;
And to the LORD I made supplication:
9 "What profit is there in my blood,
When I go down to the pit?
Will the dust praise You?
Will it declare Your truth?
10 Hear, O LORD, and have mercy on me;
LORD, be my helper!"
11 You have turned for me my mourning into dancing;
You have put off my sackcloth and clothed me with gladness,
12 To the end that my glory may sing praise to You and not be silent.
O LORD my God, I will give thanks to You forever.

# 7

# Life's Ups and Downs

### I Arise Today

*Through God's strength to pilot me:*
*God's might to uphold me,*
*God's wisdom to guide me,*
*God's eye to look before me,*
*God's ear to hear me,*
*God's word to speak for me,*
*God's hand to guard me,*
*God's way to lie before me,*
*God's shield to protect me.*

—SAINT PATRICK

Your world falling apart?

The truth is that some crises are more like a flash of lightning and a crash of thunder, shattering a pleasant journey. We're knocked violently from our feet, and we lie there stunned and confused. We're incapable of climbing to our feet to resume the journey.

That's how Helen Barnhart felt.

Helen works faithfully for our television and radio ministry in the *Turning Point* office. She's one of those persons who would prefer to work quietly in the background. However, I've prevailed on her to tell you about the day when her worst nightmare broke in upon her. Here is that story, in Helen's own words.

I'm quite accustomed to the ringing of the phone at my office. I hear it three or four dozen times daily, bringing a wide assortment of messages, most of them mundane. But it was the sound of the telephone a few months ago that transformed my life forever. That was the day I was told my son had been removed from my home.

It didn't sink in at first. Someone I didn't know was trying to tell me terrible, unthinkable things about my husband. Could they possibly be true? Could they be talking about the man with whom I had lived for twenty-six years? The father of our children and the head of our household—our primary provider? My husband stood accused of unspeakable crimes. I'll never forget the feeling of those cold, merciless words sliding from the phone into my ear. This came only a few months ago, so please understand that my life still hasn't fully recovered. It's extremely difficult for me to discuss any of these things.

The youngest of our three children was in high school and living at home. He had to be taken away—that's how severe the accusations against my husband were. He was placed in the custody of his married sisters.

It was Christmastime when these things happened.

I found I had become the sole occupant of an empty, silent house. I spent the holiday season alone within its walls as the legal machinery worked through its customary functions. A court date had yet to be determined, so the law required that I could have no contact with my son and, by extension, with my daughters because they were his caregivers. I didn't even have the luxury of work to keep my hands busy and my mind occupied, because our office was closed for the holidays. I was a prisoner of grief in my own home.

I had one great prayer request, and I prayed it constantly. I asked God to reveal to everyone that the whole nightmarish crisis was simply a mistake, that my husband was innocent, that nothing had really happened. With God, all things are possible. So I prayed fervently, passionately, unceasingly for God to simply *change everything back*—to turn my world right-side up again in the cozy order that I had found so comfortable for so long. But it became clear I wasn't going to be granted that prayer request. The situation was genuine. The changes weren't going away, and sooner or later I was going to have to face facts.

The comforting cushion of the initial shock was wearing off. Through a slowly encroaching, terribly agonizing process, I began to confront the stark new realities of my life. I watched all my hopes and dreams for the future drain away during endless empty nights, and the loss of those cherished dreams left a void deep in my soul.

My husband's prison term might as well have been a life sentence. As for my son, the court system was considering not returning him to my shattered home. That meant a sentence of my own. How could I endure all this? How could I face the loss of my life partner and be deprived of the comfort of my own child? How could I explain the situation to my family and friends? What would be the effect on our son—on *all* of our children? On *their* children?

I was familiar with all the comfortable platitudes that are offered as substitutes for true comfort. I read through the psalms again and again, seeking any stray shred of relief. I told myself, "The clue will turn up here in the Scriptures. This will be the moment when God works His magic and shows me that *everything's going to be all right.*"

That didn't happen. Everything *wasn't* all right. And everything hasn't become all right since. And yet . . .

God never left—not for a moment. He's been with me all along, and I can truly say that, in the midst of the worst I could have ever imagined life dishing out, the Lord's presence was powerful. The picture of Shadrach, Meshach, and Abed-Nego in a fiery furnace came to my mind many times during those days. Someone was walking with them in the flames, and they weren't burned. And I knew that same Someone was with me, not for personal comfort, but for protection and grace.

Christian friends came, not with platitudes, but with practical help with the details of life that don't brake for crises. A new judge was assigned to my son's case and completely reversed the court's position. Praise God, my son came home! While the harsh reality of my husband's situation never stopped being real, I could see and feel the Lord in my life. Again and again circumstances took a turn, help was provided, and developments materialized to show evidence of God walking with me through the darkness.

*I will never leave you nor forsake you.* Those words of Jesus have a very personal meaning for me now. The end of my strength and wisdom are merely the beginning of His provision and grace.

---

The seminary professor was out of patience. His student had turned in a sermon with a dull, uninspired title. The professor knew the young man was capable of better things, so he stayed after him to keep working. "The title is crucial," he barked. "It must build interest in your listeners, and it must be intriguing and relevant and powerful. That's why you're going to take this sermon back to your room, right this moment, and you're going to return it to me tomorrow with a new title—one that will grab hold of your listeners and engage their attention. Do you understand?"

The young man was at a loss; he wasn't much good with fancy words and labels. "How do I come up with a catchy title?" he shrugged.

The professor sighed and replied, "It's not so terribly hard, son. I want you to picture your sermon title in great, bold letters on the signboard on the front lawn of your church. It's Sunday morning, and here comes a bus filled with people, just passing by. Son, you want a sermon title so powerful, so compelling, so intriguing that everyone on that Greyhound will come pouring down the steps of the bus. They can't resist the compelling bait of the words in that title. Got that image? I'm sure you can improve on your title, my boy."

The student thought about what his professor had said. He got the mental image fixed in his mind and thought of the words that would most stimulate and engage those bus passengers. The next day he bounded into the classroom with a new title page for the professor. It read, "There's a Bomb on Your Bus!"

When I hear a story like Helen Barnhart's, I think, *There's a bomb on the bus.* We're bumping along in life, all together on a wonderful pleasure trip, and suddenly something explodes. Everybody off the bus! The journey is suspended; how can we go on? After the explosion, we're no longer even certain where the bus is heading, and whether it will ever arrive. The meaning of things has fled, and we feel we'll never again have hearts filled with joy, only fear. Helen's home exploded;

---

*I praise Thee while my days go on;*
*I love Thee while my days go on:*
*Through dark and dearth, through fire and frost,*
*With emptied arms and treasure lost,*
*I thank Thee while my days go on.*

**—Elizabeth Barrett Browning**

---

in my life, it was my health. Perhaps your life, too, has been ripped apart by lightning on the road, shattered by a bomb on the bus.

But the road goes on, and it will rise to many more peaks and plummet to the bottom of many valleys. It will cross bridges into new lands you've never imagined. Fellow passengers will offer you deep friendships, and you will laugh together and weep together. Not even for the deepest, most devoted Christian will the journey be carefree. Depth and wisdom can only come from shadowy valleys of tears, sickness, loss, disappointment, and broken dreams.

Those deep valleys are places of spiritual dryness and conflict with God—things David faced and chronicled for us in Psalm 30.

## A Psalm of Commemoration

Beneath the title of Psalm 30, your Bible will tell you that you've come across "a Song at the dedication of the house of David." What is the background?

Scholars have researched and debated that question, and their consensus is that this psalm is connected to events arising from the day David returned the ark of the covenant to Jerusalem. We're not referring to the period later in David's life (detailed in the previous chapter) when two priests fled an uprising with David and carried the ark out of the city. This is an earlier day when David at long last became Israel's king. After waiting so many difficult years for the culmination of Samuel's promise, the crown finally rested upon David's head. His first royal initiative was to establish the ark in the city, where it would enshrine the idea of worshiping and trusting God. The culmination of that, of course, would come in the time of David's heir, Solomon, who would build the great temple.

The ark of the covenant, as we learned in the last chapter, represented the presence of Almighty God. In the Old Testament system of worship, the ark was associated with the Shekhinah glory of God. Do you remember what happened when the Philistines took possession of the ark of the covenant? They paraded it throughout their own land to celebrate publicly their victory over the Israelites. But everywhere they stopped, terrible problems cropped up. There seemed to be a curse on the Philistines who had defiled the sacred vessel, and in time they gave up and sent away the source of their problems.

Time passed. During King Saul's administration, the ark was nearly forgotten. The king didn't spare it a thought, and the people reflected his lack of spiritual awareness. But David understood the true significance of the ark; he knew it merited placement in a central, visible location in Jerusalem as a reminder of the glory and power of God.

David made one mistake, however. When he sent for the ark, he assigned the project to a group of men who weren't exactly well-versed in Old Testament law. Maybe you've relocated to a new home and used reckless moving men. Imagine relocating the most sacred object on the face of the earth. The movers ignored the precise and critical instructions from the Book of Numbers, where dealings with the holy ark of the covenant are set forth. These were apparently that breed of men who hate to read the directions. They talked it over and decided the most convenient way to move the great golden box was to drop it into a common oxcart.

They thought that should do the trick, but the whole misadventure resulted in a few tricks they hadn't anticipated. At one point along the route, they came to a threshing floor, and the cart began to wobble. A man named Uzzah reached out without thinking and grasped the ark to steady it. It was a forbidden thing for human hands to do, and God struck Uzzah dead on the spot for carelessly handling holy artifacts. The touch of the ark simply consumed him.

David's eyes were wide; the Bible tells us he was both angry and afraid. If you'd seen a man removed from the ranks of the living simply by touching a golden box, you might have been in awe too. He suddenly realized the enormous gravity of his responsibility. David remarked, "How can the ark of the LORD come to me?" (2 Sam. 6:9).

The newly nervous king didn't dare to move the ark even one more dangerous step, so he had it put aside in the home of a man named Obed-Edom the Gittite for three months. During that period, while the ark of the covenant was present in their household, the family was blessed in remarkable ways. David's view was, "Let's just keep the thing in storage. I'd rather not tamper with anything that dangerous while I have a kingdom to establish. I'll get around to moving the thing into Jerusalem one of these days." And he turned his attention elsewhere.

But after the ark of the covenant had been in the Gittite's house for about three months, word trickled back to Jerusalem that Obed-Edom had become a kind of King Midas—everything he touched seemed to turn to gold. His every endeavor was crowned with success. The presence of the ark meant blessing and goodness for his family. And David took another look. He began to revise his thinking about the box—it was dangerous, but it was wonderful as well.

The king dug into the Old Testament law, reviewed it carefully, and gave great attention to the strict commands for moving the ark. He then proceeded to bring the ark carefully from the home where it rested. After the movers took six paces, they halted and offered a great sacrifice of oxen and sheep. And David worshiped the Lord with great joy and intensity, even dancing before the Lord "with all his might" (2 Sam. 6:14). David had always looked to this day, but after

his personal observations of the great powers of God's law—for blessing the benevolent or cursing the careless—his feelings about the ark
of the law were even deeper. And it was at this point, many scholars
believe, that David channeled his heartfelt gratitude into the song we
now know as Psalm 30.

David's entire life, as we have seen, was an emotional and spiritual
roller coaster. Even in this one story, we see David moving from anger
to fear to joyful dancing. On the one hand he saw the damage caused
by the mishandling of God's law, and on the other he saw the power
for blessing when that law is properly respected.

We ride that roller coaster ourselves: the upward surges of joy and the
deep plunges into depression. The higher the roller car races, the deeper
and faster it will plunge. The psalm we'll be exploring together offers five
contrasting experiences connected to life's ebb and flow. The psalmist
begins in the first four verses—and picks up with verses 8–10—with the
climbing, cresting, plunging cycle that moves from hurting to healing.


## From Hurting to Healing

Before anything else, there is a profoundly moving theme of healing
in this psalm. We can't be specifically certain what healing David
might have required. We do know the story of bringing the ark to
Jerusalem, but there may have been other issues and challenges in the
life of the new king at this particular time. It may have been that he
experienced some kind of illness. We do find clues, spread through
other psalms, that David had to cope with physical health problems at
times. Here in Psalm 30:8, we read David's prayer to move from hurting to healing.


### *Prayer for Healing*

As David prays in his sickness, he argues with God. In more contemporary language, we can hear David saying, "Lord, allow me to plead

my case with You for a moment. Why do You keep me ill? Why must I hover near death? What good could I possibly be to You as a dead man? Will my dust praise Your name? I believe I can worship You better in a state of life, dear Father."

Let's say this for David: His argument isn't totally self-serving. He's quite sincere in his concern for God's glory—if a bit calculated. He is saying, "If You'll save me, O God, You'll have one more worshiper in this world to bring honor and glory to Your name." We often approach God with the same agenda: *Don't You want to bless me, Lord, so I can serve You better?*

But finally, David realizes his inadequacy in negotiating with the Creator of the universe. He puts all that behind him and simply pleads to God for mercy. In verse 10 he says, "Hear, O LORD, and have mercy on me; LORD, be my helper!" No bargaining; no "Here's what I can do for You, Lord"; no rationalization; simply a heartfelt plea for mercy. And isn't that where we all end up? If you've ever been seriously ill, here are the words that finally find their way to your lips. You'll surely pass through the stages of deal-making and angry protest. But the time comes when you find yourself at the bottom line of hope or despair, and you become a small, frightened child approaching his father.

And you say, "Lord, I need Your mercy. Please, please help me!"

### Praise for Healing

So David prays for healing. Then in the next four verses he offers up praise for healing. He's had a narrow escape with death, and he says, "I will extol You, O LORD, for You have lifted me up." The phrase "lifted up" from the Hebrew language is the same expression that is used for dipping a bucket down into a well and drawing water. David has this picture in his mind: "Lord God, You reached down to the darkest depths and pulled me right out of the grave. I was almost gone."

Or think of it this way: "I lift *You* up, O Lord, because You lifted *me* up."

This is a thought that comes naturally in the aftermath of a brush with the grave. When you know that you'll see the sun rise again, just when it looked as if you were facing the night of death, you begin to wake every morning thanking and praising God. You thank Him for the morning. You thank Him for sunlight, and for the simple but profound privilege of taking another breath of oxygen in this world. You need no reminders to thank God and worship Him, for you see everything in deeper colors and brighter lights. You hear the music of God's wonderful lovingkindness, and you wonder how you missed hearing such a lovely melody before. This is the joy you feel, and this is the joy David felt as he wrote this psalm.

That joyful, thankful perspective is essential to a positive life. The reason you are reading this book with the strength to turn its pages and the eyes to take in the light that illuminates it is that God has a purpose for you. He loves you, and He keeps you alive. He gives you life and strength and breath. Could it be that in those times in which you nearly died on the freeway or had some other brush with death that God reached out and preserved you—as He did with David? As He did in granting me the opportunity to write this book?

Absolutely! You and I are here on the good pleasure and indulgence of Almighty God. Shouldn't that make you see things through different eyes when you rise tomorrow? Shouldn't you begin the day on your knees with a great smile spread across your face—and maybe a tear on your cheek—as you whisper, "Lord God, thank You for keeping me alive through another day; thank You for preserving me through another night. I lift up my voice and my hands to You in praise for Your goodness. Now let me lift up my life today in service for Your purposes!"

### Purpose for Healing

David moves from hurting to healing. Then he reflects upon the purpose for his healing. In verse 4, he says, "Sing praise to the LORD, you saints of His, and give thanks at the remembrance of His holy name."

Yes, healing has a purpose. We don't often get far enough to take that in, for too often we're like little children taking the candy from the hands of a parent. We scamper off without even saying thanks. But the truth is that when God answers a prayer and provides healing, He

---

*Sweet are the uses of adversity,*

*Which, like the toad, ugly and venomous,*

*Wears yet a precious jewel in his head;*

*And this our life, exempt from public haunt,*

*Finds tongues in trees, books in the running brooks*

*Sermons in stone, and good in everything.*

**—William Shakespeare**

---

has revealed something about His purposes—a precious clue about His wonderful workings in this world. He has intervened for a good reason, and we now have the same responsibility to offer praise as the responsibility we had when we prayed for healing. We prayed, "O Lord God, heal me and I will praise Your name." When the wonderful thing has come to pass, we cannot and must not forget our heartfelt promises.

So David exhorts the people: "Now let's all praise God—I'm talking to all of you who are His saints! Offer your gratitude and remember His name! Never, never forget what He has done for us on this day."

## From Weeping to Joy

Psalm 30 can be seen as a study in contrasts. The first one David cites takes us from hurting to healing. Next he takes us from weeping to joy. We come to a beloved verse in which David says, "For His anger is but for a moment, His favor *is* for life; weeping may endure for a night, but joy comes in the morning" (v. 5).

In the general sense, weeping and joy don't accompany each other.

There are exceptions, of course—I know some people who cry when they're happy. But normally we associate weeping with sadness and laughter with joy. And David speaks of the great gulf that exists between the height of the peak and the depth of the valley. And yet we can experience both of those things in a brief span of time. We can be filled with joy one moment and find ourselves in tears the next, because the road can bend just that quickly.

But we can look at the inevitable movement from tears to joy from two perspectives.

### This Is an Everyday Truth

The fact is, we understand the roller-coaster ups and downs of life simply through the lens of experience. Whether you're a believer or not, when someone you know is going through a difficult thing, you're likely to say to that person, "You know what, my friend? It's not going to be like this forever. Just hang in there and wait for your life to take a turn for the better. Don't give up! You'll get through this."

I heard about a wry individual who was asked to name his favorite verse in the Bible. He quickly replied, "And it came to pass." It didn't come to *stay*; it came to *pass*. I realize the man misinterpreted the familiar words, but I rather like his misinterpretation, don't you? It says something about the way life really is. Pain is so painful partly due to its feeling of permanence; it seems wrapped in the eternalness of hellfire. But as we open to the midsection of our Bibles, there is our old friend David, who puts his great bruised hand on our shoulder and comforts us. "Grief and misery come creeping up in the blackness of night," he tells us in this verse, "but hold on tight, for joy comes in the morning."

I see proof of David's words nearly every day as a pastor. We gather at the graveside on a somber afternoon to pay tribute to someone we've loved and lost. I stand before the grieving family, observing the deep sadness in their faces, and I think, "It will never, ever be the same for these dear people." But a year passes; I watch the family closely, and I can see that somehow God has brought them back from the depths. He has restored a measure of joy and gladness in the morning.

Our children are perhaps capable of bringing us the deepest grief of all. I know a pastor and his wife who have lived through the truth of that, enduring tragedy with one of their children. I'll never forget the words of that pastor's wife. She quietly said to her husband, "I wonder if we'll ever smile again." That's exactly how we all feel as the storm rages: *This is forever. I'll never be the same.* We can't remember what the sky looked like when it was blue, and we can't imagine the sun will ever break through the clouds again. But God has given us a far more powerful capacity for healing than we can possibly realize, and His powers of comfort and strengthening and revival are unlimited. The morning will come again, and with it, joy.

### *This Is an Eternal Truth*

It's an everyday truth, but it's also an eternal one.

In the Old Testament account of creation, we find words that raise an eyebrow if we're listening closely. After describing God's creative work, the Bible says this: "So the evening and the morning were the first day" (Gen. 1:5). That pattern is repeated for each of the days of creation, with evening always preceding morning. Isn't that a backward statement of things? Doesn't the morning come first?

This brings us to a valuable little principle you should seize in your daily life—one of those treasures of common sense that can bless you immeasurably.

Begin your day *before* the morning comes. Begin it on the preceding evening with prayer, planning, pondering, and preparation, and the next day will be far more successful and effective for you. Instead of weighing your spirit down with the late news or the banalities of a talk show on television, lift them with a visit to God's Word. Inject the power of His wisdom into your mind before you rest your head on the pillow. Apply His Word to your plans, ready yourself for the day to come, and ask God to bless the day that will soon follow.

You'll be amazed at how well you'll sleep, as your Father takes what you have just offered Him and organizes and renews your mind, doing all the daily mental maintenance work that makes you the kind of servant He needs. When the sun rises, you'll be startled to discover how much confidence will fill your spirit, and how energetic and effective you'll be in the workings of your daily life. The evening and the morning will be your day.

We hear much about seeking God in the earliest hours. Maybe we should be seeking Him even earlier. Give it a try.

But the concept of the evening and the morning penetrates even deeper into the meaning of life. You and I are living in the evening of creation at present. The sun may shine, but our world is darkened by sin and rebellion. The Bible assures us that a morning will dawn bright and glorious someday. All the sorrow and sadness and difficulty we've known in the darkened skies of life will vanish. The Lord will return for us at the daybreak of eternity, and there will be no more weeping, no more pain or suffering, no more broken hearts. There will be no more valleys plunging away from the peaks.

He will dry every tear, and there will be joy in that great morning.


## From Prosperity to Poverty

In the sixth and seventh verses of this psalm of contrasts, David takes us once again to the highest reaches and lowest depths. He says, "Now in my prosperity I said, 'I shall never be moved.' LORD, by Your favor You have made my mountain stand strong; You hid Your face, and I was troubled."

Those are the words of the New King James Version. Let's take a more contemporary look at what he really means. David is confiding a painful truth to us, something he has learned the hard way. He says, "I thought back on my life to the time when I had everything I'd ever dreamed. And I said to myself, 'I'm set for life—and set in stone. I've got it made! I'm a bigger man than anything life can throw at me.'"

These are the thoughts of a king who had everything going for him as he looked out from his throne of worldly power. Like Dr. Seuss's Yertle the Turtle, he says, "I am the king of all I can see!" But painful experience has taught him differently. He has realized the great danger of prosperity—that of confusing "invaluable" with "invulnerable" or ultimate wealth with permanent strength. As Yertle learned, how quickly it can all come tumbling down!

You and I see David's bitter lesson and initially feel a bit smug. We say to ourselves, "Worldly power is an illusion? Well, *I* could have told him that! What a fool that David was!" But can we be certain we wouldn't have slipped if we'd been in his place? Wealthy and powerful people are victimized by the Grand Illusion every day. They feel that they've discovered how to master and exploit so many things in life—money and power and fame and people—that they assume they've mastered it *all*. They're the kings of all they can see, but what about the things they can't see? There are more things in heaven and earth, as Shakespeare said, than they've dreamed of in their philosophies.

"Therefore let him who thinks he stands take heed lest he fall" (1 Cor. 10:12). Pride indeed goes before a fall. A simple ringing phone, combined with a single sentence from the doctor or the lawyer or even a stranger, and all our earthly security goes up in flames. It's a fine thing to have the fruits of our labor in life, as the writer of Ecclesiastes tells us; and it's important to secure our finances and have sturdy locks on our doors. But ultimate security cannot be purchased by any of these things. Worldly life is fragile. Eternal life is a gift from God, free and yet not for sale at any price.

The Old Testament tells us the story of a man who got it all wrong. His name was Nebuchadnezzar, and he was the king of all he could see in the great empire of the Babylonians. Daniel, who knew the king well, tells us of the bright and cheerful day when King Nebuchadnezzar was strolling through the palace in Babylon, admiring everything he'd established and the kingdom in his power. Listen to what he said: "Is not this great Babylon, that I have built for a royal dwelling by my mighty power and for the honor of my majesty?" (Dan. 4:30). He was thinking, *Not a bad spread I've built here, if I do say so myself.*

But the Bible tells us that "while the word was still in the king's mouth, a voice fell from heaven: 'King Nebuchadnezzar, to you it is spoken: the kingdom has departed from you!'" (v. 31).

But God wasn't finished with Nebuchadnezzar. No, He still needed the poor misguided king for several purposes, one of which was to provide an illustration for you and me, and a fairly interesting illustration, as you're about to discover. You may not believe the following story, but just open your Bible to the Book of Daniel if you're incredulous, and read for yourself. God's Word tells us that Nebuchadnezzar became arguably history's first recorded werewolf. He spent the next seven years eating grass out in the field like a beast, whether or not a full moon was out. In fact he was quite an odd exhibit for any zoo, for "his hair had grown like eagles' feathers and his nails like birds' claws" (v. 33). How the mighty had fallen!

We can only assume the king learned his lesson—the hard way, as usual. His belly filled with grass, and having endured a molting season or two, he was restored at the end of seven years. Daniel 4:37 shows us a king who is no longer foolishly proclaiming his own power and majesty: "Now I, Nebuchadnezzar, praise and extol and honor the King of heaven, all of whose works are truth, and His ways justice. And those who walk in pride He is able to abase."

That last sentence was something the king could heartily testify to from firsthand experience. Eat enough grass, and your world-view will change. Nebuchadnezzar finally realized that when you're flying high, filled with your own prosperity, God is more than able to burst your bubble.

## From Mourning to Dancing

Prosperity to poverty may seem like a negative transition, but it can be positive indeed—it can if it brings us back to God. Whatever it takes to get us there, once we come to our senses and find our way back to Him, then we can identify with David's words: "You have turned for me my mourning into dancing; You have put off my sackcloth and clothed me with gladness" (v. 11).

This is the verse that provides scholars with their primary clue that Psalm 30 is the companion chapter to 2 Samuel 6. The reference to dancing binds the two passages together. Do you remember the rest of the story?

Here is King David, entering his city with the ark of the covenant carried by the priests. It's a victory parade, the kind when everyone

---

*Remove falsehood and lies far from me;*

*Give me neither poverty nor riches—*

*Feed me with the food You prescribe for me;*

*Lest I be full and deny You,*

*And say, "Who is the LORD?"*

*Or lest I be poor and steal,*

*And profane the name of my God.*

**—Proverbs 30:8–9**

---

turns out with ticker tape to honor the dignitaries. The band is playing, and the people are cheering. The king is decked out in his clerical robe, wearing his linen ephod, the godly apparel of the priest. And David dances with all of his might before the Lord (2 Samuel 6:14). Certain pastors and Bible readers avert their eyes with decorum when they come to this verse. Dancing! That's usually not on the program for a joyful church celebration these days.

But there's no way to explain away this account from God's Word. It means what it says. Keep in mind that we're not talking about ballroom dancing, break dancing, or disco. This was godly dancing—a physical expression of abounding excitement for God's mighty deeds. The ark was among the people, and this was no time for somber, quiet assemblies. There are times when we can best express our emotions toward God and His faithfulness by having a godly party! David simply couldn't contain his joy, and we should have times when we feel that same way.

God turned mourning into dancing and sackcloth into ephod. Life before Him is a study in contrasts, in ups and downs.

## From Silence to Singing

The final verse of Psalm 30 leaves us with one last profound truth. The message is that we should never keep silent in light of God's blessings: ". . . to the end that *my* glory may sing praise to You and not be silent. O LORD my God, I will give thanks to You forever."

Please don't leave the thirtieth psalm without this firm understanding. If your life is filled with joy, give thanks to God; if you're enduring pain and tears, give thanks to God. In all things, offer your praise. Life's ups and the downs are only yard markers on the playing field of circumstances. Joy and sadness are temporary conditions, but praise and thanksgiving are permanent expressions.

When we finally come to understand that truth and begin to praise God in the midst of *all* things, we often find that circumstances themselves change in our favor. Godly faith changes the world around it, for we can live triumphantly, knowing that the pain is temporary and the end has been predetermined; it's an ending of reunion with the Father and an eternity in His loving presence. Why react in any other way than to lift your voice in praise?

## Knocked Down, but for Good Reason

I must confess that one particular animal fascinates me. I consider this creature among the oddest God ever created. He's called a giraffe. He is a strange and homely creature in appearance; his movements seem awkward and peculiar. And then there's the matter of giraffe childbirth. What? You say you haven't read many books on giraffe childbirth? Well, I'm here to enlighten you. Gary Richmond wrote an article on giraffe calves that caught my attention, and I hope you'll indulge me as I pass on some facts from it.

Gary had been invited to a zoo where a captive giraffe was about to give birth. He said, "The moment we had anticipated was not a disappointment. A calf, a plucky male, hurled forth, falling ten feet and

---

*I would willingly endure all the sufferings*
*of this world . . . to possess the smallest increase*
*of the knowledge of God's greatness.*

**—Teresa of Avila**

---

landing on his back. The mother giraffe gives birth to its young standing up, and the distance from the birth canal to the ground is about ten feet."

Are you still reading? Think of this—ten feet is approximately the appropriate height for dunking a basketball, *plus* about four extra inches. So the calf fell out of its mother ten feet above ground, and landed on its back. It lay there for a few moments, and then, according to the story, it scrambled over to get its legs underneath it so that it could take a look around and check out the world it had just entered.

Gary Richmond continued his account. The mother lowered her head to see the baby, then she moved until she was towering directly above the calf. About a minute passed, then came the shocking surprise. The mother giraffe swung her great, long leg outward and booted her baby through the air. The calf sprawled head over heels across the ground, puzzled and protesting.

Gary was astounded to witness that display. He turned to the zoologist and said, "What's that all about?"

The zoologist replied, "She wants him to get up—and if he doesn't get up, she's going to do it again."

Gary continues, "Sure enough, the process was repeated again and again. And the struggle to rise was momentous, and as the baby grew tired of trying, the mother would again stimulate its effort with a hearty kick. Amidst the cheers of the animal care staff, the calf stood up finally for the first time. Wobbly, for sure; but there it stood on its little spindly legs. Then we were struck silent when the mother kicked it off its feet again."

Gary's zoologist friend was the only person present who wasn't astonished by the mother's brutal treatment of her newborn calf.

"She wants it to remember how it got up," he explained. "That's why she knocked it down again."[1]

*To remember how it got up.* Doesn't God nurture us in just the same rough way sometimes? And if we're ignorant as to His methods and purposes, the actions can seem cold and even cruel. We finally struggle to our feet, and it seems as if we're kicked again. But our heavenly Father knows that love must be tough—and it must take the long view. God knows the world will fall apart, and we must be sturdy travelers to stay on our feet. We must not forget how we got to where we are.

Have you ever felt that God kicked you when you were down? Perhaps, like Helen Barnhart, you've received one blow after another, and you've wondered if you should even try to get up again. One of the reasons for some of the challenges in our lives is that God is toughening us up, preparing us for warfare against forces intent on destroying us. I wouldn't be honest if I didn't admit to feeling kicked and abused at times, all the while hearing the voice that says, "Get up. Get moving. Get with it! And don't forget how you got up."

Our God created the principle of rigorous discipline. I hope that by now you can understand why it's necessary. I hope you will face your next great disappointment with a new perspective—that the next time things look down, you'll look up. I hope you'll gird up your heart, reach for renewed strength, and say, "Lord, I've been taken by surprise. Life has thrown me a curve, and it's a hard thing for me to cope with. Even so, I praise Your blessed name. Whatever comes my way, joy or sorrow, I will stubbornly and confidently praise Your name. No matter how circumstances may appear, I will praise Your name.

"For I know You are wise and loving, and that no mere circumstance can change that. Whether this current road leads to exhilarating peaks or gloomy canyons, I praise You and I thank You. You are my Father, and You love me enough to train me and remake me, and only You can turn my mourning into dancing."

# Psalm 142

*A Contemplation of David. A Prayer when he was in the cave.*

1  I cry out to the LORD with my voice;
  With my voice to the LORD I make my supplication.
2  I pour out my complaint before Him;
  I declare before Him my trouble.
3  When my spirit was overwhelmed within me,
  Then You knew my path.
  In the way in which I walk
  They have secretly set a snare for me.
4  Look on my right hand and see,
  For there is no one who acknowledges me;
  Refuge has failed me;
  No one cares for my soul.
5  I cried out to You, O LORD:
  I said, "You are my refuge,
  My portion in the land of the living.
6  Attend to my cry,
  For I am brought very low;
  Deliver me from my persecutors,
  For they are stronger than I.
7  Bring my soul out of prison,
  That I may praise Your name;
  The righteous shall surround me,
  For You shall deal bountifully with me."

# 8

# Praying under Pressure

*Be not dismayed whate'er betide,*
*Beneath His wings of love abide,*
*God will take care of you,*
*Through every day, o'er all the way;*
*He will take care of you,*
*God will take care of you.*

—CIVILLA D. MARTIN,
"GOD WILL TAKE CARE OF YOU"

Achilles, the great warrior of Greek mythology, was 99 percent invincible in battle. His armor was immaculate. But he had one area of vulnerability: his heel. Today we speak of a person's "Achilles heel" as being his or her obvious weak spot, the place among all his or her defenses that is most open to attack. For a significant number of us, our Achilles heel is found in our precious offspring. We would be willing to endure any personal injury if we could take their place in enduring it. We would gladly die for them, so deep-rooted is our parental love.

Glenda Palmer had that particular Achilles heel.

Glenda had a son named Kent who was in the prime of youth. He radiated all the infectious joy and energy of any twenty-two-year-old. Kent was an active, healthy young man, and his mother adored him.

When her son's life-threatening tumor came along, she never saw it coming. She recounts for us the story of her world falling apart.

———

Those who know me well will quickly tell you I've always been a crier. I cry during happy weddings and sad movies. I cry at church when we sing "How Great Thou Art." It really doesn't take much to coax tears from me.

But that particular year—the year of turmoil, the year of our son's cancer—I didn't cry very often. I believe there are sorrows and agonies that penetrate to depths within us where tears are simply insufficient.

Our year of turmoil began when Kent began to complain about his back. It wasn't like him to worry about sore muscles or aching bones, because little injuries here and there were commonplace to him— something to shrug off. He worked in construction and stayed active in sports competition. Still, I didn't particularly worry. Finally one day Kent said, "My back hurts so bad, I don't think I can surf." So I called for a doctor's appointment. I figured my son had probably pulled some minor muscle on a recent ski trip.

The doctor performed a few tests, then he called me on the phone. The surgeon wanted to admit Kent immediately for an operation. "It looks like a large tumor," he said. "It may be malignant."

I hung up the phone and sat silently, trying to take in the terrible medical words I had just heard. I closed my eyes and began to plead before God. "Dear Lord," I wept, "please, oh please, don't take my baby away from me."

But there were no more tears after that. I didn't cry after the surgery, as the doctor stood before us using the words I had prayed with all my might not to hear—words such as *disappointed* and *chemotherapy* and *nine-pound tumor*. Nine-pound tumor? I remembered that Kent had weighed only six pounds at his birth.

During the next months, Kent, his brother, Scott, my husband, and

I simply did what we had to do. We stood firm as best we could and focused on getting through the crisis. Oddly enough, we laughed a lot.
We didn't shed tears, but we laughed. During my darker moments in
the past, when I'd contemplated the unthinkable possibility of losing a
child, I'd imagined that I would weep continuously. But that didn't turn
out to be the case for me. We bottled up our grief and occasionally released it through laughter together.

I turned to my Bible and dug deeply into its wisdom and consolation
early each morning. The words I found there became my rock in the
storm as well as my marching orders for the day. I used hymns and
songs of praise as a channel for hearing God's voice, as well as lifting
my voice and my feelings to Him. And the Lord sent people—special
people He used as His angels. They ministered to me and prayed without ceasing for Kent. As terrible as the time was, it was also filled with
irrefutable evidence of the presence and grace of God.

Yes, His grace was sufficient! I had heard it in countless sermons, but
now I knew it was really true. I had a fresh certainty that, whatever the
outcome, my Lord would be with me and His strength would be
enough.

Kent checked into the hospital five times for chemotherapy—one
week in, one week out. He lost all his hair. Each treatment was more
and more painful and filled him with unbearable anguish. I suffered
with him.

I shed a few tears during those days, but only a few.

During the cycle of into-the-hospital and out-of-the-hospital, Kent
took classes to become a real-estate agent. He kept his eyes on the future, not on death or morbid thoughts, but on life and on hope. I admired his attitude.

The season of chemotherapy came to an end, but two small tumors
remained on his aortic artery. Kent's doctor suggested a surgeon in Indianapolis who specialized in that kind of intricate cancer surgery.
This was a crucial turning point, so I began praying and fasting. We
prepared ourselves for the next battle in the war against the elements
for our son's life.

Six weeks before our trip to Indianapolis, I lost my mother. This was a moment we'd known was inevitable, for she suffered from an extended illness. Daddy asked me to read Psalm 23 to her, and those rich words of David were on my lips as she left this life: *Yea, though I walk through the valley of the shadow of death, I will fear no evil, for You are with me.* The words had a deeper meaning for me than ever before. Mother was my best friend in this world.

But I didn't cry very much.

We went to Indianapolis. The surgeon stood before us, and we couldn't believe our ears. Was it a dream? "I removed the tumors," he said. "They aren't malignant." Almost before he could finish the sentence, I was hugging him and weeping freely.

The tears finally came. But I couldn't cry for long, for there was a long list of people to call. They needed to hear about our great and mighty God whose grace is sufficient.

All of that was ten years ago. I feel great joy in telling you that Kent is alive and well, with the tumors only a distant memory. He is happily married, and he works as a mortgage lender. God has been so good.

I find that I'm able to cry again—oh, yes! I cry at weddings and during sentimental movies. But most of all, I cry when I sing "How Great Thou Art."

David was a man of faith. That much is perfectly clear from all we know about him in the Scriptures. He was a man of vision, a wise military and governmental leader, and even a man gifted in music and poetry and dancing, but like many people who love and trust God—people like Glenda Palmer—he was also a man who struggled with discouragement and depression.

David coped with a plethora of turbulent emotions during his fugitive years. He had to flee for his life from the wrath of King Saul. He had to bolster strength and courage through devastating days and fear-laden hours. Facing many of these things alone, he turned for solace to music and worship, as well as the comforts of writing about his feelings. In fact, students of the psalms believe that David wrote at least eight different psalms during his season of flight.

The superscription beneath the heading of Psalm 142 tells us we've

---

*Fits of depression come over most of us.*
*Usually cheerful as we may be, we must at intervals be cast down.*
*The strong are not always vigorous,*
*the wise not always ready,*
*the brave not always courageous,*
*and the joyous not always happy.*
*There may be here and there men of iron ...*
*but surely the rust frets even these.*

**—Charles Haddon Spurgeon**

---

come to "A Contemplation of David. A Prayer when he was in the cave." In this chapter we'll also briefly consider Psalm 57, a song arising from the same historical setting. Its superscription reads like this: "A Michtam [that is, a teaching psalm] of David when he fled from Saul into the cave."

We already know that David was running away from the most powerful man in his world, nearly always outnumbered, and without the support of anything close to the armament of his enemy. As we look in on this episode of his life, David has finally stumbled across a refuge where he can find sanctuary. In the midst of the wilderness, he has come to a place where he can lay low, pour out his heart to God, and sort out the shattered fragments of his life. He has found a cave. And he has entered the darkness of the cave of despair.

Many of us have descended into the cold, darkened reaches of the cave of despair. Glenda Palmer was there during her son's illness. You and I have paid our own visits. The cave has its own twists and hidden passages, and we can feel lost. We begin to imagine that God has forgotten us, that His comfort doesn't extend to these dark passages. Or perhaps we feel in our honest moments He just doesn't care.

It helps us to follow David's story. If nothing else, we can discover that we aren't the only ones who have experienced discouragement. One of the reasons we wear out the pages of the psalms is that it helps us simply to know that somebody has gone before us—even thousands of years before us. We find comfort in recognizing the emotions we're feeling here and now displayed in a man who lived so long ago. And we can't read the psalms without finding words somewhere along the way that fit the situation directly before us.

What a treasure we have in our hands. David preserved all these honest emotions and wise prescriptions. He maintained an invaluable journal that has never lost its power or its richness. We should begin to realize the value of keeping our own journals. I feel very strongly about that particular spiritual discipline, and I will discuss this more in depth later in this chapter. As a matter of fact, I intend to share excerpts from my own journals in the last two chapters of this book. I hope you're taking time to regularly record your thoughts and your prayers before God. Journals are precious.

David went beyond simple journaling. He went beyond simply recording for us the events of his life. He wrote out his prayers to God, then kept an account of God's workings. Here in our Bibles, we can actually chart the course of David's life as he moves through his series of crises and emerges victorious on the other side.

David is now seeking solace in a cave named Adullam. We need to clarify the point that this is one of two caves in the young man's life; the other is the cave of En Gedi, the place where David cut off the skirt of Saul's robe. You can find that account in 1 Samuel 24.

It's interesting to place the psalms and the historical books side by side to seek the full context of the psalms. We can discover, for example, how Psalm 142 seems to flow from the life of David:

David therefore departed from there and escaped to the cave of Adullam. And when his brothers and all his father's house heard it, they

went down there to him. And everyone who was in distress, everyone
who was in debt, and everyone who was discontented gathered to him.
So he became captain over them. And there were about four hundred
men with him. (1 Sam. 22:1–2)

What was happening? Most scholars believe King Saul had levied a
heavy tax on the people of Israel. It would then be clear that people
were flocking to this cave of Adullam to be with David in their anger
and rebellion over the unfair taxation. They were poor and had very
little, and many of them were the very people who had insisted before
God that they needed a king. Be careful what you pray for—Saul was
that king.

Many others of the four hundred were, no doubt, old friends of
David who gathered to lend their support. Goliath's conqueror was
still admired by most citizens of the nation of Israel. As word leaked
out concerning their hero's flight, more and more of them decided to
join David in his hiding place. In fact, in the next chapter of 1 Samuel,
we discover that the number grew from four hundred to six hundred.
Needless to say, this cave was no foxhole on the side of the hill. It was
a huge cavern with a forty-foot opening.

So we have David, fleeing his problems, fleeing Saul, fleeing life.
Finally he has come across a place of respite, and suddenly there are
great crowds of people flowing toward him from every direction.
What kind of people are these? Not exactly the best or the brightest.
These are the debtors, the troublemakers, and the discontented who
are flocking to the side of David. How do you think he feels about all
this company? Keep in mind that David is sick and discouraged. I believe he sought a cave not only for safety, but also for solitude. The
fact is that misery doesn't always love company. The last people we
want to be with in our despair are those with problems to match our
own.

That's why I can't imagine what this massive social call must have
been like for David. He is struggling just to cope with his own turbulent emotions, and now all the outcasts of Israel are straggling to his
side in the cave of Adullam.

Some commentators cast David as the Robin Hood of his day. W. Graham Scroggie, an Old Testament commentator, has this to say about the men who resorted to David: "What a crew! The three d's have formed many an assembly since then [the debtors, the distressed, and the discontented], but such are ill to get on with, and a man like David would feel lonely among such!"[1]

Thus David, having entered a cave to be alone, finds himself surrounded by the most distressed citizens of Israel. I imagine he has taken a hard look at his life and his place among the people of Israel before coming to his journal to write this psalm. David is introspective. He is emotional and very transparent with those emotions. His feelings flow out in psalms and music and praise and tears.

Do you feel that Christians shouldn't show emotions? Some believers seem to have adopted that very peculiar notion. "Christian deportment," according to the grim stereotype, is a calm, plain-vanilla demeanor characterized by a pleasant smile that never wavers even when the lions are chasing us around the Roman arena. Supposedly putting on a "happy faith" is the visual proof of godliness. But David, a man after God's own heart, vented his emotions in violent colors and operatic crescendos. We wince when we read some of his work! You need only take a close look at the psalm before us. The journal entry never denies honest emotion; there can be little doubt that the author is a man whose very soul is in distress.

## The Discouragement of David

Let's take a closer look at the discouragement of David.

### David Feels Disoriented

David confesses to us in Psalm 142:3 that his spirit within is "overwhelmed." The Hebrew words literally mean "the muffling of my spirit." What vivid terminology—have you ever felt a muffled spirit?

David has come to a place where he has begun to distrust his powers of judgment. He is no longer certain where to turn or what course to take. Life has become a great flood rushing in upon him, and he struggles to stand firm against the current.

David's muffled spirit is a picture of disorientation. He is pursued by two armies, one made of soldiers and the other of sufferers. His life is entangled in a knot of problems—which thread should be loosened first? If you read his story, you discover that he has recently made a serious mistake; his entanglement has distracted him from the will of God for a period of time—with tragic results. As punishment for harboring his prey, Saul slaughtered the village of Nob, which cared for David during his prodigal journey from God's will. David realizes that he is spiritually responsible for the mass slaying of an entire village, and he is nearly driven insane with guilt. He has entered the darkened depths of the cave to better contemplate the darkened depths of his soul, but the crowd will prevent the solitude his grief now craves.

I have often imagined David slumped within the silence of the cave, his head in his hands, reflecting on the place to which his life has brought him. Shadows flicker at the edge of his vision, and he hears the approaching echo of voices. His gaze travels to the passage of the cavern. There, a rough assortment of people is beginning to swell the passageway. They are shouting about taxes and family problems and a thousand other worries.

David closes his eyes with a sinking heart. He puts his head farther down in his hands and whispers, "O Lord God, what now? What would You have me do?" He feels lost, disoriented. But that's not the only emotion he's feeling.

### David Feels Deserted

We come to the fourth verse of our psalm. In my estimation, it's one of the saddest verses in the Bible. David writes, "Look on my right hand and see, for there is no one who acknowledges me; refuge has failed me; no one cares for my soul." Can you imagine any words more desolate and despairing?

This is the same David who wrote in Psalm 16:8, "I have set the LORD always before me; because He is at my right hand I shall not be moved." There had been a time when he felt the Lord God always at his right hand. If God was for him, who could be against him? Life was rewarding and victorious; no matter where he was or what he was doing, the Lord was always there.

But the pit into which his soul has plunged is a dark one. He sits in the one most appropriate, most symbolic place for his mood—a cold, foreboding cave. And even with a mob of "supporters" closing in, he is more convinced than ever that nobody really cares about him. They care about what he does for them, for the defeating of giants and the fighting of battles; but they don't care about *him*. He has turned to his right hand, and there is nothing but the wind.

He is alone in terms of people too. Have you ever felt alone in a crowd of four hundred? It may seem a contradiction in terms, but anyone who has ever been lonely will confirm that the greater the number of people present, the more intense can be the feeling of loneliness. This is why large, thriving cities are pockets of despair and alienation. A cave filled with the echoes of demanding voices can be lonely too. The psalm suggests to us that David saw the friendly mob and felt the fundamental difference between them and himself. Suddenly his sense of isolation was a knife in his heart. No one knew the depth of his emotions; no one cared what he felt or how he suffered.

Have you ever visited such a cave?

Problems tend to isolate us. I am the kind of individual who is certain to turn inward when the problems come. Like a turtle, my head snaps quietly back into the thick, protective shell. I want to sort it all out for myself without outside interference. I think this is a particularly strong tendency for those of us who are male. We seek the nearest cave that might offer protection from the world and its questions. We believe no one else has ever experienced such a problem as the

present one, and even our wives and children are unlikely to understand—or such is our feeling. So we bury ourselves in a cave.

Scripture commentator Alexander MacLaren offers this description
of the process: "The soul that has to wade through deep waters has always to do it alone. . . . We have companions in joy, but sorrow we
have to face by ourselves. . . . Unless we have Jesus with us in the
darkness, we have no one."[2]

---

**Laugh and the world laughs with you, weep, and you weep alone**

**—Ella Wheeler Wilcox**

---

It matters not how many people are around; you may be in the center of a crowd of thousands, but you'll believe you're hopelessly isolated. Elijah suffered from this misconception. It was he against the
world; he was firmly convinced that he was the only prophet left who
believed in God. It took the Lord to remind him that He, the Creator,
was still in control—and that there were a few thousand more soldiers
in God's army, than the prophet had calculated.

Problems encourage isolation, and isolation nurtures misconception.

### David Feels Depressed

In the sixth verse, David says, "I am brought very low." Isn't that what
the condition of depression is all about?

We've come to a very sensitive topic for contemporary Christianity.
I've actually heard preachers claim that if you're in a state of depression,
then you can't be a Christian. *Real* Christians, they say, don't experience
depression. My first question for these preachers is whether they've
read all of the Word of God. How are we supposed to approach Elijah,
who was depressed? How are we supposed to understand Jonah, who
was depressed? And what about Moses? He, too, faced depression.
Then we come to the matter of King David, a man deeply loved by

God, a man of profound spiritual experience and wisdom, who also grappled with depression throughout his life. The word that David uses for *depression*, interestingly enough, is the word for *indentation*. He applies that condition to his soul. Therefore David is saying, "I'm suffering from an indentation in my soul. I am depressed."

As a pastor, I've occasionally counseled believers in the midst of depression, and I know what a heavy burden it is for people to be "brought very low." I've known people who have suffered such intense depression that they eventually ended their own lives. They looked into the future and saw nothing but emptiness and hopelessness and despair. Heartfelt expressions of hope or encouragement were no longer enough to reach them. Life simply didn't seem worth living anymore, and they chose to forfeit the precious gift of life.

David felt a depression that may have approached such a zone of desperation. All of his hope and joy were gone; his thoughts had turned inward. At one time, the problem had been a simple one—the king was hunting him down to kill him. But now David's plight was something more abstract, something considerably more complex, something whose source was David's own heart. He had allowed his circumstances to drive him inward instead of upward. He had come to fall back on his own resources, and those resources were now spent; the well had run dry. There was nowhere else for David to turn. He no longer sensed the presence of God in his life.

But did this mean David was no longer a child of God? Of course not. Believers do indeed enter the dark cave of depression at times, and this is particularly true of godly leaders. These are men and women who dwell in the world of momentous expectations and great, ponderous burdens of responsibility. They wear the mantle of greatness with unease. And quite naturally, great expectations can lead to great depression.

## David Feels Defeated

In the grip of his low spirits, David cries out to the Lord, "Deliver me from my persecutors, for they are stronger than I" (v. 6). He turns his focus to his enemies.

David is in a place where he can see nothing but grim prospects. He is wearing dark glasses that tint the entire world in shades from gray to black. He does what most of us do when we're feeling low. He sits within his cave with a yellow legal pad and proceeds to take inventory of his life, placing each element in one of two columns

---

*Man's despair is not despair of God at all,*

*but despair of all that is not God.*

*Beyond that certain despair lies Christian hope,*

*the certainty that God alone is enough for man.*

**—William McNamara**

---

marked *good news* and *bad news*. When he gets to the bottom line, he takes a look and concludes, "I've got some bad news and some more bad news." Nothing good seems to be visible through dark glasses in a dim cave. The assets are zero, and the liabilities are endless. One of those itemized listings would have read, "My enemies are stronger than I am," and you can be sure that's a man's depression talking. David would like to be counting his blessings, if only he knew where they all went.

Depression is certainly not the best venue for formulating objective conclusions. Sober reasoning is impossible. David goes on to compare himself to a man in prison in verse 7. And so he is; he is a prisoner of his own perspective. He has locked himself into the dungeon of despair and thrown away the key. We can only be thankful to God that he made his escape.

## The Defeat of David's Discouragement

There can be no doubt that discouragement defeated David. There had been a time when he had sent a stone into a giant's head; now he had encountered a giant that could get into his own head. But for the people of God, there is never a pit too deep to escape. There is never a cave too dark for His light to illuminate. And finally, as the Scriptures attest, David defeated discouragement.

David traveled a path to liberation from the imprisonment of his mind, and he left a map for all of us to follow when we feel hopelessly lost in our despair. We simply need to listen to the Word of God.

### David Verbalized His Problems to God

Have you ever asked the following question? *Why should I tell God my problems? If He knows everything, why should I bother to go into all the details?*

All I have to offer you is the biblical answer to that question, and I believe it is sufficient for us. We tell God about our problems because He has commanded us to do so. That certainly seems reason enough for me; how about you?

Even so, I can think of a few other reasons to open up before God. One of these can be found at the beginning of this psalm. Let David spell it out for you—not once, but three times:

- "I cry out to the LORD with my voice" (v. 1).
- "I cried out to You, O LORD" (v. 5).
- "Attend to my cry" (v. 6).

Perhaps David is a man after God's own heart because he is willing to share his own heart with God. He pours it all out before his Father, doesn't he? When David feels that he'd really love to see his enemies all die violently, that's exactly what he says. When he feels terribly sorry for himself, he shares exactly that. If you or I wrote a book of psalms, just how accurate a map of our souls would we lay out? Our map of the geography of David's heart, after thousands of years, is precise down to the smallest detail.

Prayer should be a time of no-holds-barred, straight-ahead communication with God. We cut to the root of the problem, and we're not afraid to name names. And when that happens, we feel a tremendous sense of unburdening ourselves before the most intimate Friend imaginable. He is listening, He cares, He responds, and we can tell Him anything at all.

Yet we have this lingering impression that God, as the CEO of the universe, is too busy and industrious to take time for our problems. We can't talk to the president, we can't talk to the governor, and maybe not even the mayor. Our calls will be screened by a small army of support personnel. So why should we expect the God of creation to take a call from us? Why should He care about our little problems? When we think along those lines, we're likely to sink deeper and deeper into depression.

Cast human logic and bureaucratic conventions aside. God has said we are to cast all our cares upon Him—period. If we hold back any burden, we short-circuit the healing process that He is so eager to bring about within us. We also shield ourselves from truths that we need to face honestly—truths that will suddenly become bright and clear the moment we bring them into the light of God's presence.

I found an enthusiastic endorsement of that truth in an unlikely place, an airline magazine. During a recent flight, I was thumbing through the usual pages of advertisements when I came across a little article on a topic that interested me: journaling. I went on to read the following:

> Battling illness and pain with pen and paper may be unorthodox, but it may also spell relief. "People who write for twenty minutes a day about traumatic events reduce their doctor visits, improve their immune systems and, among arthritis sufferers, use less medication and have greater mobility," says James W. Pennebaker, Ph.D., a professor at the University of Texas at Austin, who has conducted studies on the topic. . . . Why the relief? Suppressing negative emotions can weaken the immune system and arouse your fight-or-flight system, churning up blood pressure and heart rate. . . . Writing about conflict or trauma helps organize the experience. The net effect is that people can move beyond the stressful event.

The author quotes another Ph.D. Mark A. Lumley an associate professor of psychology at Wayne State University in Detroit. This scholar theorizes that the positive results of journaling have something to do with the nature of pain. "Writing . . . about stressful events relieves the emotional part of pain. That's when the patient says, 'I can still feel it, but it doesn't bother me as much.'"[3]

It is interesting to me that as science stumbles along in the modern world, it tends to come across truths that we've had for thousands of years in the Word of God. This particular article concluded that it's important for us to honestly express the issues of our lives. *Amen.* That's what the Lord has been trying to tell us all along.

If a candid journal can be a healthy thing, how much more can an honest prayerful expression be, when we bring our concerns before the Lord? Insert Almighty God into the equation of that magazine article, with all its research experts, and the effectiveness of what they're prescribing is elevated far beyond anything a psychologist can possibly imagine.

When you find yourself within the dark, cold walls of the cave, feeling isolated and depressed, aren't you glad we have the kind of God whose patience has no limits, whose love cannot be exhausted, and whose tender mercies never come to an end? Aren't you glad you can write down your thoughts then lift your voice and say, "Lord, here, I've expressed it! This is exactly what I'm feeling. And I know I can offer it to You without fear or shame."

When you do that, God begins the process of recovery.

## David Recognized His Presence before God

David says, "When my spirit was overwhelmed within me, then You knew my path" (v. 3). David has verbalized his problems before God. He has unrolled them as if they were a great scroll holding all the secrets of his mind and heart. Suddenly he makes a startling realization: All this time he has been pouring out his heart, God was already at work with David on his discouragement. Every moment David felt overwhelmed by problems, God was busy dealing with them. Every second David despaired over the lack of God's presence, God was right there, as close as ever.

A friend of mine asked his little granddaughter, "What did you learn in Sunday school about God?"

She said, "What I learned is that God never says, 'Oops!'"

We laugh because we feel it's a charming little story. Then we realize it's a profound theological truth in disguise. God makes no mistakes. You never find yourself in a place that's not exactly where God

---

*At times when we feel forsaken, may we know*

*the presence of the Holy Spirit who brings comfort to all human*

*hearts when we are willing to surrender ourselves.*

*May we be convinced that even before we reach*

*up to Thee, Thou art reaching down to us.*

**—Peter Marshall**

---

expected you to be. David could never find a cave where God wasn't waiting for him, just as Jonah could never charter a boat capable of cruising outside the Lord's jurisdiction.

God knew about David and his depression and every single problem he'd ever had or would have in the future. God knows. Our term for that is *omniscient*. It means He knows every detail of your life and your feelings. Isn't that a comfort?


### David Realized His Provision in God

He says, "You are my refuge, my portion in the land of the living" (v. 5). David has remembered he is praying to the Creator of heaven and earth. And now he begins to rejoice in the provision that God has made for him. An old African-American preacher once commented unforgettably on this verse: "There's no living in the land of the living like living in the living God!"

The land of the living is not a reference to eternity or heaven. It is a reference to living *right now*. Aren't you glad the Bible has been writ-

---

*There has to be a song—*
*To make our burdens bearable,*
*To make our hopes believable,*
*To transform our successes into praise,*
*To release the chains of past defeats,*
*Somewhere—down deep in a forgotten*
*corner of each man's heart—*
*There has to be a song.*

**—Robert Benson**

---

ten for people who are living in the land of the living? It's about so much more than "pie in the sky in the sweet by and by." The Bible is written for the rough realities of life, the nitty-gritty of the here and now. It is intended to help those of us who rise every morning, drive to work, and punch the clock to face genuine challenges. Its pages are filled with real-life solutions for real-life problems.

### David Resumed His Praise to God

David writes, "Bring my soul out of prison, that I may praise Your name; the righteous shall surround me, for You shall deal bountifully with me" (v. 7). David has moved from the depths to the heights in these few verses, and he is ready to praise God again. Prayer will do that for us. We can pray our way right through the pressure. We can pray our way right through the sickness. We can pray our way right through the crises and the losses and the fears. If we will only come before Him honestly, He'll meet the needs in our lives—every one of them.

David has traveled from prison to praise. He recorded the journey in his masterpiece known as Psalm 142. And I like to imagine that he wrote a sequel. I enjoy picturing him recording the final word of Psalm 142, then turning the page of his journal to begin Psalm 57— another psalm written in that cave.

This piece is "a [teaching psalm] of David when he fled from Saul into the cave." Most scholars believe that Psalm 57 was written at the same time or in the same setting as Psalm 142. But this one is much more like a song. It's closer to the hymns we sing in joyful worship of God. It's structured in two verses and one chorus. The two verses play out, and after each verse, the chorus can be sung.

Be merciful to me, O God, be merciful to me! For my soul trusts in You; and in the shadow of Your wings I will make my refuge, until these calamities have passed by. I will cry out to God Most High, to God who performs all things for me. He shall send from heaven and save me; He reproaches the one who would swallow me up. Selah. God shall send forth His mercy and His truth. My soul is among lions; I lie among the sons of men who are set on fire, whose teeth are spears and arrows, and their tongue a sharp sword.

Now here is the chorus:

Be exalted, O God, above the heavens; Let Your glory be above all the earth.

Then David starts to sing verse 2:

They have prepared a net for my steps; my soul is bowed down; they have dug a pit before me; into the midst of it they themselves have fallen. Selah. My heart is steadfast, O God, my heart is steadfast; I will sing and give praise. Awake, my glory! Awake, lute and harp! I will awaken the dawn. I will praise You, O Lord, among the peoples; I will sing to You among the nations. For Your mercy reaches unto the heavens, and Your truth unto the clouds.

And then the chorus comes around again. Why not read it out loud?

Be exalted, O God, above the heavens; let Your glory be above all the earth.

Next time you read Psalm 142, continue on to the rich music of Psalm 57. It makes a fitting doxology to the honest emotional journey of the first cave psalm. We can just imagine David's beautiful singing voice, the first voice to sing so many of these immortal psalms, echoing through the cold, stony walls of the cavern—a beautiful melody dispersing the darkness. In an echo chamber, it doesn't take a loud voice to be heard for many miles:

*"Be exalted, O God, above the heavens . . ."*

Imagine the setting. The voice is clear and beautiful, soulful as befits a singer who has known years of deep turmoil. Nothing but the one voice can be heard in those rocky corridors. Then, suddenly, a rough, untrained voice joins him in unlikely harmony. The duet continues along. And just like that, one by one, a choir of four hundred ragged, rejected, and unloved singers is lifting one mighty choral voice together. Debtors and derelicts are making beautiful melody, accompanying a king in exile. There has never been such a concert, and there may never be another, unless it will occur in a Roman coliseum or a German prison camp—in a place where music and hope and laughter were thought to have been cast out forever. It is the music of the miraculous.

Tears and melody are now mingled without shame in a purity that is revealed whenever believers sing against all worldly expectation, when, for example, Glenda Palmer weeps through her chorus of

"How Great Thou Art." In a cave of exile, David and his choir pour out a song of praise. Their concert hall is a natural geological sound chamber, one whose acoustics were designed by God long ago, for this very earthshaking, despair-breaking moment.

The people sing on, praising God, their voices penetrate the massive stone of the natural ceiling to drift to the very portals of heaven, and perhaps even the angels stop to listen.

*"Be exalted, O God, above the heavens . . ."*

# Psalm 107

1   Oh, give thanks to the LORD, for He is good!
    For His mercy endures forever.
2   Let the redeemed of the LORD say so,
    Whom He has redeemed from the hand of the enemy,
3   And gathered out of the lands,
    From the east and from the west,
    From the north and from the south.
4   They wandered in the wilderness in a desolate way;
    They found no city to dwell in.
5   Hungry and thirsty,
    Their soul fainted in them.
6   Then they cried out to the LORD in their trouble,
    And He delivered them out of their distresses.
7   And He led them forth by the right way,
    That they might go to a city for habitation.
8   Oh, that men would give thanks to the LORD for His goodness,
    And for His wonderful works to the children of men!
9   For He satisfies the longing soul,
    And fills the hungry soul with goodness.
10   Those who sat in darkness and in the shadow of death,
    Bound in affliction and irons—
11   Because they rebelled against the words of God,
    And despised the counsel of the Most High,
12   Therefore He brought down their heart with labor;
    They fell down, and there was none to help.
13   Then they cried out to the LORD in their trouble,
    And He saved them out of their distresses.
14   He brought them out of darkness and the shadow of death,
    And broke their chains in pieces.

15 Oh, that men would give thanks to the LORD for His goodness,
And for His wonderful works to the children of men!
16 For He has broken the gates of bronze,
And cut the bars of iron in two.
17 Fools, because of their transgression,
And because of their iniquities, were afflicted.
18 Their soul abhorred all manner of food,
And they drew near to the gates of death.
19 Then they cried out to the LORD in their trouble,
And He saved them out of their distresses.
20 He sent His word and healed them,
And delivered them from their destructions.
21 Oh, that men would give thanks to the LORD for His goodness,
And for His wonderful works to the children of men!
22 Let them sacrifice the sacrifices of thanksgiving,
And declare His works with rejoicing.
23 Those who go down to the sea in ships,
Who do business on great waters,
24 They see the works of the LORD,
And His wonders in the deep.
25 For He commands and raises the stormy wind,
Which lifts up the waves of the sea.
26 They mount up to the heavens,
They go down again to the depths;
Their soul melts because of trouble.
27 They reel to and fro, and stagger like a drunken man,
And are at their wits' end.
28 Then they cry out to the LORD in their trouble,
And He brings them out of their distresses.
29 He calms the storm,
So that its waves are still.
30 Then they are glad because they are quiet;
So He guides them to their desired haven.
31 Oh, that men would give thanks to the LORD for His goodness,
And for His wonderful works to the children of men!

32   Let them exalt Him also in the congregation of the people,
    And praise Him in the assembly of the elders.

33   He turns rivers into a wilderness,
    And the watersprings into dry ground;

34   A fruitful land into barrenness,
    For the wickedness of those who dwell in it.

35   He turns a wilderness into pools of water,
    And dry land into watersprings.

36   There He makes the hungry dwell,
    That they may establish a city for habitation,

37   And sow fields and plant vineyards,
    That they may yield a fruitful harvest.

38   He also blesses them, and they multiply greatly;
    And He does not let their cattle decrease.

39   When they are diminished and brought low
    Through oppression, affliction and sorrow,

40   He pours contempt on princes,
    And causes them to wander in the wilderness where there is no way;

41   Yet He sets the poor on high, far from affliction,
    And makes their families like a flock.

42   The righteous see it and rejoice,
    And all iniquity stops its mouth.

43   Whoever is wise will observe these things,
    And they will understand the lovingkindness of the LORD.

# 9

# When You Are at Your Wits' End

*The Lord's our rock, in Him we hide,*
*Secure whatever ill betide*
*A shelter in the time of storm*

*The raging storms may round us beat*
*We'll never leave our safe retreat,*
*A shelter in the time of storm.*

—IRA SANKEY

When I was first diagnosed with cancer, I went to certain special people for counsel and comfort. One of these was Dr. Marv Eastlund of Fort Wayne, Indiana. I knew he was a man who would fill three critical roles: first, as a close, trusted friend of many years; second, as a career physician of excellence; third, as a fellow struggler who had grappled with serious illness in his own life. I leaned on his support, advice, and brotherly encouragement; I'll never forget his ministry to me.

Dr. Eastlund's bend in the road was a pancreatic disorder. I've asked him to tell you about the medical misadventure that landed him flat on his back for several weeks at the Mayo Clinic.

There are certain kinds of change none of us ask for, and none of us receive with open arms. In my life, pancreatitis was an uninvited visitor—

the last item that would ever have appeared on my agenda. I was thoroughly miserable when the doctors broke the news to me about it.

The dreadful disease moved into my life like a tornado, demolishing my control over my life, my career, and all my plans for the future. My first reaction was intense anger, to be honest. I resisted this outrageous medical intrusion and fought it with all the energy I could muster. One of my main weapons was denial. I insisted on keeping my usual schedule and simply ignoring the pain.

That was a losing battle, as I'm sure you can imagine. The pancreatitis won. I soon reached my pain threshold, and I could no longer pretend that my body was fine and healthy. I was filled with anger. Who could I blame? I could find no scapegoat, so I blamed myself. Anger gave way to discouragement and self-pity. I wallowed in my own misery for extended periods of time, fully realizing that I was sick—really sick—and that my life would never again be the same. What response was there for me but despair and gloom? I became consumed with my own problems. And if there was any small thread of hope left within me, the repeated hospitalizations snuffed it out.

Discouragement gave way to depression. There were days I could do nothing but sit and stare. My family tried desperately to encourage me, but I made certain they didn't succeed. I was investing a good bit of energy in my negative emotions, and I didn't want to cheer up. Life was unfair. The future was hopeless.

And yet deep within me, there was the nagging question of my faith. I couldn't give up the life commitment I had made to God. He meant too much for me to simply turn away from Him. So I was being torn by great spiritual conflict: How could a believer experience the thoughts and emotions I was feeling? Why had God let me sink into anger, discouragement, and depression? If my faith was as strong as I'd always thought it was, why, then—how, then—could I now be questioning His very existence? Where was He? Why didn't He answer my pleas?

My faith was on very rocky ground indeed. Physically, mentally, and spiritually, I had come to my wits' end. I had nowhere to turn. So I lay down on my back one day, sighed deeply, and stared up at the ceiling.

And as I did that, I realized that my eyes were fixed in the right direction—up. I was looking toward heaven. *Up* was the only direction a bed patient could look. And with new resolution, I realized I had to be faithful to Him and keep trusting Him. I could not turn away. As

---

*From this side of glory we see the tapestry from*
*underneath, and it is full of knots and twisted threads*
*and frayed ends that lack meaning and beauty.*
*From God's perspective, it is all under control.*

## —Charles Swindoll

---

distant as He seemed at times, I realized that my pain and despair only served to draw me closer to Him than health and happiness could ever have brought me.

Through the pain, I began to know Him better. I found a friend in God, a *genuine* Friend I had never known before.

I see my problems differently now. When life closes in, I know that the only way out is the way up.

*God is a genuine friend*—Dr. Eastlund found that out, and the psalms repeat that rich theme over and over.

## Pictures of Helplessness

Psalm 107 celebrates the friendship and the faithfulness of God. It's a beloved hymn of thanksgiving for His deliverance. We can find, in the section spanning verses 4 through 32, four word pictures of circumstances faced by God's people along their journey. These four separate pictures have a common overlapping theme: the human feeling of helplessness.

We'll be taking a close look at these fine pictures. As we do so, I invite you to imagine you and me walking through the Bible's great gallery of art. It is a fabulous museum, filled with inspiring portraits and fantastic renderings in every corner. We've begun with the beautiful landscapes of the tranquillity of the Garden of Eden, the towering summit of Sinai, and the pastoral beauty of Canaan. We've seen portraits of prophets, priests, and patriarchs. Finally, as we enter the building known as the Book of Psalms, we come to Room 107. It's a thought-provoking gallery. We'll need to spend some time here in contemplation.

Here are four paintings carefully rendered by the artist whose goal is to portray four great challenges of life. I'll be serving as your tour guide for this particular room, and I ask you to keep up with the group and, please—no flashbulbs! As we study the paintings, I will pause briefly at the first three to make some general comments. Then we'll engage in an in-depth exploration of the fourth and final painting. This one is the culmination of the other three, a masterpiece filled with emotion and symbolism that will astonish you. We will spend the majority of our time there, and I predict you'll be coming back to gaze at the painting on your own time and again.

But let's begin our tour, shall we?

### Painting #1: *The Desert*

The first painting is a landscape, but it's not one you're likely to see from the brush of your typical painter. This landscape happens to be a desert.

We might call this one "Wanderers in the Wilderness." The title would draw its inspiration from a description found in verses 4 through 9 of Psalm 107. There we read about the experience of being lost in the desert. Of course, we realize that not all deserts are composed of sand, and we can be lost without losing our physical bearings. Listen to the word picture painted by the psalmist: "They wandered in the wilderness in a desolate way; they found no city to dwell in. Hungry and thirsty, their soul fainted in them." We grow thirsty just hearing these words.

Many have lost their way in a dry wilderness, devoid of meaning and purpose. For some, the desert is loneliness. Others are lost in a cycle of routine futility. Still others become dislocated in a desert of affluence, which turns out to be a drier and thirstier land than they ever expected. The wanderers trudge through the sand without hope or help, seeking the true spiritual home that always eludes them.

As we move to the next portico, we find a different scenario.

## Painting #2: The Prison

The desert may have seemed an odd subject for a painting, but verse 10 offers one even less likely. It is a group portrait of prisoners, "those who sat in darkness and in the shadow of death, bound in affliction and irons."

Leonard Griffith writes, "People are like prisoners, trapped in the dungeon of their own moral folly, the victims of evil rather than the doers of it. They started out with freedom of choice, but they continued to choose the wrong thing." But that freedom will be fleeting when we choose evil. The wrong choices become patterns of behavior that finally master those who made the choices. "The drug addict would give anything to be set free from the chains of his habit, but it has him hooked and he knows that the end of it will be his death. . . . In his sober moments, the alcoholic hates himself for the hell that he creates in his own home, but his bottle is like a chain, and he knows that he cannot break loose from it."[1]

So there are prisons of addiction—gambling, drugs, and alcohol—but there are also prisons of abuse or of improper relationships. People are taken prisoner by their own conduct.

Not all prisons are of our own making, however. Some of us are trapped by difficult circumstances from which there seems little hope of escape. These prisons might have been constructed by other people's evil, by persecution, or by matters over which they have no control. We don't have to be at fault to become hopeless captives. Our painting shows the desolation of imprisonment, and it saddens us to look upon this canvas. We take one more look, and we move on.


### Painting #3: *The Hospital*

Now we come to the portrayal of a familiar but forbidding setting, that of a hospital. In verses 17 through 22, we find something not too different from an ICU. Are you surprised to find that in the Bible?

---

*In me there is darkness, but with Thee there is light.*

*I am lonely but Thou leavest me not.*

*I am feeble in heart, but Thou leavest me not.*

*I am restless, but with Thee there is peace.*

*In me there is bitterness, but with Thee there is patience;*

*Thy ways are past understanding,*

*but Thou knowest the way for me.*

**—Dietrich Bonhoeffer**

---

Look closely at the picture painted for us in these verses: "Fools, because of their transgression, and because of their iniquities, were afflicted. Their soul abhorred all manner of food, and they drew near to the gates of death" (vv. 17–18). This is a ward of illness and affliction, and it serves as a corridor that opens into the darkness of death.

Not every illness, of course, is caused by sin. But the people here have poisoned themselves with their own transgressions. They are suffering, ready for the release brought only by death. There in the ward they lie, waiting only for their final moments on this earth. That's the story laid out for us in the third of the four paintings. We take in its gloomy canvas and move to the last picture. This one is larger than the others, and it captures our full attention.

*Painting #4: The Storm*

The picture causes us to catch our breath. It captures perfectly the power of nature in all its unleashed fury. As our eyes move across the canvas, we know what it means to be clinging to the deck of a ship that is caught in a terrible storm. We take the forces of nature for granted—until we become their helpless prey.

We know how the disciples felt, violently tossed in the nighttime waves and fearing death before Jesus came. We know how the passengers of the *Titanic* felt on a far calmer night—but one in which the greatest ship ever built was no match for a stray block of ice. We're gazing at the portrait of a furious tempest:

> Those who go down to the sea in ships, who do business on great waters, they see the works of the LORD, and His wonders in the deep. For He commands and raises the stormy wind, which lifts up the waves of the sea. They mount up to the heavens, they go down again to the depths; their soul melts because of trouble. They reel to and fro, and stagger like a drunken man, and are at their wits' end. Then they cry out to the LORD in their trouble, and He brings them out of their distresses. He calms the storm, so that its waves are still. Then they are glad because they are quiet; so He guides them to their desired haven. Oh, that men would give thanks to the LORD for His goodness, and for His wonderful works to the children of men! Let them exalt Him also in the congregation of the people, and praise Him in the assembly of the elders. (Ps. 107:23–32)

## A Closer Look at the Storm

*The Place of the Storm*

These sailors realize their small stature, their seeming insignificance, out on the open sea. There is no land in sight. There is no one to rescue those in peril on the sea.

You may never have crossed the ocean on a large ship, but the picture will remain just as powerful for you—for we all know what it's like to be caught in one of life's many storms. You realize immediately that towering waves and billowing storms can come in many forms.

When I've encountered the storms of my own life, I've taken encouragement from this psalm. It has always been when I've ventured out onto the open sea, when I've been taking a great step of faith and moving beyond the borders of safety, that I've been caught by the treacherous winds. I feel certain that I'm pursuing the will of God for my life, but my faith is sternly tested by the wind and the rain. That's when I have thought about the assurances of Psalm 107. At the end of this chapter, I'll tell you how this psalm became permanently etched on my soul.

For now, let's consider Jesus and the small circle of men around Him. They understood the terror of the tempest. They also understood the mystery of deep waters. We know this from Luke 5:4–6, when Jesus commanded Simon Peter to "launch out into the deep and let down your nets for a catch." Simon grumbled a little about this, reminding the carpenter from Nazareth that the professionals—men who knew their trade—had been fishing all night, and they hadn't caught a thing. Nevertheless, Simon said, if that's what Jesus wanted, the boys would take one more shot. And you know the rest. After one more trip, the nets were overflowing, literally bursting with fish.

The message? Great works are done in deep waters. If you're diving for pearls, you have to move out of the shallow end. Many of us never learn that lesson; fear restricts us to the comfort zone, where we miss out on untold adventures. But Jesus tells us to launch out into the deep—in risk taking, in the pursuit of excellence, and in the knowledge of Him. We walk to the edge of all our light, and that next step into the blackness holds the destiny God has for us. But it also holds whatever dangers lie in the darkness. We know that, we realize the risks, and perhaps we'll never take that one terrifying step that makes the miracle possible.

It's not simply biblical sense—it's common sense as well. If you're in the business world, you realize that. Play it safe, and you'll never build a business. Launching a new firm is launching out into the deep. The storms are certain to come, and the winds will howl. You'll be out on the edge, all by yourself in an unsteady boat. Perhaps your business will fail despite all your best efforts and intentions. But you'll never know unless you cast the net.

No one ever said it would be easy out in the deep waters. No one ever guaranteed fair weather and smooth sailing. It's your choice—stay along the shore and you'll always be safe from drowning and disaster. But you'll also never know the blessings of the deep things of God.

## The Producer of the Storm

What's wrong with this picture? What seems unusual about the storm depicted in this psalm?

"For He commands and raises the stormy wind, which lifts up the waves of the sea" (v. 25). The pronoun *He* is capitalized. Now we realize the striking thing about this storm. As great as the power of the wind and the waves may be, there is something—Someone—more powerful in the background, behind it all. It is God—the God who sends the rains.

Did you step back from the canvas when you realized that detail? Are you shocked? We're much more comfortable crediting God with calming storms than with causing them. And yet we must take the Scripture at its word. The Bible teaches us that He is Lord of all—and that includes the storms that serve His purposes along with everything else.

Let's take care before blaming God for every storm, however. Sometimes we've done just fine on our own bringing on those dark clouds. We make the mistakes, and God's place is simply to let us discover how deeply we need Him when we're just about to go under the waves. So we're not referring to those self-induced tempests. We're talking about storms brought about expressly by divine intention. And those do exist.

Job understood that. He had a disciplined understanding that character is a function of trial, and even trials were deeply tied to His friendship and faith in God. He said, "He knows the way that I take;

when He has tested me, I shall come forth as gold" (Job 23:10). *He knows.* Job found strength in the knowledge that God knew him intimately, and he set out with the understanding that tests would deepen that friendship. When the storms came, he was prepared. Even during the most excruciating pain, Job knew God was in control of his problems. He knew that pain had a purpose.

Listen to this expression of the same understanding in Psalm 66: "You brought us into the net; you laid affliction on our backs. You have caused men to ride over our heads; we went through fire and through water; but You brought us out to rich fulfillment" (vv. 11–12). Have you felt people "riding over your head" at your workplace recently? Have you been through fire and water in family problems? A devoted believer will pray for God's deliverance from problems, but a wiser one will pray for God's use of them.

Even Jonah—rebellious, dispassionate Jonah—knew Who was behind the storms. When God sent him on a mission, he booked passage on a ship and headed in the opposite direction as quickly as he could. The belief that he could run away demonstrated an appallingly limited view of God. His God was too small! But the ensuing tempest enlarged his perspective. Here was a God who could trouble the sea. Job realized that he could run, but he couldn't hide. The Lord sent the storm just as He sent Jonah. Jonah was God's messenger to the Ninevites, but the storm was God's message to Jonah.

Why did He send the storm in your life? Is it intended to cut off your flight from God, as in the case of Jonah? Is it to draw you closer, as in Job's life? If you're weathering a storm, you can be certain the winds are no random weather front. They blow for a clear purpose. As you're caught up in a tempest, ask God to help you be caught up in His purposes.

## The Peril of the Storm

"They mount up to the heavens, they go down again to the depths; their soul melts because of trouble. They reel to and fro, and stagger like a drunken man, and are at their wits' end" (Ps. 107:26–27). What an image God paints on the canvas of our minds here!

In his masterful paraphrase, *The Message*, Eugene Peterson rewords the passage like this: "You shot high in the sky, then the bottom dropped out; your hearts were stuck in your throats. You were spun like a top, you reeled like a drunk, you didn't know which way was

---

*Usually prayer is a question of groaning rather than speaking,*
*tears rather than words. For He sets our tears in His sight,*
*and our groaning is not hidden from Him*
*Who made all things by His Word*
*and does not ask for words of man.*

**—Augustine of Hippo**

---

up." This is a riot of mixed metaphors, of course, in the service of a strong point—the "you" in this passage is spinning wildly out of control! Have you ever lost control of an automobile on an icy highway? If so, you know this feeling well. These passengers of the rocking ship are at their wits' end.

By the way, did you know where the expression "at your wits' end" came from? Right here in the psalms. These people have been outwitted. They've come to the end of all their ideas and strategies. The tempest has mastered their vessel. The ship has set off to navigate the winds and the waters, but that's all been turned upside down. The wind and the waters are now navigating the ship. The passengers can do little but watch—and pray.

### The Prayer in the Storm

Unfortunately, prayer seems to be our last port in a storm. It should be the first. But the people of this passage do turn to God in verse 28: "Then they cry out to the LORD in their trouble, and He brings them out of their distresses." Have you ever noticed the inverse relationship between depth of crisis and length of prayer? You could almost create a mathematical formula to demonstrate that the calmer things are, the lengthier and more eloquent our prayers tend to be. But the greater the storm, the shorter and simpler we pray—starting with this classic prayer adopted by many devout and troubled believers over the centuries: "Help!"

When we were living in Fort Wayne, Indiana, the driveway of our little house emptied out into a busy highway. For us, a simple trip to buy groceries was a guaranteed adventure. One day, I was sitting in the passenger seat while Donna backed out into traffic—and never saw the approaching car. But I did, right at the last moment. I looked up, anticipated the collision, and blurted out, "Lord—help!" Yes, the car hit us; but it barely missed the side of the car where I was seated, and I escaped a serious injury. I assure you I have several prayers more inspiring and articulate than "Lord—help!" But it was just the thing for that occasion—precisely the right length.

The seafarers of the psalm may have called out the same words, and probably more than once. Their circumstances have certain similarities to the characters in the other paintings. Let's look at the first picture again. The desert wanderers, hopelessly lost, "cried out to the LORD in their trouble, and He delivered them out of their distresses" (v. 6).

How about those prisoners in their cell? What are they saying? "Then they cried out to the LORD in their trouble, and He saved them out of their distresses" (v. 13).

Meanwhile, back in the sterile, deathlike hospital ward, what are the patients saying? "Then they cried out to the LORD in their trouble, and He saved them out of their distresses" (v. 19).

In the storms, in the wilderness, in captivity, and in illness, people desperately seek an escape. And Dr. Marv Eastlund has said it for all of us: The only way *out* is the way *up*. No matter what the problem may be, no matter what trouble may ensnare us, there is only one path to safety. The only hope is to reach beyond ourselves to Someone stronger than we are, and stronger than the shackles that bind us. Only One can fill that requirement. And even the proverbial atheist in the foxhole realizes it in the depths of his heart. Even the most thoroughgoing skeptic will finally come to that point of absolute desperation and look up to the heavens to cry, "Lord—help!"

God's part in the storm is a sensitive topic for us right now—it hits a little too close to home, for many of us are being tossed around by ill winds at this very moment. We fear that if we stopped to consider that God may be the Author of the storm, we might be overcome with anger at God. And yet I imagine arriving in heaven when my day comes, and hearing my Lord admit that He has used storms quite frequently to drive me to my knees. I'll be capable of handling the knowledge of it then, and He'll smile and say, "That one was a real corker, wasn't it, David? That crisis you went through that particular year? I really had you going! But now you can see that it brought you back into My camp at just the right time. You weren't paying as much attention to Me in those days, remember? You were drifting, and where might you have finally ended up if I hadn't stepped in and done something to get your attention? Remember how it all paid off? I'm sure you never realized how that whole crisis prepared you for the good things to follow!" And for the first time, I'll be able to laugh about some sore spot or other; we'll laugh together, but in a joyful way.

God certainly hates everything that causes us pain, whether it may be imprisonment or illness or a storm of some kind. But He knows that lesser pain is a necessary part of avoiding far deeper pain later. It hurts to pull out a thorn, but the pain of leaving it would cause the deeper agony of infection. God knows that He has to pull out a few thorns occasionally, and we'll cry out in pain and even anger at Him. But it's all for a purpose.

God knows, even if we don't, that we're not self-sufficient. He loves to bring us to our knees in fresh dependence on Him. If only peacetime prayers carried the intensity of storm-tossed prayers! If only we could seek Him with the passion that possesses us when we feel trapped and desperate. God hears those passionate prayers. And He provides the peace that can be found nowhere else.

## The Peace in the Storm

"He calms the storm, so that its waves are still. Then they are glad because they are quiet" (vv. 29–30).

Have you ever noticed the wonderful purity of silence after a prolonged cacophony of noise? The tyranny of sound suddenly loses its hold on us, and the ensuing quiet seems to liberate the spirit. It's truly a peace that passes understanding. We refer to this phenomenon as "the calm after the storm." It's about comfort and relief. Deep inside us, we realize that the Bringer of the storm is also the Master of it; He can take it away in the blink of an eye. When we realize He is great enough to send and remove storms, we fall down in worship.

When the people of the psalm were being battered by the storm, they cried out in fear and helplessness. And God responded. He calmed the storm and stilled the waves. And that idea quickly reminds us of the stories of Jesus. The events played out in Psalm 107 foreshadow the remarkable episodes we find in the Gospels. The disciples, having chosen to pursue the Teacher and the adventure He called them for, found themselves in the middle of turbulent experiences, challenges for which they must have felt ill-prepared. We can read these accounts and realize the Lord was allowing the storms to break loose because He wanted them to learn lessons that would serve them well later. They would face persecution. They would face hostility and terrible odds against an intimidating goal. They could not learn the lessons and build the strength in any other classroom than the stormy seas.

On one occasion, the disciples climbed into a boat to travel across the Sea of Galilee. Jesus boarded with them, crawled into the back, found a nice spot, and went to sleep. As they traveled far out to sea, suddenly the weather changed. A storm front quickly rolled in, and it looked like a serious one. Here were the disciples, hopelessly far from safety; surely they were going to die together. According to Matthew 8, Jesus awoke, took a good look around, and asked why His friends were so worked up. He also dropped in a stinging remark about the weakness of their faith. Then he stood in the boat, rebuked the winds and the sea, and watched the calm settle as far as the eye could see.

That's Matthew's story. But it's rewarding to discover what Luke adds to the picture. Always the astute observer of human emotions, he shows us the dimension of fear the disciples experienced. It is in Luke's account that we find out how some of the men came to Jesus and jostled Him awake, gasping, "Master, Master, we are perishing!" (Luke 8:24).

These fishermen and tax collectors and assorted commoners were shaking the arm of the Lord of glory, the One who created the winds and the waves and the sea that had them so frightened. If they had realized the full import of this, they wouldn't have demonstrated so much panic in the way they roused Him. They might even have been looking forward to the show Jesus was capable of putting on as He stilled the storm. But they were fully expecting to die. I've always been impressed by this story, and years ago I scribbled a little note next to it in the margin of my Bible. My note reads, "We are far more secure in the storm with Jesus in our boat than we will ever be on the shore without Him."

And I still believe that. If you've opted to pursue the adventure of following Jesus, you've already discovered that the journey doesn't occur in a luxury limousine. He will lead you to and through some rough places. It may be that you've found yourself in the "old gospel ship," rocked by the waves and thrashed by the downpour as lightning and thunder boomed all around you. The moment may come when you say, "I didn't sign up for this! I know I sang, 'Wherever He leads, I'll go,' but can't we at least check the weather report first? How could He lead me into a storm like this one?"

Just cling to the knowledge that you could be in no safer place than a storm of His making. You are safer and more secure in the tempest with Jesus than you could ever be in the calmest place without Him. That calm, you'll come to realize, is an illusion; and the storm is for a good purpose and a short duration.

Speaking of storms, my friend Ron Mehl tells about a woman who was caught in a frightening storm in the middle of the Atlantic Ocean. She was aboard a luxury liner carrying a large number of children. The woman saw that everyone else was panicking, running to and fro through all the passages. All this was upsetting the children, so she gathered them together and began telling them Bible stories to keep them calm. The children became quiet, captivated by the wonderful stories.

The ship made it through, safe and sound. As the captain made his rounds, he saw the woman laughing and talking with the children. She had stayed calm through the storm, and she was calm now. He was puzzled. "How did you keep your cool when everyone else was falling to pieces?" he asked her. "Have you been through something like this before?"

"It's simple," said the woman. "I have two daughters. One of them lives in New York and the other one lives in heaven. I knew I would see one or the other of them in a few hours and it didn't make any difference to me which one."

Does that story seem a trifle sentimental and unrealistic to you? It shouldn't. It simply describes the mind-set of the serious believer—the follower who takes Jesus at His Word. If you feel such a story is simply sentimental, you may feel the same way about heaven and the concept that God is in control. Grace through the storm is a function of believing that the Creator of the storm is also the Deliverer from it. He is also the One who can bring us peace and strength when all those around us are falling to pieces.

He is our Deliverer, and that fact is gloriously portrayed in living color in every canvas of the eternal gallery known as Psalm 107. The first painting shows desert wanderers—those who can't find the path. "And He led them forth by the right way, that they might go to a city for habitation" (v. 7). *A city for a habitation*—the very words that define hope and peace when you've been lost in the desert.

Then we revisit the darkened prison. What happens to the captives? Someone comes to unlock their cell and show them the sunlight again. "He brought them out of darkness and the shadow of death, and broke their chains in pieces" (v. 14).

Over in the hospital, patients hover near death—only to be healed miraculously. "He sent His word and healed them, and delivered them from their destructions" (v. 20).

Downpour or desert, dungeon or disease—the specific facts of the crisis ultimately don't matter. For God is in control. Wherever we are, whatever we may be up against, when we cry out to God in our trouble, He will hear us. He will calm the waters. And the time may come when He will even let us know the reasons He unleashed them.

## The Purpose of the Storm

"So He guides them to their desired haven" (v. 30).

The Lord didn't stop at delivering the people from the storm. He took them where they needed to go. There's only one twist: The storm may change our idea of a destination. Crises never leave us the same as they found us. Those of us who love and trust God through the worst times—those of us who are receptive to what He might be trying to teach us—find that our hearts have changed by the time the stillness replaces the storminess. We will be far more in tune with His desires. Our goals will have moved closer to His own.

If you doubt that point, you might want to ask Jonah a few questions. Was he a different man after the whale spit him up onto the shore? Were his purposes closer to God's purposes after he discovered what can be wrought from disobedience? He came out of the belly of a whale and hit the ground running. There were no roads that could deliver him to Nineveh fast enough.

God changes our *want-to* in the midst of His storms.

## The Praise after the Storm

What is there for us in that time when the calm returns but to praise our God? And how we wish everyone we know, and all men and women on the face of the earth, would join us in worship and exaltation. He is greater than any of the forces of nature.

"Oh, that men would give thanks to the LORD for His goodness, and for His wonderful works to the children of men! Let them exalt

Him also in the congregation of the people, and praise Him in the assembly of the elders" (vv. 31–32).

We've been hopelessly lost in the barren wilderness, and suddenly we find ourselves in an oasis. What do we do? We give thanks. "Oh, that men would give thanks to the LORD for His goodness, and for His wonderful works to the children of men! For He satisfies the longing soul, and fills the hungry soul with goodness" (vv. 8–9).

We've been imprisoned by addiction or abuse or past memories or another cruel master—when we discover a Master who is loving and who frees us. What do we do? We give thanks. "Oh, that men would give thanks to the LORD for His goodness, and for His wonderful works to the children of men! For He has broken the gates of bronze, and cut the bars of iron in two" (vv. 15–16).

In the first two word-pictures in Psalm 107, we offer thanksgiving to the Lord for what He has done. But in the last two pictures, the image changes.

We've been desperately ill, waiting only for death. How do we respond to healing? We come together for worship. "Oh, that men would give thanks to the LORD for His goodness, and for His wonderful works to the children of men! Let them sacrifice the sacrifices of thanksgiving, and declare His works with rejoicing" (vv. 21–22).

And finally, we make it through the storm. God brings us through, and what do we do? We assemble for thanksgiving, praise, and worship. "Oh, that men would give thanks to the LORD for His goodness, and for His wonderful works to the children of men! Let them exalt Him also in the congregation of the people, and praise Him in the assembly of the elders" (vv. 31–32).

Is it really important to include other people in this celebration? Shouldn't it be enough simply to thank God quietly, in the privacy and sincerity of our own hearts?

I hear that sentiment more and more frequently these days. "I don't really need to worship God in a church," people say. "I can worship Him just as well by myself, working in my garden on a Sunday morning, or up at my lake cottage."

It sounds convenient, but it's not very biblical. We're told all through Scripture to come together in the assembly for the exaltation of God together. "In the presence of the elders," that is, of the leaders, we give praise to God. Together we become something greater than we could ever be individually. Together we offer an entirely different brand of worship than we offer in solitude. Together we are the living body of Christ.

## From Raging Storm to Rejoicing

I have turned to Psalm 107 in my Bible through the years, and its meaning for me grows as I advance in age. This psalm, I feel, has my name written on it. I've felt that way ever since something that happened early in my ministry at our current church.

---

*Almighty God, Father of all mercies, we, Your unworthy servants,*
*give You humble thanks for all Your goodness and loving-kindness*
*to us and to all men. We bless You for our creation, preservation,*
*and all the blessings of this life; but above all for*
*Your incomparable love in redemption of the world*
*by our Lord Jesus Christ; for the means of grace, and for*
*the hope of glory. And, we pray, give us such an awareness*
*of Your mercies, that with truly thankful hearts we*
*may make known Your praise, not only with our lips,*
*but in our lives, by giving up ourselves to Your service,*
*and by walking before You in holiness and righteousness*
*all our days through Jesus Christ our Lord, to whom, with You*
*and the Holy Spirit, be all honor and glory through all ages,*
*Amen.*

*—A General Thanksgiving,*
*Book of Common Prayer*

---

I've been pastor at Shadow Mountain Community Church for more than nineteen years. But in the early years of my time here, I held two jobs. I accepted a call not only to pastor the church, but also to become the president of Christian Heritage College. I had a strong feeling of God's leading in holding both positions. But I never saw the storm front that was moving in. Eight years ago, the college was seriously ill, hanging on by a thread.

During one particular summer we had run out of resources, the tuition money was gone, and existing funds were insufficient to carry us through to the fall. The church had underwritten us, but now those resources were no longer available. The church had simply given all it could give. Nearly every week, I attended meetings in which we agonized over what to do. Slowly but surely, we were edging toward the idea of simply closing the doors of the college. We even met with another Christian college to explore the possibility of a merger. I remember wondering if this was what God had in mind—but I could feel no peace about it.

One day I was filled with a sense of the storm. I felt like the waves were crashing over us, and that we were drowning in the waves. I didn't know what to do. I gathered our senior staff, and we all traveled to a local Christian camp called Pine Valley. It was vacant, and the caretakers allowed us to use one of their conference rooms. Our group gathered around the table to pray, but I still felt a deep sense of despair and hopelessness. No options were appearing; our prayers weren't being answered, or so it seemed. We'd tried everything we could think of trying.

And then I came to Psalm 107.

It was the storm. My feeling of enduring a storm reminded me of the imagery in the psalm. So as we sat there in the conference room at Pine Valley, I opened my Bible and I read this passage to the group. I told the senior staff, "There is one crucial thing we can never forget. Together we have chosen to do business in the great waters—deep waters. Not many churches have schools, but we have several. We have a preschool, three elementary schools, a junior high school, a high school, and a college. We've pursued these out of obedience to

God's leadership. It's not supposed to be easy. We've launched out into the deep, and we shouldn't be surprised to find ourselves caught in the storm."

We talked about the challenge at hand, and I returned to the theme of the psalm. "What we have to do is to *cry out to the Lord*. We have to ask God to move into the midst of this situation and do something that only He can do."

I've experienced few events like that one, and I'll never forget what followed. We began to pray around the table with very intense, heartfelt emotion. It was one of those powerful, spiritually charged atmospheres that come about when needy Christians get serious about seeking God's deliverance. There were tears; there was pleading. There was a knock at the door.

It was the proprietor of the camp. She motioned for me to come out into the hall, where she told me, "You need to call your office."

I found a pay phone and called Glenda at the church office. She said, "Are you sitting down?"

I said, "Glenda, I'm in a phone booth."

"Well if you can't sit down, hang on," she began. And this is what she told me. She said the women down in the college mailroom had been routinely opening mail. They came across a strange envelope— it contained no letter. No letter at all, but it did have a check inside— *a check for half a million dollars.*

I went back into the meeting with my eyes filled with tears, and everyone was anxious. They wanted me to tell them who had died. I said, "No one has died! Let me tell you what has happened. We've been sitting here in this room, in the midst of a storm. We've been crying out to God for His help, and He heard our pleas. He reached out to us in our trouble and brought us into a place of peace."

To say that we began to praise God would be an understatement. When you come out of a storm in which all had seemed lost, and God does something magnificent, the worship is unforgettable!

That's known as a happy ending. Do you still have doubts that your story will have one? Perhaps the storm is raging for you as you read these words. Perhaps you're lost in a wilderness of shattered hope, or shut away in a prison of debt. Perhaps you face a hospital ward of health concerns, or family problems are rocking your boat and you feel you'll be lost forever.

Wherever you are, whatever the crisis may be, there is an important principle at work. If you feel helpless, you've become eligible for the assistance of God. You need only cry out for His salvation. He will do the rest in His time, *and He'll do it well.*

When the storm is over, you'll be a new creature—wiser, stronger, and ready to serve Him. The sea will be calm, the breeze will be soft, and the silence will present itself as a sanctuary for you to exalt His name and sing His glorious praises. If He can control the storm, what other wonderful works might He bring to pass in your life?

With that exciting thought, you'll cast off and launch out into the deep waters.

# Psalm 46

*To the chief musician.*
*A Psalm of the Sons of Korah. A song for Alamoth.*

1 God is our refuge and strength,
  A very present help in trouble.
2 Therefore we will not fear,
  Though the earth be removed,
  And though the mountains be carried into the midst of the sea;
3 Though its waters roar and be troubled,
  Though the mountains shake with its swelling. Selah
4 There is a river whose streams shall make glad the city of God,
  The holy place of the tabernacle of the Most High.
5 God is in the midst of her, she shall not be moved;
  God shall help her, just at the break of dawn.
6 The nations raged, the kingdoms were moved;
  He uttered His voice, the earth melted.
7 The LORD of hosts is with us;
  The God of Jacob is our refuge. Selah
8 Come, behold the works of the LORD,
  Who has made desolations in the earth.
9 He makes wars cease to the end of the earth;
  He breaks the bow and cuts the spear in two;
  He burns the chariot in the fire.
10 Be still, and know that I am God;
  I will be exalted among the nations,
  I will be exalted in the earth!
11 The LORD of hosts is with us;
  the God of Jacob is our refuge. Selah

# 10

# Triumph over Trouble

*A mighty fortress is our God*
*A bulwark never failing,*
*Our helper He amid the flood*
*Of mortal ills prevailing.*

—MARTIN LUTHER,

"A MIGHTY FORTRESS IS OUR GOD"

It was October 1998. I was on my way to Charlotte, North Carolina, where I'd been invited to preach for a prayer ministry. I have a friend in that city, Pastor Page, who has struggled with a very rare variety of leukemia. We've compared notes over the last couple of years, sharing back and forth about my cancer and his leukemia.

By the time I arrived in Charlotte, I was quite weary. Cross-country flights have that effect. But the schedule was tight, and there was no time to catch my breath. In little more than the blink of an eye, I was sitting at a banquet, talking with the pastor and his wife about stem cell transplants. Pastor Page has endured two rounds of that procedure, and he and his wife cataloged all the highlights for me. But there was a strange feeling in the back of my mind. Have you ever had the odd impression that you should listen closely to some-one—that this person's words could very likely become important to you in the future? I felt this distinctly. It wasn't a pleasant thought, but I wondered if I was being prepared for something that lay in my future.

The evening, however, was a fine one. My preaching time was well received, and afterward I lingered to meet and mingle with the friendly people. All of this happened on a Friday night at the end of a busy autumn week. But I had miles to go before I could sleep. I still had to drive to Boone, North Carolina. I looked forward to attending my son's college football game there on Saturday.

By the time I found my way to the condo where I was to stay the night, I didn't want to think about how late it was. I believe it was at least 2:00 A.M., following a full day of packing, flying, speaking, and driving. The Appalachian air had a bite to it, so I climbed wearily into bed and coiled myself into blankets and bedding, more than ready to sleep like a rock.

But it didn't happen that way.

It was in the middle of the night when I awoke. Perspiration was flowing and my bedclothes were drenched. It was as if I'd just come in from the rain, and I had to get out of bed and change into something else. This was a completely new experience for me, but I had no doubt about the meaning. The doctors, you see, had been preparing me for this possibility. Every time I'd been in for a checkup, I'd heard the stern question, "Have you had any night sweats?" While my answer had always been no, I'd learned that this was one of the sure symptoms of lymphoma.

Through the night and early morning, I lay alone in a condominium thousands of miles from home, knowing my earthly body had lost one more crucial battle with the armies of disease. All my fears were revived, and I knew for certain that drifting back to sleep was out of the question. So I sat up and began to pray, pouring out my anxious heart to God. I talked over every aspect of my condition with Him. It was really the only option I had, wrapped in blankets in that North Carolina condominium.

Somehow I managed to get up and get myself to the football stadium the next day. College games, of course, are loud and spirited and require plenty of energy. I flew home Saturday night in order to be there to preach my regular Sunday schedule. Now if there's any day in which it's difficult for a pastor to rest, it's Sunday. The marathon went on and on—and brought me the next day to the office of my chiropractor, whom I told about the pain I had begun to experience in my left shoulder. He gave me the gift of yet another appointment, sending me to my oncologist. It was his opinion that something was amiss in my left collarbone area.

I made the appointment to see my oncologist, but getting an answer would have to wait. The oncologist wanted to get a biopsy of the swelling, and that surgery would have to be scheduled for the future. A week and a half had passed since I'd first realized something was wrong. I was tired both physically and emotionally, and the demands on my body and my soul seemed never to reach an end.

While I waited for the surgery to be done, I returned to North Carolina to see my son play another game. But I had another purpose for making this jaunt across the country. I have a friend in that area, Dr. Furman, who is among the finest doctors in his field. He is a tho-

---

### From My Journal

*Lord, I cannot rid myself of this nagging fear. Deep in my heart, I know the disease has crept back in. I can feel it stealthily going about its work of destruction in my body. Please help me to do whatever I can to nurture my immune system. Show me how I can rebuild the strength that has drained away from my weary vessel.*

*Today I've been tired and listless. I simply can't continue feeling that way. Please lift my dying spirits, Lord—You are the only true Healer and I put my trust entirely in You. I await Your loving hand, nursing me back to strength and service.*

---

racic surgeon, but his general knowledge of medicine is quite broad. Dr. Furman was good enough to take a look at my weary body. It was his opinion that the swelling in my collarbone was nothing for me to worry about. That was the good news.

The bad news was the swollen nodule Dr. Furman found in my neck. And it really was bad news, for in all likelihood it meant a recurrence of the cancer I had fought off before.

I knew Dr. Furman had the correct diagnosis. My cancer was back, with a vengeance, and that was nearly impossible for me to accept. I had celebrated a victory over the dread disease. I had put it behind me, assigning it to the closed files of my unhappy memories. I had determined to live happily ever after. But the road had come to another bend—if anything, an even crueler one. It felt almost like a mockery to my sense of gratitude to God for bringing me through it before. My mood went black. Could I survive another weary bout with the giant? What was the meaning of being forced into the battle again? Wasn't once enough?

It was the darkest night of my soul, a nightmare with no hope of waking. I can't even begin to tell you.

The psalms are dotted and drenched with more tear stains than any other part of the Bible. Music is a direct portal to the soul, and the Book of Psalms is the hymnal of the Old Testament. Every conceivable emotion from ecstasy to anger to despair can be found in these pages. Many of the most beautiful verses ever written are gathered in this collection of the hymns and poems of the kingdom of Israel. What Paris's Louvre museum might be to art, the Book of Psalms is to poetry.

If there is a single great message here, it is that our pain is real, but God's presence is just as real. The psalms bear witness to the fact that we aren't the first to walk down the difficult roads of disappointment and persecution and bitterness. Here we find hope in the time of storm, even when the thunder and lightning cause us to run for shelter. As we read the Book of Psalms, we feel as if our story has been recorded before we have lived it. And if the problems have been there before us, the solutions must be there for us too. There can be no more powerful healing balm than the wisdom we find in this book positioned strategically in the center of the Bible.

Whenever I have suffered, the psalms have provided my medicine. When I have been wounded, they have bandaged me and pointed me toward healing. When I've most needed these verses, no commentaries or scholarly notes have been necessary. The simple and heartfelt words I've found here have always been enough. I've drunk deeply of them, bathed in them, and let them wash over me until I've felt the dust of the world cleansed away by the hope and peace of God's presence in the music of the psalms.

But at other times, I've yearned to swim to deeper depths in these verses. I've wanted to go farther beneath the surface to understand something of the writers and the context and the problems that inspired these songs. It's no different than I've felt about the classic Christian hymns. I have in my library four or five volumes that chronicle the stories behind the great hymns. What inspired the composer? From the setting of what life encounter was he writing? As I read how these timeless melodies came into existence, I can never sing them thoughtlessly again.

It's just the same with the psalms. We get a "backstage pass" and discover what was happening in David's life or what Israel was enduring when a psalm came to be written. And the words and the music of these pieces seem to come alive with new meaning.

I think you'll be interested in how Psalm 46 came about.

The year is 701 B.C. The king of Assyria is a man whose name strikes terror in the hearts of those in the Mediterranean world—Sennacherib. He is obsessively intent on expanding his kingdom, which has rapidly risen to dominance. He has led his army on a ruthless

---

**From My Journal**

*I've been thinking lately—wondering if I'll ever feel one hundred percent well again. I'm sure it's quite normal for me to feel this way, but I also realize I've been learning one of the toughest of truths: "When I am weak, then I am strong." Help me not to forget the lessons of the bend in the road.*

---

march throughout the Mediterranean world, heading south now toward Judah. Like a swarm of locusts, the Assyrians have consumed and conquered everything in their path. Among the rising and falling dynasties of the ancient world, this empire is a cruel and mighty one, merciless in its drive toward conquest.

In his great journey of capture and enslavement, Sennacherib the conqueror has come across a curious little kingdom called Judah. This kingdom revolves around the hub of a city the people call Jerusalem. And Sennacherib's military intelligence tells him that Judah is ruled by a man by the name of Hezekiah. They say he is a godly man who came to the throne when he was young.

Judah shows signs of having been through great unrest and civil discord. Many of the previous rulers, it is said, ruled foolishly and weakened a once proud and powerful state. But Hezekiah is different. Hezekiah has shown the same regard for reform and spiritual rule as Sennacherib has shown for conquest and domination.

For example, these people have an ancient tradition they call the Passover. Under past rulers, the ancient practice has been virtually discarded and forgotten, but Hezekiah has reclaimed it and lifted it to its original place of prominence and spiritual significance. He has pointed his people back to the temple and the work of the priests and of godly sacrifice. He has been absolutely intolerant toward idols and pagan practices inconsistent with his God, and the shrines and statues have been toppled and smashed during his regime.

The historians will record this description of Hezekiah:

> He did what was right in the sight of the LORD, according to all that his father David had done. . . . He trusted in the LORD God of Israel, so that after him was none like him among all the kings of Judah, nor any who were before him. For he held fast to the LORD; he did not depart from following Him, but kept His commandments, which the LORD had commanded Moses. The LORD was with him; he prospered wherever he went. (2 Kings 18:35–7)

An interesting man, this King Hezekiah; he is a foe Sennacherib cannot take for granted. The Assyrian monarch has already conquered Israel, the kingdom to the north that was once part of a unified nation that included the province of Judah. The inhabitants of Israel have been conquered, shackled, and marched off in captivity to spend the rest of their lives as slaves. And word of this has spread southward like wildfire. The people of Judah realize the ravaging, merciless forces of Sennacherib are marching toward Egypt at this very moment, and Judah lies squarely in their path. Confrontation is a certainty—and destruction is almost as sure.

Soon, Assyrian troops surround the walls of the city. Their foreign voices can be heard outside the gates, hurling ridicule and threats. "We've heard about the God you serve," they taunt. "We're here to find out how special He is. Why don't you send Him out to defend you? We've destroyed many tribes, and none of their gods put up a fight."

They also attempt a shrewd and deadly maneuver.

> Thus says the king: "Do not let Hezekiah deceive you, for he shall not be able to deliver you from his hand; nor let Hezekiah make you trust in the LORD, saying, 'The LORD will surely deliver us; this city shall not be given into the hand of the king of Assyria.'" Do not listen to Hezekiah; for thus says the king of Assyria: "Make peace with me by a present and come out to me." (2 Kings 18:29–31)

"Never mind what your leader says," they're saying. It's a line as old as the snake in the garden and as new as a bumper sticker that reads, "Question authority." *Ignore your leader. Do what is right in your own eyes. Have we got a deal for you!*

The Assyrians especially target Hezekiah's idea that God should be trusted and obeyed. "Come on out now with a nice gift for your new boss, Sennacherib," they're saying. "Hezekiah and his naive faith are finished." All this time, the policy of King Hezekiah is not to deal with terrorists—to ignore the taunting outside the gate.

But this city has something else interesting about it: prophets. And at present, there happen to be two effective ones named Micah and Isaiah. King Hezekiah leans on them, and he is now given a word of encouragement through Isaiah. Here's a paraphrase of the message:

"Relax. God says that everything is under control, and you're doing the right thing in ignoring the challenges of Sennacherib's men. Don't worry about him, for he has blasphemed the name of God, and he will be dealt with. Sennacherib will hear rumors that turn him homeward, and there he'll die by his own sword."

The bottom line? "It may look bad, King Hezekiah; you may see your city surrounded. But seeing is not believing—believing is *seeing*. See what your God is doing. See that He is still in control." The blasphemy of Sennacherib is this: He has mixed the name of the one true God with the names of all the false ones in that part of the world. He has broken one of the highest and holiest of commandments—defaming the name that is above every other name. His own mouth has sealed his fate.

A few days later, messengers come running in to Hezekiah holding a letter from Sennacherib. It's not a very polite letter. It's filled with ugly threats and details about how the people of Judah will soon be destroyed. And the king of Judah does something very interesting. He carries the letter with him to the temple, and he spreads the letter out before him and before God. "Read this, Lord!" he is saying.

You and I have felt exactly like that, haven't we? The problem is so great and terrifying that all we can do is run to God, lay it all out before Him, and say, "Look! Just look what I'm facing!"

Hezekiah spreads the menacing letter before God. "Well, Lord?" he says. But his prayer is much more eloquent than that. It's recorded in 2 Kings 19. He concludes, "Now therefore, O LORD our God, I pray, save us from his hand, that all the kingdoms of the earth may know that You are the LORD God, You alone" (v. 19). Hezekiah realizes the true issue—that the power and sovereignty of God have been challenged.

The king leaves it all with God. He walks back to his palace, passing by the walls beyond which foreign soldiers are still hurling ridicule and dark warnings. And he waits. It is all the king of Judah can do, wait and pray and have faith. He knows that at midnight, the attack will come. The ominous moments tick by.

You can read the climax in 2 Kings 19:35. The angel of the Lord comes by night, and he executes 185,000 Assyrians. When the break of day comes, the men of Judah return to their posts and can't believe what is laid out before them—acres of Assyrian soldiers, no longer

---

### From My Journal

*Look at me, Lord! You know me so well, and You know how terrified I am about the idea of enduring another cycle of chemical treatments. You know I can't face the idea of losing all my progress toward the five-year cure I've been counting on. But, Lord, You know me so well. I lay this before You and trust Your will for me. I need Your help as never before. My strength is as weak as it's ever been. You give above and beyond all that we ask or think, and I know I can trust You with this challenge. I also know that my fears are a waste of precious mental energy.*

---

ridiculing, no longer frightening or imposing. It's a landscape of death. Listen to the exact words of Scripture: "There were the corpses—all dead."

The Lord God has taken up the challenge of Sennacherib and his men.

Many people would have laughed at the seeming folly of Hezekiah, hurrying to the temple to show God a threatening letter. But this leader lays out his burdens before the Lord, and the Lord lays out His response outside the gates. It's just that simple. All the citizens of Judah quickly realize that this day will be forever celebrated in the history of their nation. It is a red-letter day, and a red-letter psalm is penned to commemorate it: Psalm 46. This, one of the most famous of all psalms, is actually a song of celebration written after the invaders were put down.

But who actually wrote the unforgettable words of the psalm? One candidate for that distinction is Hezekiah himself. Some scholars point to the king, who would obviously have led the worship and cele-bration. But others point to Isaiah, a poet of unsurpassed eloquence.

The author might well have been an anonymous scribe whose name is lost to the ages, but the occasion for Psalm 46 is crystal-clear: the rout of the Assyrians by the angel of the Lord.

If you've never before known the story behind this great hymn of victory, how do you feel about it now? Psalm 46 towers over us as a biblical monument to the awesome and limitless power of God. Like all monuments, it has the function of helping us to remember something precious and sustaining—in this case, that no barrier is too great for God to overcome. A city surrounded by an entrenched enemy, inches from destruction by a mighty army, cannot be of any great concern for the God who has set the galaxies in space, the God who created and continues to sustain the earth. Kings and armies seem like juggernauts from our limited perspective, but they're nothing in the great scheme of God's hold on history. The Greeks, the Romans, the Assyrians, and the Babylonians all seemed invincible for a brief time. They are now no more than colorful characters from ancient history, and God's strength has not waned.

That's why this hymn and the story behind it have always offered me such comfort and assurance. Psalm 46 radically realigns my per-

---

*God is our hiding place; He is our power.*

*Providing in trouble, He's there every hour.*

*And fear will not find us, though earth be in motion,*

*And mountains fall into the heart of the ocean,*

*Or tidal waves roar and the flood waters pour;*

*No, the mountains themselves cannot shake His devotion.*

**—Psalm 46, from Ron Suggs, My Rhyming Bible**

---

spective. It shows me that with God, all things are possible. It persuades me that victory is always within reach for anyone who is willing to spread out their concerns before God. It is not the might of the enemy but the strength of God's power that wins the day.

## When Trouble Comes, Retreat to Your Refuge

Psalm 46 divides neatly into three sections, each of them punctuated by one word: *Selah*. Each stanza is built around a powerful, godly concept that will strengthen and reassure us in times of trouble. We have so many treasures to unlock from the wealth of this chapter.

The first three verses set the tone for the psalm.

### Our God Is an Awesome Refuge

The first and most dominant image from Psalm 46 is the picture of a hiding place: "God is our refuge and our strength." The Hebrew word for *refuge* invokes a quiet place to go for protection. Hezekiah finds refuge in the temple. And it's not a place for leaving his problems outside—the king brings them in to spread before Almighty God, revealing every detail.

This idea is sprinkled throughout the Old Testament. Listen, for instance, to Deuteronomy 33:27: "The eternal God is your refuge, and underneath are the everlasting arms." We are placing ourselves in His comforting hands and our hope in His powerful arms.

Psalm 91:2 says, "I will say of the LORD, 'He is my refuge and my fortress; my God, in Him I will trust.'"

Psalm 18:2 offers us, "The LORD is my rock and my fortress and my deliverer; my God, my strength, in whom I will trust."

I hope you've learned through experience, as I have, that God is your guaranteed refuge. We try many other alternatives. At the first sign of trouble, we rely on our own resources. Then, when we fail to solve the problem, perhaps we'll call on family or a close friend. Friends, of course, are notoriously unreliable in giving the right advice or dependable support. They can even aggravate the problem. We may go see a godly counselor or, if worse comes to worse, even a minister. The ultimate answer is not to be found in any of these options, some of which can provide a Band-Aid or a cup of cold water. The answer is in the midst of us. Our Lord is our refuge, a very present help in trouble.

October 31, 1517, is often called the Fourth of July of Protestantism. On that day there were the first tremors of a spiritual earthquake of worldwide proportions when a quiet, obscure monk named Martin Luther nailed a parchment to the door of the University of Wittenberg in eastern Germany. His document contained ninety-five theses, or points for debate. He raised questions that ignited an ecclesiastical revolution. The great idea at the center was salvation by faith, not by works; being a good church member is insufficient to pay the price of our sins. The movement launched by Luther also reestablished that we have direct access to God through Christ, our high priest.

But there were other wonderful ideas that rose out of the Protestant Reformation. One of these was the rediscovery of congregational singing. Luther had strong convictions about the power of sacred music, and he expressed his convictions in a number of statements. For instance, he wrote, "If any man despises music, as all fanatics do, for him I have no liking; for music is a gift and grace of God, not an invention of men. Thus it drives out the devil and makes people cheerful." *If you dislike music, you're a fanatic.* I didn't say that—Martin Luther did.

He also declared, "The devil, the originator of sorrowful anxieties and restless troubles, flees before the sound of music almost as much as before the Word of God." And since I'm a preacher and I love music so much, I gravitated toward this quotation: "I would allow no man to preach or teach God's people without a proper knowledge of the use and power of sacred song."[1]

It's clear that Luther, who helped to redefine modern, faith-based Christianity, carried a high opinion of the place of music in worship. And which hymn was most central to the Reformation? That one's easy—"A Mighty Fortress Is Our God," a song Luther wrote based upon Psalm 46. This hymn became the battle cry of God's people during the Reformation, a great source of strength and inspiration, especially among those who were martyred for their convictions. This hymn has been translated into almost every language, and there are more than sixty different English translations of the text itself.

When difficulty or discouragement came upon Martin Luther and his friend Philipp Melanchthon, the two key architects of the Reformation, sometimes Luther would say, "Philipp, come, let us sing the Forty-sixth psalm." The two of them would bring out the metric version Luther had written, and they'd sing the words together. If you travel to Germany and visit the place where Luther is buried, you'll find the first line of the psalm engraved on the great man's tomb.

A mighty and awesome refuge is our God—for our time, for Luther's time, for any time.

## Our God Is an Accessible Refuge

Our God is "a very present help in trouble" (v. 1).

*Trouble*—that's a word that needs no introduction. As used here, the more precise meaning would be "in tight places." Have you been in tight places recently? We speak of being stuck between a rock and a hard place. We have no room to maneuver. The words *very present* convey the idea that God is easy to find. He is as real and as much there with you as He could possibly be. Some of our friends run out when trouble rolls in, but God isn't like that. He moves in closer, putting His great arms around us. When we're in tight places, He draws us tighter.

In Exodus 33:14, God's word to Moses was, "My Presence will go with you, and I will give you rest." That's exactly what He does for us all. He is very present.

## Our God Is an Ageless Refuge

Our refuge is not only accessible, but ageless. "Therefore we will not fear, though the earth be removed, and though the mountains be carried into the midst of the sea; though its waters roar and be troubled; though the mountains shake with its swelling" (vv. 2–3).

The psalmist comes to this section and asks himself, "What would be the greatest natural catastrophe imaginable?" And he invokes a flood that could wash away mountains and remove the earth itself. The earth is the most ageless thing available to our senses. It is basically the same earth that Moses and David and Jesus and Paul walked upon. But what if even the earth were to crumble? Even in all this, he says, we'd have no reason for anxiety. The world may be *ancient*, but God is *ageless*—and that's a different matter entirely. We feel as if there's no more time for God to act, but what is time to God? He created it. He is ageless.

When trouble comes, we can retreat to our refuge, who is awesome, available, and ageless. No problem is any match for Him.

Knowing these liberating truths about God our refuge strengthens us and fills us with courage. Then what should we do to face the task at hand?

## When Trouble Comes, Rediscover Your Strength

The challenge forces us into the waiting arms of God. When we realize that He is in control, we're overjoyed and immensely comforted.

---

### From My Journal

*Lord, never let me forget that my mind must be fixed on You. I think of You so much more now than the time before my cancer arrived. I have become more sensitive now to Your will and to the process of becoming holy. I want my life to honor You. I want to live for You. I want to serve You wholeheartedly.*

*In these days when I face an uncertain future, my heart would be troubled; help me to remember that "You will keep him in perfect peace, whose mind is stayed on You."*

---

But our overriding impulse, once within the stout walls of God our refuge, is simply to faint from exhaustion. We've been weakened by the anxiety, fear, and commotion of all that has befallen us. We've been functioning on sheer adrenaline, and in the sudden realization of safety, our last ounce of strength seems to flee. Our resources are spent.

Now is the time when we learn that God is more than a refuge. He is also our strength.

## We Have a Secret Power Within

In ancient times, the sentries of a city would bring news of approaching invaders. The city walls would quickly be fortified, and everyone would seek safety inside. What do you think the greatest fear would be in such a situation? It wasn't catapults or rocks or flaming spears. The people most feared being cut off from supplies of food or water. The invaders may not be able to come inside, but they could stop you from getting the things you needed from the outside.

In advance of the arrival of the Assyrians at Jerusalem, Hezekiah had time to prepare his defenses. In the Kidron Valley outside of Jerusalem bubbled a deep spring called Gihon. It provided the water supply for Jerusalem, so it was of enormous strategic importance. Hezekiah knew that above all costs it must be protected, so he redirected the spring through a conduit that was 1,777 feet long, hewn of solid rock. He brought the spring waters beneath the walls of Jerusalem into a reservoir in the middle of the city. Then he covered up all traces of the spring in such a way that Sennacherib would have no idea where the water supply was. If the angel of the Lord hadn't destroyed the Assyrians that night, the people of Judah would still have had fresh water for a lengthy period of time. Hezekiah had planned well.

There is a suggestion of this incident in the psalm. "There is a river whose streams shall make glad the city of God, the holy place of the tabernacle of the Most High" (v. 4).

The meaning and symbolism of water in the Bible run deep—no pun intended. God's Spirit is ever present in our midst to refresh us, cleanse us, and strengthen us for the journey. He is the eternal spring that never runs dry. Jesus sat by a well one day and said, "Whoever drinks of this water will thirst again, but whoever drinks of the water that I shall give him will never thirst. But the water that I shall give him will become in him a fountain of water springing up unto everlasting life" (John 4:13–14).

Soon after that, Jesus said, "If anyone thirsts, let him come to Me and drink. He who believes in Me, as the Scripture has said, out of his heart will flow rivers of living water" (John 7:37–38).

The Holy Spirit of God living within you is a secret fountain of life-giving water. People don't realize the depth of God's Spirit in residence within your soul. Through the Holy Spirit, God has come to live inside you. There's no way to overstate the powerful implications of that startling truth. Why should we look outside for help when trouble comes? Almighty God is among us and within us. He is the source of living water, springing up into eternal life.

## We Have a Secret Person Within

"God is in the midst of her, she shall not be moved; God shall help her, just at the break of dawn. The nations raged, the kingdoms were moved; He uttered His voice, the earth melted. The LORD of hosts is with us; the God of Jacob is our refuge" (Ps. 46:5–7).

"Just at the break of dawn," as we read here, God certainly did help her! That's when the angel of the Lord dealt with the Assyrians. The armies of Judah may have been outnumbered and out-armored, but there was one Warrior who tilted the scales toward a rout of the Assyrians.

The Lord stepped into time and space like that mysterious fourth silhouette in Nebuchadnezzar's furnace, as recorded in the Book of Daniel. Shadrach, Meshach, and Abed-Nego—a clear and simple total of three—were marched into the furnace to await the flames. Who was this fourth shape in the fire, "like the Son of God"? The Lord occupied the fire with His children. In tight places, He holds us even tighter. We're safer in raging flames sheltered in His arms than in the coolest and calmest climate without Him.

That same truth applied to the besieged walls of Jerusalem.

## When Trouble Comes, Redirect Your Thoughts

In times of trouble, God's advice to us is not abstract, but pragmatic. He offers not empty philosophies, but sound battle plans.

The Lord reminds us that the mind is a powerful element in our armory—both weapon and shield. Our thought patterns are crucial in the midst of our difficulties. Any soldier would tell you that the moment the enemy can be demoralized, he is beaten. Competitive athletes and even combative politicians will confirm the pragmatism of this concept. In the spiritual realm, we must go into battle with our thoughts fixed on Him.

A sanctified mind can stand against any worldly foe. How can we offer our thinking to God when we're facing a crisis?

### Review the Works of the Lord

"Come, behold the works of the LORD, who has made desolations in the earth. He makes wars cease to the end of the earth; He breaks the

---

**From My Journal**

*Our faith is being stretched, Lord—how true that is. I may not enjoy it, but I know You have a loving purpose in this. Keep us trusting You with each day and with each new twist in the uncharted road we're traveling. Lord, I know that the times allotted to me are determined by Your eternal plan—and You will surely accomplish above and beyond all that I can even ask or think.*

*I trust You, even when I am afraid.*

---

bow and cuts the spear in two; He burns the chariot in the fire" (Ps. 46:8–9).

The God of today is the God of yesterday. If we want to know what to expect from Him, we need only to review His record. How it helps us to put our minds to the task of remembering God's works! The same God who sustained you in the past, who brought you victoriously through every previous crisis, is the God who stands with you here and now, in the midst of this fresh testing of your spirit.

That's why God's salvation of Judah during the crisis of Sennacherib was infinitely precious to God's people—it created a milestone for them. The dramatic mass destruction of the enemy became a kind of "memory monument" so tall it would never be forgotten. Parents would tell their children, children would tell their grandchildren, and of course the event was memorialized in God's Word to astound and inspire countless generations to come. The people of God could always look back, even from bondage, and say, "Remember how the angel of the Lord slew the Assyrians? Surely He is among us, and surely He will protect us." The power of memory—for good or for evil—is formidable indeed.

This is a good place to put in yet another request for you to start keeping a journal—and now you can see a good reason for doing so. Journaling memorializes the blessings of God. My mind will often wonder, "What was going on in my life on this day in 1994?" The pages of my journal sit open and ready to fill in the details. After I read and refresh myself, I'll nearly always smile and say, "Amazing! I'd forgotten all about that. God did a wonderful thing for me, and I had let it pass from my mind." Your journal provides spiritual fuel, made up of the ingredients of your past, to add power and hope to your life.

Time is the loving creation of our God. That's why the great enemy of time and memory is the devil. Satan loves to trap our minds within the present calamity, where the problem can expand to massive proportions, stripped of the context of God's purposes. Our Lord would use time and crises to mold us in wisdom and maturity to the image of Christ. But the evil one prefers that you not dwell on that fact. Doesn't he whisper in your ear that this new bend is the end of the world? Doesn't he tell you that God has forgotten you, that you're all alone against the wheels of fate, and that none of this has any meaning other than to break you against that wheel? If those sentiments sound familiar, just remember who it is that whispers them to you. Satan has managed to impress that philosophy upon the majority of our writers, filmmakers, and cultural minds. Your life is being lived in a lonely, meaningless vacuum, according to that tragic mind-set.

But from the victorious perspective of heaven, today's trouble is a blip on the eternal horizon—a "wisdom upgrade" to boost you toward the place where you ultimately want to be. And when you come to doubt the stated philosophy of that view, it will help you to take a look at the record. You need your Bible. You need your journal. You need those sanctified memories that convince you that God is in control. Gird yourself against the foe with the weapon of memory, by reviewing the mighty works of the Lord.

### Reclaim the Words of the Lord

Have you heard these golden words before, this timeless call to worship? "Be still, and know that I am God; I will be exalted among the nations, I will be exalted in the earth! The LORD of hosts is with us; the God of Jacob is our refuge" (Ps. 46:10–11).

"Be still!" If we stripped them from their present context, you'd identify those two words as an exasperated admonition to your young children. "Stop that! Be still!" And don't you think God sees us as rambunctious children sometimes? Can't you imagine Him leaning over the banister of heaven and calling down, "Be still!"

He is calling some important message to us, as everything from the lips of God is important. But we can't hear Him. We're too busy squabbling and playing games and doing everything but listening. So He cries out for us to slow down, silence our voices, and listen.

A refuge, after all, is a place of quietness. When we seek safety, silence is our friend; it hides us from the enemy, allows us to listen for important information, and affords us the opportunity to regather our strength. It allows us to be still and know that He is God.

This is the closing message of this immortal psalm. We're enjoined to be silent that we may become aware of His presence and His purposes. Whatever their specifics may be when translated into our lives, they all converge in the ultimate one: that He should be exalted among the nations and exalted in the earth. The nations begin with the people as individuals, so we can be certain that He will be exalted in our personal circumstances—if only we will be still and know that He is God.

For the second time, the psalmist says, "The LORD of hosts is with us." We have a tendency to let our eyes hurry over such phrases as if they were so much conventional religious jargon. But in fact, they're crucial to the meaning of this section of the psalm. Read them and take them in, for the author has seen fit to speak them twice. "The LORD of hosts is with us; the God of Jacob is our refuge."

Who is the Lord of hosts? In the Hebrew it is *the Lord of Sabaoth*: the Lord of the angels, the Lord of the hosts of heaven. Why is this worthy of consideration? Think about the story from 2 Kings. The angel of the Lord—*one* angel of the Lord—was dispatched from heaven to defend the city of Jerusalem. That angel destroyed 185,000 Assyrians who were bent on the destruction of God's people.

The people of Judah needed only one angel, but the Scriptures promise us we're not limited to one angel. We have the Lord of them all with us.

Keep that in mind the next time you hear one of those trendy angel stories—you've noticed how angels have been all the rage in contemporary culture lately. We hear of angels at dangerous intersections, angels in hospital wards, even angels helping you find a good parking spot. We'd have to conclude the angels have gotten very busy lately, and they're now more involved in highway safety than in defending the walls of Jerusalem and 185,000 invading soldiers. Perhaps this is so. I've personally not been the recipient of any obvious, visible angelic encounters—but I do believe we have angels watching over us.

Perhaps guardian angels are provided for us. But would you rather have your own angel than the Lord of Sabaoth as your God? He is the One who created and empowers the angels. And that same mighty God lives within our hearts. Perhaps when our hearts are troubled, we should spend less time looking for angels and more time speaking to the awesome God within our hearts, telling Him, "O Lord, God of creation, I know You are present with me. Give me strength and power to face this moment."

There is a wonderful word in the Old Testament. It is *emanu*, which simply means, "with me." Perhaps the most astounding fact of all astounding facts about our great God is that He is "with me." There can be no greater geometric line than the one defined by the distance between those two points—my lowliness and His omnipotent perfection. And yet He is "with me."

That word *emanu*—"with me"—travels through time and becomes something deeper and wiser, just as all of us hopefully do. *Emanu* ultimately gives birth to a new word, *Emmanuel*: "God with us." And He will be called Emmanuel, for God is with us.

Hannah Whitall Smith was one of our greatest writers of devotional literature. Many of her works of spiritual depth came from the crucible of terrible emotional pain from the loss of children, the infidelities of her husband, and the loss of many of her close friends. One of her greatest works is called *Living Confidently in God's Love*. When she wrote it, she had been experiencing terrible pain and unanswered questions. She didn't know where to turn or whom to seek for counsel. It seemed to her, just as it seems to you and me, that no one had ever been on the path she was traveling. No one could possibly understand what she was experiencing. Here are the words she used to describe her feelings:

There happened to be staying near me just then for a few weeks a lady who was considered to be a deeply spiritual Christian, and to whom I had been told I should go for additional help to get through my trouble. So I summoned up my courage, and one afternoon I went to see her. I poured out my troubles before her, and I expected, of course, that she would take a deep interest in me and would be at great pains to do all she could to help me. She listened patiently, did not interrupt me, but when I finished my story, and I paused, expecting her to respond in sympathy and consideration, she simply said, "Yes, all you say may be very true, but then in spite of it all, there is God."

I waited a few minutes for her to say something else. But nothing came, and my friend the teacher had the air of having said all that was necessary, and I knew she was done. But I continued, "You don't understand how very serious and perplexing my difficulties are."

"Oh, yes, I did," replied my friend. "But then, as I tell you, there is God."

I could not induce her to make one other answer. It seemed to me most disappointing and unsatisfactory. I felt that my peculiar and really harrowing experiences could not be met by anything so simple and so mere as the statement, "Yes, but there is God."

[But] . . . from wondering, I came gradually to believe that being my Creator and Redeemer, He must be enough. And at last, a conviction burst upon me that He really was enough. My eyes were opened to the fact of the absolute and utter all-sufficiency of almighty God.[2]

What do we mean when we say, "God is enough"? Let's be honest and agree that it sounds suspiciously like the language of piety and self-righteousness, just a tired cliché.

But in reality, those three words are so much more than jargon. God *must* be enough, in fact, for if He isn't, where do we find ourselves?

---

### From My Journal

*I believe that You and You alone are the answer, O Lord. My doctors are merely tools You will use. Lord, it is to You alone that I look for healing.*

*You are Jehovah Rophe, and You can heal according to Your will.*

---

Where do we go for Plan B? If the God of heaven and earth, who is mightier than all the world's armies, who can cause the earth to melt into the sea, who is "with us"—if that God is not Lord of your crisis, you're in deep trouble, and so are the rest of us.

Praise His name that we need not worry about that possibility. The fact is that God *is* sufficient. Our God is in control. He holds the destiny of the galaxies in His hands, all the while knowing the precise number of hairs on your head. He has preserved His people time and again, performed miracles on battlefields and in cattle fields, among prophets and priests and plumbers. Above all else, He loves you and chose to measure that love out not in words, but in blood. He loves you enough to give you the greatest gift conceivable. Would such a love allow you to suffer without a purpose? Would such a love neglect to have a wonderfully happy ending lying in wait for you?

God has never run away from you, so you must never run away from Him. Run into His waiting arms, for that's what He most desires. He is your refuge—your city wall, your cool and refreshing stream, and your impenetrable defense from the enemy. He is a very present help in times of trouble.

# Psalm 16

*A Michtam of David.*

1  Preserve me, O God, for in You I put my trust.
2  O my soul, you have said to the LORD,
   "You are my Lord,
   My goodness is nothing apart from You"—
3  And to the saints who are on the earth,
   "They are the excellent ones, in whom is all my delight."
4  Their sorrows shall be multiplied who hasten after another god;
   Their drink offerings of blood I will not offer,
   Nor take up their names on my lips.
5  You, O LORD are the portion of my inheritance and my cup;
   You maintain my lot.
6  The lines have fallen to me in pleasant places;
   Yes, I have a good inheritance.
7  I will bless the LORD who has given me counsel;
   My heart also instructs me in the night seasons.
8  I have set the LORD always before me;
   Because He is at my right hand I shall not be moved.
9  Therefore my heart is glad, and my glory rejoices;
   My flesh also will rest in hope.
10 For You will not leave my soul in Sheol,
   Nor will You allow Your Holy One to see corruption.
11 You will show me the path of life;
   In Your presence is fullness of joy;
   At Your right hand are pleasures forevermore.

# 11

# The Best Is Yet to Come

*While we walk the pilgrim pathway,*
*Clouds will overspread the sky;*
*But when trav'ling days are over,*
*Not a shadow, not a sigh!*
*Let us then be true and faithful,*
*Trusting, serving ev'ry day.*
*Just one glimpse of Him in glory*
*Will the toils of life repay.*

—E.E.HEWITT

*The worst is behind me,* I thought. What a relief!

I had survived the greatest trial and most paralyzing fear of my life, and my faith had stood firm. And it wasn't merely intact, but deeper and more resonant. For I felt that I had a tight handle on just what was occurring spiritually in my life. God was using my serious illness to draw me into a deeper knowledge of Himself. I was grateful for what I had learned and for the rewarding new insights I had into His ways. Best of all, the crisis was over!

Then the nodule was discovered.

So much for having all the answers; my bubble was burst. I was despondent.

That was late in 1998. I checked into the hospital and had the nodule surgically removed from the base of my neck. The doctors sent it away for pathology studies, and I had to wait and brood over the freshly revived question of my mortality. When I returned to see my oncologist, Dr. Saven, he confirmed what I already knew—I was facing a recurrence of lymphoma. The only good news was that the lymphoma was still in the quadrant of my body in which the cancer had originally appeared. It had been contained and prevented from spreading.

Then the doctor told me I was a candidate for a stem cell transplant. "Stem cell therapy may not be what you had in mind for the months ahead," he said, "but it's the best opportunity we're going to have to drive out this disease once and for all."

I thought of my conversations with Pastor Page, detailed in the previous chapter. He had been through two rounds of stem cell transplants, and his experiences suddenly became very relevant. Now I understood why I had been led to take such a great interest in his medical history. I realized that God had prepared me for this crisis by providing me with a friend who had walked down this road ahead of me.

I was soon to meet Dr. Mason, who heads up the stem cell transplant department at Scripps Clinic. Dr. Mason is a leader in the field of outpatient stem cell transplant. His research has helped to shape what we know and can expect in this new medical frontier. And I was grateful, because I entered this new experience with many qualms. I had the impression that a stem cell transplant had frightening side effects. I had heard that the white blood cell count plummets, and you're open to every kind of infection and illness. I pictured myself quarantined in the hospital, unable to see visitors, wearing a mask on my infrequent visits to the outside world, and desperately playing defense against the normal germs of the air.

Dr. Mason painted quite a different picture of what was ahead for me. He explained that patients living within twenty minutes of the hospital have the advantage of living at home throughout the procedure. Only those from distant addresses had to check in and stay.

I learned that, before anything else, I had to qualify for the treatment. I had to receive more standard chemotherapy to determine whether the tumors would shrink. In other words, as the doctor put it,

"If the little hammer doesn't work, the big hammer's not going to work either." So it was up to my body to demonstrate that it was still sensitive to the chemicals in question. The tests took several weeks and, by this time, Christmas had come and gone. We were into the year 1999.

Needless to say, "happy holidays" weren't operative for me in 1998. I felt very burdened by the new tests and the procedures that lay ahead. There was also a speaking tour on a cruise to the Bahamas scheduled for January 1999. Was I taking a risk by heading for the other coast for a cruise and extended biblical teaching responsibilities? Dr. Mason smiled and urged me to carry on my life as it should be lived. He counseled me to do everything I normally would do, even though I was taking chemotherapy and my hair was beginning to come out.

The success of the stem cell transplant could also be boosted if I built up my strength by taking daily exercise. That was just the kind of thing I was eager to find—a rare opportunity to take my prospects into my own hands, at least in a small way. I immediately immersed myself in a program of one hour per day on the treadmill. By the time I entered the hospital in March, I could count no more than four or five days when I hadn't walked 4.2 miles on the treadmill. Even on the cruise ship sailing in the Bahamas, I logged my hours in the exercise room and kept up my program. That treadmill was my road to wellness, and I was hurrying down it daily.

If there was anything I could do—anything at all—to increase my chances of success in the ordeal that lay ahead, I was determined to give it my very best shot.

*March 22, 1999.*

The day had a great, red, nervous circle scribbled around it on our family calendar. After arriving at the hospital, I was taken through all the pretransplant procedures. I had already provided many stem cells during my first episode of chemotherapy. There were eighteen bags of stem cells in cold storage waiting for me.

During the procedure I was attached to a Groschond catheter. This was placed in my chest during a surgical procedure, to provide access to my veins both for blood testing and injecting of the chemotherapy.

After that procedure, the medical team began the flow of toxic chemicals. They selected four of the most powerful toxins ever injected into the human body.

It was a long and demanding day, and I was able to rest during the following one. But the stem cell transplant began. During this process,

---

*So much depends on me, yet all I have for this task is whatever health and energy You give me. . . . I eat carefully, rest, exercise, and think positive thoughts, and still this wretched lump of clay fails me. You have Creator's rights on my body. You formed every miraculous part. What You take away is Your business. I will do what I can with whatever capability You give me. It's Yours. . . .*

*The days end as the years end, with never enough time for all the good that could be done, only just enough for Your priorities, if I get them right. You created time, and it does not limit You. But I do not have a thousand years today, God. I have only now.*

*So this day is Yours; I am Yours; these people are Yours; the resources are Yours. The challenges we face are Yours, as is anything we hope to accomplish.*

*It's Yours, God. It's not mine.*

— **Richard Kriegbaum, Leadership Prayers**

---

the toxic chemicals bring the white count down to the lowest possible number by which your body can survive. In such conditions, as I'd been told, there is no defense against infection or disease. The body simply doesn't have the resources to fight back.

The doctors then reintroduced the white cells from the stem cell collection back into my body—in my case, about eighteen bags of stem cells were returned to my system. At this point, the toxic chemicals began to take their toll, and I became gravely ill. The toxicity of the chemicals ate the lining away from my throat, all the way down my esophagus to my stomach. I couldn't swallow my own saliva. I couldn't eat. If I had not been on morphine, I wouldn't have been able to sleep. It was an excruciatingly painful time to be alive. I had been forewarned, but I had never dreamed that any procedure in modern science could be so miserable and uncompromising.

I'll never forget Easter Sunday. I was back in my hotel room after having blood work done at the hospital, and I was beginning to feel truly uneasy about what lay ahead—and whether I had run out of options. I knew that the wonderful people at church, buoyed by the hope of the resurrection, were pouring out their intercessory prayers for my health and well-being. My white blood cell count had yet to begin its rebound.

But we were in for a shock. The day after Easter, I went to the hospital with an anxious heart, preparing myself for the latest results. I couldn't believe my ears. The incredulous doctors told me that on Sunday, my white count had soared from two hundred to twenty-eight thousand! This was in the realm of the miraculous. With a heart filled to bursting with joy and relief, I thought about the prayers of God's people on Resurrection Sunday. What power they had unleashed! How wonderful to know that on the day of celebration for Christ's defiance and defeat of death, my body had seen a resurrection of its own.

I had come through the night season—just like David, the psalmist, sufferer, and singer. David knew about the night seasons, and Psalm 16 is our evidence of that.

Once again, by the words beneath the title, we know that we've come to one of David's very special psalms. Scholars suggest this one may have been written during a brief interlude of peace—a welcome respite in the hectic world of David, who was suddenly granted a vacation from fearing for his life. David had found himself holding the life of Saul at the point of a spear. A quick thrust and a twist, and his problems would have been over.

But the anointed slayer of Goliath refused to exploit the opportunity before him—and Saul, in the light of such mercy, didn't have the heart to keep hunting the one who had pardoned him. The whole story is played out on the pages of 1 Samuel 26.

Saul and three thousand of his best soldiers were hot in pursuit of David. They had camped for the night in the Wilderness of Ziph, without having any idea of the proximity of their prey. For David was in the immediate area. He came to the place where the army of Saul was encamped, and he could see they had settled in for the night. They had relaxed their guard. David decided to embark on a sponta-neous fact-finding mission, joined by Abishai, who was the brother of Joab, the general of his army.

David and Abishai crept up to Saul's camp in the dark of night. They could see Saul himself, sleeping soundly with his spear em-bedded in the ground beside his head. This was the ultimate in vul-nerability—a resting warrior's greatest nightmare. Abner and all of Saul's finest were in close reach. It could be a rout—a slaughter. That's the way Abishai saw it. He put his mouth near David's ear and whis-pered, "Why not kill him now and get it over with? We'll never have to run or hide again!"

Here is David's reply: "Do not destroy him; for who can stretch out his hand against the LORD's anointed, and be guiltless?" (1 Sam. 26:9)

David saw what lay before him in terms greater than his own self-serving options. He looked at things as God would see them, and he realized that he wasn't in a spiritual position to remove from this earth the one God had anointed. Instead, he did something very clever. He took hold of Saul's spear, protruding from the ground by the king's head, as well as a bottle of water lying nearby. He walked away with both items. This was calculated to cause more than a bit of concern in Saul's camp. How would you feel if the spear that guards your life was within easy grasp, and you woke to find it removed? As it happened, however, nobody awoke because God had placed the whole camp into a deep sleep.

The second half of 1 Samuel 26 tells the whole story. David and Abishai made their way out of that clearing and across the valley. Once he found himself at a safe distance, David stood atop a hill and shouted toward Saul's encampment. David's character is consistently fascinating. Here was a man who has been godly enough to do the right thing when he had the opportunity to take the life of his tormentor, yet he was human enough to have a little fun with the situation. He couldn't resist toying with Abner, Saul's right-hand man—letting Abner know about his brush with death.

Here's what David, in so many words, was saying: "Hey, Abner! Looks to me as if you're not a very good bodyguard! I was standing right beside your king a few minutes ago, and I could have taken him

---

*To seek aid in time of distress from a supernatural Being*

*is an instinct of human nature. I believe in the truthfulness of this*

*instinct, and that man prays because there is something in prayer. As*

*when the Creator gives His creature the power of thirst, it is because*

*water exists to meet its thirst; and as when He creates hunger there is*

*food to correspond to the appetite; so when He inclines men to pray it*

*is because prayer has a corresponding blessing connected with it.*

**—C. H. Spurgeon**

---

out in the blink of an eye while you were snoring. Next time you might want to watch your back, and your king's too!"

Saul was startled to hear David's voice, and he called out, "David, is that you?"

David basically replied, "Yes, it's me. King Saul, why do you insist on tracking me down? What have I ever done to you? Please listen closely to what I'm about to say. If God has led you to do all this, then praise God—let's lift up an offering to Him. But if it's a matter of people polluting your heart with all this plotting and conspiracy, those people are cursed in the Lord's eyes. I have an inheritance from God, and these people have tried to push me out of the picture and force me into the service of false gods. My king, I ask you not to spill my blood, as God is our witness. Think about it—you, the king of Israel, mobilizing your forces against a mere flea."

Saul was clearly moved by this speech. His words in verse 21 can be paraphrased in this way: "You're right—I have sinned. Come home,

David, my son. Today you spared me and counted my life as precious, and it's time for me to return the favor. I've played the fool—I can see that now. And I'm ashamed of myself."

The phrases we find in 1 Samuel 26:19–20 offer the clue that unlocks the connection with Psalm 16. The wording almost precisely matches the wording in Psalm 16:4–6. That psalm reaches across history to us today, reminding us in our crises to reflect on the goodness of God. We may feel our world is coming to an end. We may feel so tightly entangled in the problems of this world that there's no escape. But when we pause to reflect on the power and majesty and love of God, everything begins to change. There's an awesome power unleashed by a simple action when you "count your many blessings, name them one by one."

I read a book recently that analyzes where modern counseling has gone wrong. The author was making the point that psychiatrists often urge us to dredge up any and every unhappy event from the past. These negative memories then receive all the blame for our problems. I've had people tell me that after taking the tour of every unhappy event in memory, they felt worse than they did before seeing the counselor.

The author I was reading had a countersuggestion. Instead of taking inventory of the negatives, why not total up the positives? What if the counselor said, "Let's take a few moments to review your life, and see if we can find eight or ten genuinely good things that have happened to you. Let's reflect, review, and accentuate the positive. See if that doesn't make you feel better."

Of course, that strategy is unworkable in the therapeutic community. Once put into practice, it would be so effective that people wouldn't need the expensive therapy! The cure would be bad for business.

Maybe that's too cynical a view of the psychiatric profession, but we can be certain of one thing: Celebrating the blessings of God is wonderful therapy for the spirit. The Word of God never ceases reminding us to review the mighty works of the Lord. Try these two examples:

"I will remember the works of the LORD; surely I will remember Your wonders of old. I will also meditate on all Your work, and talk of Your deeds" (Ps. 77:11–12).

"Bless the LORD, O my soul, and forget not all His benefits" (Ps. 103:2).

*Never, never forget the things He has done.*

But we do forget, don't we? Industry is the enemy of reflection— and we modern people are nothing if not industrious. We become so busy hustling to get things done, watching life become more and more complex, getting ourselves caught up in anxiety, that we simply forget all the good things God does on a daily and even momentary basis. You and I know people who are enormously blessed with health, wealth, beautiful families, remarkable talents, and exciting occupations. Blessings are breaking out all over them. Then we're not at all surprised to find those same people consumed with anxiety. They would stand out more in this world by displaying an attitude of gratitude than they would by needing a checkup from the neck up.

And that's during normal circumstances, when the waves are calm. When the storm comes, the winds are blowing, and the waves are high, we've lost our reference point with the blessings of God. We can't find our way back to Him, and the black clouds and high tides are more than we can handle. We've lost that invaluable perspective. For if we were to measure our lives against those of people in the rest of the world, we'd find ourselves crying out, "Thank You, Lord—I'm so blessed!"

David finds himself in a temporary oasis of tranquillity. He's not running for his life, and he's able to enjoy peace of mind. He takes the time to reflect upon all the good things he has received from the Lord. Psalm 16 is the record of his spiritual inventory.

## Remembering Who God Is

"Preserve me, O God, for in You I put my trust." That's how David begins the psalm we'll be exploring in this chapter. "O my soul, you have said to the LORD, 'You are my Lord, my goodness is nothing apart from You.'"

There are psalms in which David comes around to remembering who God is, and we see his entire perspective transformed within a few verses. But in this chapter, we can say that David begins right at

---

*There is no music in a rest, but there is the making of music in it. In our whole life-melody, the music is broken off here and there by "rests" and we foolishly think we have come to the end of the tune. God sends a time of forced leisure, sickness, disappointed plans, frustrated efforts, and makes a sudden pause in the choral hymn of our lives.... but how does the musician read the "rest"? See him beat the time with unvarying count, and catch up the next note true and steady, as if no breaking place had come between. Not without design does God write the music of our lives. Be it ours to learn the tune, and not be dismayed at the "rests." They are not to be slurred over, not to be omitted, not to destroy the melody, not to change the keynote. If we look up, God Himself will beat the time for us. With an eye on Him, we shall strike the next note full and clear.*

**—Mrs. Charles Cowman, Streams in the Desert**

---

the beginning—by acknowledging who God really is. And he sees God in several profound dimensions. Let's examine them.

### Seeing God in His Personal Presence

David turns his attention toward the presence of God in his personal life. In the first two verses we find three different names for God. If we were to read it directly from the original Hebrew language, it would go something like this: "Preserve me, *Elohim*, for in You I put my trust.

O my soul, you have said to *Jehovah*, 'You are my *Adonai*, my goodness is nothing apart from You.'"

David is fully aware of the magnificent and manifold presence of the awesome God. He sees the God of the covenant, who deals with His children with love and grace. He sees the powerful *Elohim*, who presides over all creation. He sees the personal *Jehovah* God who knows the most intimate details of our hearts and minds. He feels the perfect presence of *Adonai*, and he cannot help but be overwhelmed that the God who is all this and more would surround him with love, protection, wisdom, and strength.

God is with us. From the womb to the tomb, we are always in His presence and we're never apart. The distractions of the world will rob us of the full implications of this, and that's why we need to pause whenever and wherever possible to simply soak it in and allow it to transform us: We live in the presence of *Elohim, Jehovah, Adonai*.

At the end of the psalm, David looks within himself and gravely observes that he finds no goodness apart from God. That is no simple thing; it's actually among the most profound revelations that can ever come to us. Have you reflected seriously upon the fact that there is no good thing in your life—your family, your talents, your possessions, your friendships, your potential—that doesn't have a string leading back to the love and grace of God? There is no good thing within us or about us or connected to us that doesn't come from Him. "Every good gift and every perfect gift is from above, and comes down from the Father of lights, with whom there is no variation or shadow of turning" (James 1:17). Choose any good thing, large or small, and follow it back—follow it back as far as you can.

> Back of the loaf is the snowy flour,
> And back of the flour, the mill
> And back of the mill is the field of wheat,
> The rain, and the Father's will.[1]

You say, "I make my own bread." *Oh, is that right? Where did the flour come from?*

"Well, I got the flour at the mill." *Where did the mill get the flour?*

"They got it from the grain." *Where did the grain come from?*

"It came from the ground." *How did it grow?*

It grew because God allowed the sun to shine, and because He sent the rains to shower down upon the earth where the grain was planted. Every good and perfect gift is from the Father of lights—not *some* of the good gifts and *some* of the perfect gifts, but *every* one of them is a specially chosen, lovingly crafted gift from the Creator of all.

Romans 8:32 tells us that receiving the Lord Jesus Christ as our Savior makes us the recipient of even more than eternal salvation. He will bless us bountifully in every way. "He who did not spare His own Son, but delivered Him up for us all, how shall He not with Him also freely give us all things?" And Jesus said, "I have come that they may have life, and that they may have it more abundantly" (John 10:10). Why? Simply because He is a Father who adores His children, despite all their imperfections.

We are blessed by the presence of *Elohim*. Of *Jehovah*. Of *Adonai*.

## Seeing God in His People

David's thinking first takes in the greatness of God, and then he moves to the subject of his friends, whom he calls "the saints who are on the earth." During his time on the run, David has been surrounded by dedicated friends who put their lives on the line to help protect him. And he is profoundly moved by the thought of it.

He says, "They are the excellent ones, in whom is all my delight." Do you ever stop to simply delight in your friends? Do you let them know they are "the excellent ones" in your life?

David may have had his wonderful, devoted friend Jonathan in mind. He may have been thinking about Abishai, who had stolen quietly into the camp with him that night and risked his own life just to help a friend. He may have been thinking about both these men and others as well. While David had been through more than a few harrowing experiences, God had never failed to provide a friend to go alongside him. David had never had to be alone.

That's an important spiritual principle. Do you go it alone when times are tough? God never intends you to do so. Read 1 John closely, and you'll see the premium placed by God upon our place in the family of God. John says it so simply and so eloquently: Loving people and loving God are closely related. In 1 John 3:14, the apostle writes that we know we have new life in Christ by the way we love our brothers and sisters in fellowship—and if we feel no love for others, it's a sure sign that we are abiding in death.

John goes on to say, "Beloved, let us love one another, for love is of God; and everyone who loves is born of God and knows God. He who does not love does not know God, for God is love" (1 John 4:7–8). John is writing a commentary that extends from what he had

---

**My friend Joe Ivey sent me this wonderful letter**
**after hearing of my sickness:**

I personally feel that God has you in a very specific place in your kingdom work here on earth. Just before writing you, I was meditating on Psalm 103:1–5: "Bless the LORD, O my soul; and all that is within me, bless His holy name! Bless the LORD, O my soul, and forget not all His benefits: who forgives all your iniquities, who heals all your diseases, who redeems your life from destruction, who crowns you with lovingkindness and tender mercies, who satisfies your mouth with good things, so that your youth is renewed like the eagle's."

I know this is a familiar passage to you, brother. It starts out in blessing the Lord but then continues with He "heals all [our] diseases." That is our prayer for you.

---

given us in John 3:16. For "if God so loved us, we also ought to love one another" (1 John 4:11).

He also gives us a warning in 1 John 4:20–21: "If someone says, 'I love God,' and hates his brother, he is a liar; for he who does not love his brother whom he has seen, how can he love God whom he has not seen? And this commandment we have from Him: that he who loves God must love his brother also."

Jesus said it first, in John 13:35: "By this all will know that you are My disciples, if you have love for one another."

Can the scriptural imperative be any clearer? You are not alone.

So David reflects upon his relationships with the people of God. Have you ever stopped for a moment when you are in the midst of difficult times and counted up the true, godly Christian friends that God has given to you? One of the best things about going through a little storm, or even a big one, is that all of a sudden the true nature of God's people becomes clear to you. You find out that God has given to you some fantastic, godly friends.

## Seeing God in His Principles

In verse 4, David observes, "Their sorrows shall be multiplied who hasten after another god; their drink offerings of blood I will not offer, nor take up their names on my lips." Here David has moved from the roll call of beloved friends to the relationships that are a bit more troubled. David is always honest about the fact that there are a few flies in the ointment of his life.

During his frantic tour of the countryside, David has seen the idols of Moab and the idols in Philistia. He serves the true God and knows the competition. He is also aware, from the existing Scriptures, of the tragic idolatry in the history of his own people. He is thinking, *I know the goodness and love and majesty of God. And I've seen the alternative. How thankful I am that I have never fallen into idolatry, that I serve the one true God, and that He counts me as worthy to worship and serve Him.*

God does so many things for us. He blesses us coming and going, right and left, when we awaken and when we sleep. But if He never gave us any other blessing, He would be worthy of our constant praise just for His constant presence among us. To know God and to be known by Him—this is an indescribable blessing. It means that we need never be truly lonely. It means that we are never isolated. It means that we are significant, circled points on His map.

But David doesn't stop there. In the heart of this psalm, he takes a look at God and at what He is doing at the present time.

## Rehearsing What God Is Doing

God never sleeps. Isn't that comforting?

He is always at work, always fine-tuning the minute details of our lives—not that He provides us with a detailed agenda. There are many times when we're puzzled about what He is up to. We look ahead and wonder if He hasn't forgotten us, because nothing seems to be happening in the way we expect.

Other times we become Monday morning quarterbacks, second-guessing His decisions and the directions He allows life to take. These are the symptoms of spiritual immaturity, as natural as they are for us. Rejoicing in what God is doing—whether we like it and understand it or not—is a way of worshiping Him. It is an act of obedience and a sacrifice of praise.

### The Lord Is Our Completeness

"You, O LORD, are the portion of my inheritance and my cup" (v. 5). Old Testament language combines these Hebrew words, simply saying that the Lord is the One who makes us complete, who provides for us whatever we need. It is the answer to that part of the Lord's Prayer that says, "Give us this day our daily bread."

How blessed we are as God's people to know that few of us in the Western world have ever gone hungry. God has generously provided for us. When you bow at the table to thank God for your next meal, be sure you're thanking Him from your heart. Realize what a blessed privilege it is to be provided with the essentials of life. Know that He gives them to you to provide the strength you need to serve Him.

### The Lord Is Our Certainty

"You maintain my lot," David says. What he means is that God takes care of his circumstances. And how can the psalmist doubt it? For years he has lived as a nomad, fleeing from hiding place to hiding place from a powerful king and an army bent on finding and destroying this one man. And he has lived to tell the tale.

David has lost nearly everything—his freedom, his home, his family, and his good name. Yet he is able to praise God in the midst of it all and say to God, "You maintain my lot. You provide for me in my time of need."

### The Lord Is Our Contentment

The sixth verse offers us a beautiful statement of faith. David says that the Lord is his contentment: "The lines have fallen to me in pleasant places; yes, I have a good inheritance."

What are those "falling lines"? David is saying, "Lord, as I look back across the years, I realize that I've led a good life, and I have been given good things." Can you say that?

I can. I was born in a Christian family. I was reared on the gospel, nurtured on the milk of the Word of God, and educated in Christian schools and a Christian college. I was blessed with godly friends. I've been deeply influenced by people who stayed in our home and people who came along at certain times and in certain places to speak to me, mentor me, and bless me. I was given good friends capable of providing solid counsel when I needed it. I was divinely protected from the things that could have—and perhaps *should* have—happened to me when I was running wild as a young man.

I have no choice but to look back and say the lines have fallen to me in pleasant places. In no way do I deserve the blessings I've been given. The good things showered upon me would have been sufficient for 150 years, and I've received them in this brief lifetime. And that's exactly what David is saying in the sixth verse.

How is it that we come so often to feel just the opposite? How is it that we throw regular pity parties, with a guest list of one? We brood in solitude, thinking that we have the worst fortune, nothing ever goes our way, we never win the prize, and everyone else has it better. I have those moments just as you do. Self-pity throws everything out of perspective—upside down, to be precise. If we don't feel we're getting what we deserve, we should stop and think about what it is that we *do* deserve—after a moment's reflection, perhaps we won't want "justice" so much. If we think nothing ever goes our way, we need to check the record. If we think everyone else has it better, we need to think about some of those wealthy people and whether or not, in the truest sense of the word, they really "have it better." We need to clear up our vision.

We can clear it up by taking time to meditate on how greatly God has blessed us. We need to learn the joy of contentment in what we've already been given. The Word of God tells us how to do that (Phil. 4:11). Did you know that contentment is something we have to develop intentionally? It doesn't happen automatically. All babies are born discontented.

We learn contentment through conditioning our minds to dwell on our blessings, and to turn to expressions of gratitude. David, like Paul, learned to be content.

## The Lord Is Our Counsel
"I will bless the LORD who has given me counsel; my heart also instructs me in the night seasons" (v. 7).

What a blessing it is to know our Creator and Sustainer on a first-name basis and to be able to approach Him night or day. The Word of God tells us that when we lack wisdom, we should simply go ask God for it (James 1:5). It never tells us that when we lack wisdom, we should go through the appropriate channels. It never tells us to call technical support and wait on "hold." It never tells us that we're on our own and should fend for ourselves. The Word of God says for us to go directly to the Source. We can fearlessly approach God, and He will be overjoyed to see us! He will pour out wisdom and blessings we never thought to request. He will urge us to come to His side again and again. No question is unwelcome.

God is always available. We may be deep in sleep, yet He is available—watching over us, gently handling our minds, dealing with the problems we've been facing. It is as if God does His holy maintenance work on our minds and hearts as we rest. You climb into bed at night

---

### From My Journal

*Dear Lord, I pray that this might be my final visit to this insidious disease. I pray that I might not ever have to undergo the trials of chemotherapy again. I ask that You would continue to give me good health as I strain to recover my strength and resume my life. I need You, Lord, and I pray that You would be the sole source of strength in my life. I love You for what You have already done for me!*

---

thinking about the challenge weighing down your heart, and you lay it before God before drifting off. During the night, a quiet miracle comes to pass. You wake up feeling entirely differently about things. How could you have not seen it this way before? God has brought it all together in your mind and resolved yesterday's care.

I believe David had that experience. "My heart also instructs me in the night seasons," he tells us. The Lord is our completeness, our cer-

tainty, our contentment, and our counsel. But David isn't quite finished. He ends this little section by adding one more attribute to the
magnificent collection.

### The Lord Is Our Confidence

David reviews the blessings of God and says, "I have set the LORD always before me; because He is at my right hand I shall not be moved."
What a powerful statement that is, declaring that with God in our
sights, the world and all its forces can align against us, and we will be
unstoppable. David, who has faced armies, has more than earned the
right to tell us that.

David's agenda for Psalm 16 is becoming clear to us. First he has reviewed who God is. Next he has rehearsed what God does. And now
he brings Psalm 16 to a joyful and victorious conclusion by rejoicing
at what God is going to do. Before us we have one of the most spec-
tacular portions of the Old Testament, because it provides a ringing
demonstration of the supernatural quality of God's Word. Here is
David, gazing into the future through the eyes of faith and seeing
things he has no right to see. He comprehends things that have never
been communicated to him, as far as the Scriptures tell us, except by
the Holy Spirit.

And he lays out what he sees accurately—so accurately that when
New Testament writers, far in the future, will discuss these events,
they will prove their points by quoting the writings of David in Psalm
16.

## Rejoicing in What God Will Do

We never cease to be astounded by the foresight of Old Testament
writers revealing future events. How can anyone doubt the validity
and authority of the Scriptures when they observe this trait? Prepare
to be astonished by the prophecy of David.

### Rejoicing in the Resurrection

First, *David rejoices in his own resurrection.* He says, "For You will not leave my soul in Sheol." You may recognize the ancient word *Sheol.* It was used to refer to the abode of the dead or the grave itself. David continues, "Nor will You allow Your Holy One to see corruption" (v. 10). In the text, the words *Holy One* are capitalized because they refer to the Lord Jesus. But we should be clear that before David foresaw the resurrection of Christ, he saw his own resurrection. While he doesn't understand completely what is going to happen, David has rehearsed for us all of the good things God has done for him, and is doing for him, in his life. He reflects on all these uplifting truths, and in his incredible spiritual insight he comes to the realization that surely such a loving and protective God will continue to care for him in his death and beyond.

David's view into the world of eternity is a startling one—it surpasses even the prophets. Allow me to give you an example. We all know, at some time or other, a family that loses a small child. People become deeply concerned about the eternal fate of an infant who dies. How does God deal with a soul too young to have had any chance to accept the gospel? Will a doomed infant be saved?

When someone brings that question to me, I always return to the story of the first child born from the union of David and Bathsheba. The Bible says that while this newborn was dying, David fasted and wore sackcloth. He mourned; he pleaded with God. But the baby died, and David rose and dressed, anointed his body, ended his fasting, and returned to normal life. Seeing the grief he had endured while the child was still alive, no one could understand his acceptance of the child's death. Some of the servants asked him to account for his behavior.

David explained it, and his answer has tremendous implications for us. "While the child was still alive," he said, "I fasted and wept; for I said, 'Who can tell whether the LORD will be gracious to me, that the child may live?' But now he is dead; why should I fast? Can I bring him back again? I shall go to him, but he shall not return to me" (2 Sam. 12:22–23).

Did you catch that last sentence? David knew he would see his child again one day. In other words, the infant would be in the place David knew he would someday go—into the arms of his loving Father. He knew what we know, that there is a place known as heaven; but he also knew that God cares for His helpless little ones. David had seen his own resurrection.

But, yes, he had also foreseen the resurrection of the Messiah.

*David rejoices in Christ's resurrection.* David has said, "For You will not leave my soul in Sheol, nor will You allow Your Holy One to see corruption" (v. 10). One phrase stands out here, and it takes this verse to a whole new level—one that becomes one of the great, victorious peaks of the Old Testament. While David has been talking about his own death, he finds himself thinking in deeper terms—supernatural terms that wander far beyond the reality of himself, his time, and his place.

David would never refer to himself as "the Holy One." It's totally out of character with the David of the rest of the psalms—the David known for a deep humility and a sense of his own unworthiness before God. Never does he even approach claiming for himself holiness of any kind. But as he speaks of victory over the grave, the Holy Spirit lifts a corner of the curtain and gives him a glimpse into the future and the cornerstone of human history—and the first Christians were quick to notice it.

The amazing, farseeing words in verse 10 are carefully selected and quoted on two occasions in the New Testament. The first of these came when Peter was preaching on the Day of Pentecost—without a doubt one of the most amazing, Spirit-empowered sermons ever preached. Three thousand souls entered the kingdom of heaven and the fellowship of Christ in the wake of that lightning bolt of a sermon. In the grip of true inspiration, Peter describes Jesus:

. . . whom God raised up, having loosed the pains of death, because it was not possible that He should be held by it. For David says concerning Him: "I foresaw the LORD always before my face, for He is at my right hand, that I may not be shaken; therefore my heart rejoiced, and

my tongue was glad; moreover my flesh will also rest in hope, because
You will not leave my soul in Hades, nor will You allow Your Holy One
to see corruption. You have made known to me the ways of life; You
will make me full of joy in Your presence." (Acts 2:24–28)

Empowered by God's Spirit, Peter confirms that David had been
speaking of Christ's resurrection. Even so soon after Christ's ascen-
sion, His followers realize the full implications of David's written
words so long ago. Did David himself know whereof he spoke? As
journalists say today, just what did he know and when did he know it?
We can't be certain David grasped the full meaning of the events to
which he was pointing; the important thing is that he spoke the truth.
He validated his inspiration by accurately foretelling Christ, and Paul
added the Holy Spirit's affirmation that Psalm 16 looks forward to
Jesus.

But these verses come into play in another New Testament context.
You'll find it in Acts 13; the place is Antioch and the agent is Paul. He,
too, is delivering an inspired sermon when he explains, "Therefore
[David] also says in another Psalm: 'You will not allow Your Holy One
to see corruption.' For David, after he had served his own generation
by the will of God, fell asleep, and was buried with his fathers, and
saw corruption; but He whom God raised up saw no corruption" (Acts
13:35–37).

Paul is very clear on this: David talked about seeing no corruption,
but he himself certainly returned to the earth, ashes to ashes and dust
to dust. "He whom God raised up," on the other hand, overcame the
terrible power of the grave. He ascended to heaven in the body.
David, Paul attests, was speaking of Christ. Peter knew it, Paul knew
it, and it must have been common knowledge among those first believers who knew their Hebrew Scriptures.

With perhaps the limitations of his understanding, from the vantage point of his particular spot in history, David may have been unable to fathom the full implications of what he was writing. But we,
with the advantage of knowing and embracing the Gospels, can see
what David might not have seen. Praise God, we need never endure

the corruption of the grave. Christ has written the last word. He has saved us from eternal death.

## Rejoicing in the Rapture

We come finally to a beautiful ending for our psalm. Try to imagine a more powerfully positive—and positively powerful—bottom line than this one: "You will show me the path of life; in Your presence is fullness of joy; at Your right hand are pleasures forevermore" (v. 11).

Once again, David is seeing into the future, to a time when there will be the possibility of a perfectly intimate relationship with our Lord. Yes, David has attested that the Lord will emerge from a guarded tomb and confirm His status as the Chosen One. But David, who has looked down the road through time all the way to the Easter event, now looks even farther and sees a certain path—the "path of life," as he calls it. This path leads through all the troubles and cares of the world and right into the holy presence of God. "I'll walk down that path one day," David says. "And I'll be in a land where joy is made full, and pleasure can be found at God's right hand."

David can sense the hope that will be made real in Christ. The ultimate pleasure is to be found in the realization of dwelling in the presence of our all-wise, all-knowing, all-loving Creator. And to realize we can spend all of eternity in the perfection of that presence is to feel true hope and joy indeed.

Do you know how to enter that presence? I know only two ways you can accomplish that. The first way, if you are a child of God, is simply to die. As Paul said, "For to me, to live is Christ, and to die is gain" (Phil. 1:21). Even death is positive if it brings us near Him.

Paul teaches in 2 Corinthians 5:8 that we will be well pleased to be absent from the body and present with the Lord. At the very instant of death, we will find ourselves in a new world—the world of being right at His side. We no longer see in a mirror dimly, but face to face. And we need never worry or shed a tear again, for our joy will be made complete.

I see that and my heart surges with joy. What a glorious day it will be to be reunited with Christ. But Paul also said, "To live is Christ." This earth need not be a place to simply escape someday. I'm hoping my years on this planet will stretch out a bit longer. I've looked cancer in the face, and I'll be honest enough to tell you my desire is to beat the rap.

I want to be here for the rapture of the church. Paul tells us, in 1 Thessalonians 4:16–17, that Christ will appear from heaven with a shout. I wouldn't mind being around to witness that event. I want to hear the trumpet Paul has foretold, and I want to see those graves open up and give forth their dead, who will joyfully race through the skies to rejoin their Creator and Redeemer. Then, as Paul says, "we who are alive and remain" (I'm counting on numbering myself among that group) will be caught up with Christ as well. It will be quite a spectacle!

And that, my friend, would be the second way to come into God's presence. Burial or rapture—we can travel to His side by land or by air.

If I had to die today, I know I would have the thrill of being immediately in the presence of my precious Lord. But if I stubbornly push this earthly vessel of my body a few more miles, and if I continue to fight the good fight against cancer and live on—well, there are the considerable consolations of living for Christ in this wonderful world: enjoying my loving wife and counseling my children in adulthood, seeing how God nurtures and develops my grandkids, enjoying the many pleasures of fellowship in the body of Christ and the simple joys of daily living.

Death or life? I agree with Paul—it's a win-win proposition, wouldn't you agree? I agree with David as well, as I realize the fullness of these things and begin to sing God's praises. I have so much to be thankful for. God is everything for me, as I hope He is for you—counselor, friend, provider, and loving Father. He has prepared a mansion for all of us—an appointed room for you, and one for me.

We are going to know joy as it is meant to be known and pleasure as we have never known it.

I want to tell you about a woman who was a staunch and faithful church member. She was ravaged by illness, and no one expected her to live much more than another week or two.

She knew her day was approaching, and she called the pastor and asked him to come help her plan the funeral. So he joined her at her

---

*No one experiences complete sanctification without going through a "white funeral" — the burial of the old life. If there has never been this crucial moment of change through death, sanctification will never be more than an elusive dream. There must be a "white funeral," a death with only one resurrection—a resurrection into the life of Jesus Christ. Nothing can defeat a life like this. It has oneness with God for only one purpose—to be a witness for Him.*

**—Oswald Chambers**

---

deathbed, and they began making arrangements. The ailing woman listed for him all the hymns she wanted sung, all the Scripture verses she wanted read, and those she preferred as the soloists.

Then she said, "Pastor, there's one thing I want you to do. You may feel this is strange, but I want you to promise me today that you'll fulfill my wishes anyway."

The pastor frowned mildly. "What's that?" he asked.

She said, "I want to be buried with a fork in my right hand."

The pastor's frown became deeper. This was quite an odd request. "That's a request I've never heard," he said kindly, "but perhaps if you try to help me understand your reasons, I can feel better about carrying out your request."

She said, "Pastor, I've been a member of our church for most of my life. And one of the great joys for me has been the potluck dinners we have. I don't think I've missed one dinner in my life. In the old days, we had them on a weekly basis. And what I remember best is how, after the first course was served, one of the hosts would always stand up and say, 'Save your fork. The best is yet to come!' So, pastor, I'm counting on you to bury me with a fork in my hand. When my loved ones pass by the casket and look at me, I want you to be standing nearby. Those people will ask you why I'm holding an eating utensil, and you'll smile and tell them that for me, *the best is yet to come.*"

Can you believe that? Can you look beyond the bend in your road and trust that, even though you can't see where the road winds, the best is yet to come?

Can you look beyond the terrible frustrations of poor health, and believe that God is preparing a sumptuous feast for you? Can you stand in the midst of family trauma, or a crisis in business, or whatever your trial might be, and praise the name of your Father, because you know He is your rock and your salvation?

David could do that, and countless souls throughout the ages have joined with him in joy that flies in the face of rational explanation—pursued as they have been by the giants of life, the jealous kings of daily experience, the limitations of relationships, and the disappointment of hopes and dreams. They have found that these very times of discouragement have not been defined by the absence of God, but somehow, by the miraculous, closer presence of Him. They have stared at the emptiness of death and realized that it held the fullness of a feast.

They have clung to Him, found His love and peace and wisdom, and joined with the great throng who sit at that banquet table. The dessert hasn't arrived, but the anticipation of it is already in the air. Perhaps in one way this is the best moment of all, the moment of anticipation—the moment when we realize the best is yet to come.

# Epilogue
## Resuming the Journey

*When through fiery trials thy pathway shall lie,*
*My grace all-sufficient will be thy supply;*
*The flame shall not hurt thee, I only design*
*Thy dross to consume and thy gold to refine.*

In the end, the doctors gave me the thumbs-up.

They told me the stem cell transplant couldn't have proceeded more smoothly, that this body of mine came through the ordeal better than we had any right to expect.

I remembered another day, in what seemed like another lifetime, when I saw the doctors smiling and giving me that same seal of approval. I had been at Scripps Clinic, breezing through a battery of tests on my physical exam. How confident I had been—how unsuspecting of what was lurking in wait for me, to be revealed on that black afternoon. What would I have thought of the endless trials, treatments, chemotherapy episodes, renewed hopes, and shattered dreams that were to dominate my life in the months and years ahead?

That day in September of 1994 seemed a lifetime ago indeed. Now, I'd made it through the stem cell transplant. I'd love to take all the credit for having done so well. After all, hadn't I exercised fanatically every single day, running for my life on a treadmill?

Or maybe I was blessed with exceptionally excellent doctors. Certainly their expertise had played a role, and I thank God for gifted medical practitioners every day. I placed my life in their hands, and they surely hadn't failed me.

But from my vantage point, there was one powerful factor that went the farthest to explain the success of my ordeal. I attribute my healing to the faithful prayers of the people of God—so many of them in scattered places. There were Christians interceding for me before God's throne around the clock. I know I felt fresh spiritual vitality from their prayers, just as I felt fresh physical vitality from my 4.2 daily miles on a treadmill. Never underestimate the power of prayer. Walking on a treadmill is refreshing, but walking with God is transforming.

Today, I live in remission. My life can be characterized as the sweet calm after the storm.

I suppose the storm passed with the stem cell transplant. I stayed briefly in the hospital to get through those first critical hours and days of recovery. Then I was sent home to begin my journey toward recuperation, and hopefully a restored, healthy life. I rested at home for several weeks during which I read, slept, and enjoyed a few visits with the people in this world who are dearest to me. Then, on Mother's Day of 1999, I returned to Shadow Mountain Community Church to preach for the first time since March.

The feeling of walking into that packed auditorium is something I'll never forget for as long as I live. Here was the throng to whom I owed so much, the loving people who had spent countless hours lifting me up before God. I honestly believe everybody who had ever attended our church was present in that sanctuary to welcome me back. And they all rose from their seats to applaud as I entered the room.

How would you have kept your composure in such a situation? One moment such as that is worth a lifetime of struggle. I was emotionally overwhelmed by the outpouring of love and acceptance. I silently thanked God from the very depth of my being, trying to maintain my composure—but I can tell you it was quite a challenge to do so, for my heart was as full, and as electrified, as the church sanctuary. What a blessed man I was—and still am.

More than anything else, today I'm grateful to God. I continue to pray that the doctors got rid of all they were looking for this time, that my days of excruciating treatments are finally at an end. But I also know that cancer is not a battle, it's a war. And I can only be thankful for battles won and land retaken in the name of Christ. I feel thoroughly undeserving of the depths of His mercy, the deep well of His strength and His infinite compassion poured out upon me. I trust you can say much the same thing.

That's why you and I face the road ahead with lighter hearts and lesser burdens. The bending path can seem like a lonely one, but we all must walk it. I hope the true stories that have been shared—mine and those of several of my good friends—will somehow serve to fortify you for the battles, conflicts, and struggles of your own life.

Even more, I hope that God's Word, as we've explored it through the wisdom of the psalms, will be your beacon in those dark times you may well be facing at the present. Never forget that He has offered us a storehouse of guidance in the field of adversity. We have the answers for how God's people can face their trials with courage, faith, and hope. That storehouse can be found between the covers of your Bible.

Let's you and I hold that Word close to our hearts and turn our eyes to the bends that lie ahead. I'm thankful that I can still walk down it with you in this body that has been through so many struggles.

This life is a remission for both you and me, don't you agree? Jesus, the Great Physician, has performed our treatment with His skilled hands, and He "got it all"! Death has been defeated. We've come through the ordeal with hearts filled with gladness and gratitude. But on earth, the skirmishes continue even after the war has been won. We continue to fight daily battles with the forces of sin, which want so badly to infiltrate our lives and spread so insidiously.

But now we know what we're up against. We set our eyes on the One who gave us our marching orders, and we march ever onward.

We travel this road for the days that God has ordained for us, taking the difficult curves, but also seeing the wonderful scenery along the way. The journey is rewarding, and the destination is the only one worth the traveling. Let's walk it with joy—together.

The Irish poet traditionally blessed the traveler with the words, "May the road rise up to meet you." Allow me to rephrase it this way as my parting words of encouragement for you:

> *May you rise up to meet the road,*
> *and all its snares and hazards,*
> *in the grace and wisdom*
> *and wonderful sufficiency of God.*
>
> *Amen.*

# Notes

## Chapter 1: A Bend in the Road

1. Gordon MacDonald, *The Life God Blesses* (Nashville: Thomas Nelson, 1994), 25.
2. Ibid., 28.
3. Source unknown.
4. MacDonald, *The Life God Blesses*, 25–26.
5. Laura A. Barter Snow, "This Thing Is from Me," (Grand Rapids: Faith, Prayer and Tract League, n.d.
6. Ron Mehl, *Surprise Endings* (Sisters, Oreg.: Multnomah, 1993), 60.
7. MacDonald, *The Life God Blesses*, 42.
8. Mehl, *Surprise Endings*, 60.

## Chapter 2: Psalm for a Dark Night

1. "Luck Rivals Worst of Sick Jokes: 'There's Hope,' New Yorker Says," *Los Angeles Times*, 19 March 1995, A28.
2. Source unknown.

## Chapter 3: I Need Your Help, Lord

1. Lloyd John Ogilvie, *Falling into Greatness* (Minneapolis: Gregson, 1984), 191.
2. William Barclay, *The Daily Study Bible: The Gospel of Luke* (Philadelphia: Westminster Press, 1975).
3. Eugene Peterson, *A Long Obedience in the Same Direction* (Downers Grove, Ill.: InterVarsity, 1980), 40–41.

### Chapter 4: When God Delays

1.  F. B. Meyer, *Choice Notes on the Psalms* (Grand Rapids: Kregel, 1984), 23.
2.  Adapted from John Phillips, *Exploring the Psalms*, vol. 1, *Psalms 1–88* (Neptune, N.J.: Loizeaux Brothers, 1988), 99.
3.  James Montgomery Boice, *Psalms: An Expositional Commentary*, vol. 1, *Psalms 1–41* (Grand Rapids: Baker, 1994), 109.

### Chapter 6: A Desert Psalm

1.  H.D.M. Spence et al., *The Pulpit Commentary*, vol. 2 (Chicago: Wilcox & Follett Co., n.d.), 25.
2.  C. S. Lewis, *Reflections on the Psalms* (New York: Harcourt, Brace & World, 1958), 50–51.
3.  Lewis Smedes, *Standing on the Promises* (Nashville: Thomas Nelson, 1998), 91.

### Chapter 7: Life's Ups and Downs

1.  Gary Richmond, *A View from the Zoo*, out of print.

### Chapter 8: Praying under Pressure

1.  W. Graham Scroggie, *A Guide to the Psalms*, vol. 4 (Grand Rapids: Kregel, 1995), 79.
2.  Alexander MaClaren, *The Psalms*, vol. 3, *Psalms 90–150* (New York: A. C. Armstrong & Son, 1894), 408.
3.  Dorothy Foltz-Gray, "Words of Comfort," *American Way*, July 1999, 36.

### Chapter 9: When You Are at Your Wits' End

1.  Leonard Griffith, *God in Man's Experience* (Waco, Tex.: Word, 1968), 108.

### Chapter 10: Triumph over Trouble

1.  Source unknown.
2.  Hannah Whitall Smith, *Living Confidently in God's Love* (Springdale, Penn.: Whitaker House, 1984), 278–80.

### Chapter 11: The Best Is Yet to Come

1.  Ray C. Stedman, *Jesus Teaches on Prayer* (Waco, Tex.: Word, 1975), 72.

# About the Author

DAVID JEREMIAH is senior pastor of Shadow Mountain Community Church and Chancellor of Christian Heritage College in El Cajon, California. He is the best-selling author of twelve books, including *Jesus' Final Warning, Escape the Coming Night* and *The Handwriting on the Wall.* Dr. Jeremiah also hosts *Turning Point,* an international radio and television program, which is released on over 1000 outlets. He and his wife, Donna, make their home in El Cajon, and they have four children and three grandchildren.

# Endorsements

*This moving book reveals how one man of God who had preached biblical principles for years stared death in the face—and found that God is faithful to those who put their trust in Him. David, his family, and his great church rose to the challenge of one of life's greatest bends in the road and let it enrich their lives.*

TIM LAHAYE
author, pastor, teacher

*David Jeremiah lifts the plumbline of God's word so high that we can more accurately measure the truth, so clear that we can more easily see the truth, and so relevant that we can more faithfully obey the truth.*

*Praise God for him!*

ANN GRAHAM LOTZ
author of *Just Give Me Jesus*

# MORE SELECTIONS FROM DAVID JEREMIAH

### Slaying the Giants in Your Life
Dr. David Jeremiah weaves gripping, real-life stories of contemporary giant slayers who came face-to-face with their own Goliaths: temptation, doubt, procrastination, and jealousy. In each, you will discover afresh the eternal unwavering promise of God to overcome those giants.

### The Things that Matter
In this study of Jesus' Olivet discourse, Dr. David Jeremiah pinpoints a believer's priorities and encourages readers to stay the path of the simpler things in life. Anyone who is overwhelmed, perplexed or anxious about the past, present or future will renew their hope for living through this small, yet powerful work.

### The Handwriting on the Wall
In *The Handwriting on the Wall,* prophecy expert David Jeremiah shows how an understanding of prophecy, specifically that in the book of Daniel, opens a pathway to dynamic, faithful living today—with confidence and hope for the future.